LOOPHOLES OF THE RICH

LOOPHOLES OF THE RICH

How the Rich Legally
Make More Money
& Pay Less Tax

REVISED EDITION

DIANE KENNEDY, CPA

WILEY

John Wiley & Sons, Inc.

Published by John Wiley & Sons, Inc., Hoboken, New Jersey.
Published simultaneously in Canada.

For general information on our other products and services please contact our Customer
Care Department within the United States at (800) 762-2974, outside the United
States at (317) 572-3993 or fax (317) 572-4002.

Wiley also publishes its books in a variety of electronic formats. Some content that
appears in print may not be available in electronic books. For more information about
Wiley products, visit our web site at www.Wiley.com.

Library of Congress Cataloging-in-Publication Data:
Kennedy, Diane., 1956-
  [Loop-holes of the rich]
    Loopholes of the rich : how the rich legally make more money and pay less tax
/ Diane Kennedy—Rev. ed.
      p. cm.
    Published simultaneously in Canada.
    Includes index.
    ISBN 0-471-71178-0 (pbk. : alk. paper)
      1. Corporations—Taxation—United States.   2. Tax planning—United States.
  I. Title.
  HJ4653.C7K46 2004
  658.15'3—dc22   2004058889

10 9 8 7 6 5 4 3 2 1

Contents

v

CONTENTS

Foreword

There are two parts to making a whole lot of money. The first is earning it and the other is keeping it. The hard part is keeping it. In this book, *Loopholes of the Rich*, you are going to legally learn how to make more, keep a whole lot more, and pay less tax. One of the things I teach is "The best thing you can do for the poor is not be one of them."

What you want to do is build a financial fortress around yourself, your family, and your businesses. Do what the rich do by having a plan and a path. You need an effortless strategy that is easy to understand. This book takes you through it step-by-step-by-step. Diane gives you not only a wealth creation system, but a wealth preservation and protection system that is invincible, unstoppable, and resolute, and works for you now and works for the future. What you want to do is create a residual, philanthropic future income that makes your church, temple, mosque, or charity of your choice infinitely better off than they were before you came. So now you have lasting value, because you knew the *Loopholes of the Rich*.

You deserve to know this information, and now Diane has written it in such an easy-to-understand way that you can make it, keep it, and have it grow. As John Wesley said, "You want to earn all you can, save all you can, invest all you can," and let me add *protect* all you can, so then you can give all you can.

> —Mark Victor Hansen
> Co-creator, #1 *New York Times* best-
> selling series *Chicken Soup for the Soul*®
> Co-author, *The One Minute Millionaire*

THE RULES HAVE CHANGED

Are You Living Your Dream . . . or Your Nightmare?

Are you one of the millions today who keep working harder and harder and receive less and less in return for their effort? Just where does that money seem to go? And, even more frightening, where does all your time go? Many today are waking up to the realization that they have somehow gotten old, and their lives so far have only been about striving—with nothing to show for all the years of work.

Where Did It All Go Wrong?

The biggest expenses for the average American are interest and taxes. Both of these expenses put *your* money in *someone else's* pocket. The interest that you pay on your home mortgage, car loan, credit cards, and the like is income to someone else. The taxes you pay go to support the government without much input from you. In other words, the typical middle-class wage earner works to pay other people. And, worse yet, the average American seemingly has no say in how the money is spent. No wonder you feel out of control sometimes!

The middle-class dream has become a nightmare. You can't work harder at your job and expect to get ahead. And, even worse, you might not know this until it's too late. You might find out that you have no future just as you're ready to retire and enjoy your golden years. That's when you find out the pension you hoped for is gone. That's when you find out your house costs you more in property tax and insurance than you can afford. And, too late, you find out you now have outdated skills for the job market. This is one nightmare that doesn't end when you wake up. You don't even know you're in the nightmare until you wake up and find out you have no money and no future.

The good news is that there still is a dream possible for you. And that future is possible no matter where you are today. It doesn't matter where you live. It doesn't matter how much money you have now. It doesn't matter how much debt you have. But the way to realize the dream, and end the nightmare, is not the way your parents taught you.

The plan of your parents—work hard, save your money, and collect your retirement—was effective for them, but it doesn't work now. *Loopholes of the Rich* was written to provide the information you need to operate in today's world. In this book you will learn the new rules that the wealthy play by. And you will learn how you can play by the same rules.

What Does It Mean to Be Average?

Five years ago, it was estimated that the average 50-year-old American had a net worth of zero. Consider what that means. It means that someone has worked for 25 or more years and has been able to accumulate nothing. Of course, that's an average; so for everyone who has assets that exceed their debt, there is someone who owes more than they own. At 50 years of age, they have another 15 years or so to work. A lot has to change if they want to recover from where they are now. They have to reverse the effects of 25 years of work in just 15 more years of work.

Last year, a new study was done. It's now estimated that an average 50-year-old American has a net worth of *minus* $7,000! It's going the wrong way!

The conventional wisdom for the average person just doesn't work anymore. If you aren't average, or don't want to get those average results (owing more than you own), then it means that you're ready to learn the secrets of tax-advantaged wealth building that the rich know.

How to Improve the Odds

Avoid being average by creating balance between financial education and proper financial action. No one person can have all of the answers. A team makes you stronger. Your team should encourage and move you in the right direction. This book will tell you how to find, evaluate, and work with the right team. With their help and advice, you can succeed!

How to Put More Money in Your Pocket Today

Taxes are the single biggest expense for the average American today. One small change in the amount of tax that you pay can create a huge change in how you and your family live your lives. This book will tell you what small changes make the biggest impact.

Even better, you'll learn strategies that can help you save taxes today! But it takes more than just learning about them. You need to also put the ideas into action. *Loopholes of the Rich* will show you how to do that as you build a team that supports your goals. But, first, we start with the basics of loopholes.

Loopholes Are Government Incentives

Loopholes are government incentives to promote public policy. They aren't something shady or shifty. In fact, the government wants you to take advantage of the legal tax loopholes that the tax law provides. So where are the loopholes? You'll find most of the loopholes in the two areas that most support the economy—businesses and real estate investing. Businesses, and particularly small businesses, provide stimulus to the economy. A growing business employs people, hires consultants, invests in equipment, and just generally kick-starts a struggling economy. In fact, look at recent tax legislation. Does it seem like the tax cuts are unfair? They are! That's because the government wants to create a change in the economy and knows that the best way to do that is by creating opportunities for businesses to grow.

Real estate loopholes are another important part of public policy. Real estate investors provide housing for people who don't currently own their own homes. The government has tried to provide that same kind of housing (called public housing), and the result is decaying tenements where no one wants to live. In fact, while property values have generally appreciated (when taking the long-range view), public housing values have generally gone down. The government therefore provides the loopholes in order to encourage real estate investors.

The first edition of *Loopholes of the Rich* was published in 2001. Since then, I've heard from thousands of people about how they have made more money and reduced their taxes by taking advantage of the tax loopholes that the government wants you to use. The loopholes are there! The government puts them there for us to use, but it's up to us to find them.

A Word of Caution

You will hear ideas and examples throughout the book that will excite you. You will likely find that the people in the examples have situations very much like yours. You will want to do something—be moved to take action. That's great! The caution is that you must follow all the steps closely. One of the fundamental, key steps is the need to have a good team. Find advisors whom you can trust to give you the best advice.

The Do-It-Yourselfer

Every so often, as I speak at seminars, participants' questions make it clear that they intend to do it themselves in attempting to find the right business structure for their businesses. I am reminded of a medical school classmate of a friend of mine.

It had become evident who the top student in the class was by the second year of medical school. In fact, this particular young man was so far advanced that he had trouble communicating with any of his fellow students and many of the professors. As his knowledge, and his conceit, grew, he began to believe that he was more competent than *anyone* else in the medical profession. This was in spite of the fact that he was only in his second year of medical school.

With that belief, he self-diagnosed a potential appendix problem for himself and determined that he should have an appendectomy. Of course, he felt that no one was as good as he was, so he also decided to remove the appendix himself.

He gave himself local anesthesia and rigged up mirrors on his narrow dormitory bed so that he could view the operating site—his own abdomen. His skill might have been top-notch, but he couldn't stanch the flow of blood quickly enough and soon passed out from the blood loss. Luckily, he was discovered before he died from the failed surgery attempt.

He was trained, he was competent, *and*
he almost died trying to do it himself!

The Bottom Line: Use trained professionals; don't try this by yourself.

What You Will Learn in
Loopholes of the Rich

Loopholes of the Rich came about as a result of my years of experience working with people who searched for ways to reduce their taxes and increase their wealth. After talking to literally thousands of people from all over the United States and Canada, from all walks of life, with different assets, educations, and circumstances, I found that there were often similar questions and stumbling blocks that they encountered. That is why this book was written—to create a common ground of understanding as a foundation on which you can build with your own personal advisors.

The first statement that I generally hear from someone just starting is "I don't know where to start!" They ask, "What do I do first?" Usually they have a stated goal of what they want, such as to pay less taxes and to protect their assets. But they might not know what it is they really want. After a few minutes of conversation, we usually discover that what they are really after is a sense of control and understanding about their own finances. They don't feel good about what they have done to date. They want to know that someday they will be able to have true financial freedom. And they want to know that they have that freedom protected. In other words, they want to be able to keep their financial freedom.

Perhaps you have longed for the same goal. As you read through this book, you will likely find some of your current ideas challenged. And, even more important, you might find that your friends and current advisors will challenge the ideas presented here. That doesn't mean that your friends are wrong and it doesn't mean that the ideas in the book are wrong. What it does mean is that we all understand things within our own framework and point of view. If something comes along that is not in that point of view, either we can reject it as incorrect or we can try to adjust our point of view to accept it. If you choose to accept different ideas, then you can experience growth and more depth of understanding. That is really what this book is about—to give you different ideas about things you might already think you know.

Above all, I have striven to present the ideas in a format that makes them easy to understand. We will be discussing tax loophole strategies and tax law. You can't learn those subjects from reading just one book. You actually can't ever say you have completely learned them, because tax law is constantly changing as new cases are decided, refinements are added by additional Treasury regulations, and, of course, the inevitable changes to the tax code are enacted by Congress.

Loopholes of the Rich Success Story

Scott had worked as a manager making a very respectable salary of about $50,000 per year. But, seven years after graduation from college, he was deeper in debt than when he had graduated. Scott talked about how he dreaded driving to work every day. He didn't know how much longer his car would last. And if it broke down, he had no money with which to repair it and no more credit available on his credit cards. So, each day he worried as he drove to and from work.

The car lasted . . . but his job did not. Scott was now faced with no income. Luckily, he soon got work as an independent business consultant. Interestingly enough, he made almost $50,000 in his first year. But he didn't make it as an employee—he made it as a business owner. And Scott had made use of the tax loopholes to set up the right business structure and take the legal deductions, so he ended up with more money in his pocket. In fact, at the end of his first year he had $10,000 more cash even though he had made the same amount of money!

Scott had used the tax loopholes that the government wants him to use. Scott is now my business partner at TaxLoopholes and D Kennedy & Associates (DKA). We both use the money we make from the businesses (after taking all of the tax-free benefits we can) to invest in real estate. Our wealth grows in the best tax-advantaged ways.

How the Book Is Set Up

The book is divided into four sections. Each section is important and builds upon the other. I suggest that you read the book through once, completely. Then go back to more closely read the chapters that are most applicable to your own circumstances. The four sections are:

I. The Five STEPS to Financial Freedom

Learn the five STEPS to financial freedom so you can achieve the ultimate in tax savings and start building wealth today.

II. Jump Start! Your Wealth

Learn the seven pillars of wealth building that use the tax advantages of the rich. This section teaches you how to maximize and coordinate business tax loopholes, real estate loopholes, and home loopholes to create wealth with leverage and velocity.

III. New Tax Strategies for C Corporations

New tax law has created brand-new opportunities for using C corporations. Learn how in this section!

IV. Take Your Loopholes and Still Sleep at Night

Set up your business and accounting to keep what you earn safe from frivolous lawsuits. Learn how to minimize the risk of IRS attack. Reduce the risk *of* an audit and reduce the risk *from* an audit.

Bonus

- Real-life tax strategy examples.
- The 300+ Business Deductions checklist.
- IRS business types.
- Sample forms.

Different Financial Strategies

Throughout the book, you will see the stories of different clients unfold. You may find that you have similarities to one of these clients. The clients are actually amalgams of real-life examples. Everything you will read about these clients and their personal experiences has happened to someone. The examples are real, but specific details have been changed. Plus, of course, the names have been changed.

For example, Ted and Ellen are based on the characters of people I have known for a long time. (In fact, I had gone to school with someone like Ellen.) They got trapped in the middle-class nightmare—working hard, not home much with their two children, and tired most of the time. They were looking for a way out. They weren't afraid to try something new, and they were bright, hardworking people. But they didn't want to risk their family's security along the way.

The people you read about are in very different situations with unique issues, but you may find elements in your own situation. Every client of mine has had many learning experiences along the way to their business success. My hope is that you can learn from these experiences as you read about them. Every lesson you learn from someone else and *apply* is one fewer lesson you won't have to learn the hard way. I don't know about you, but that sounds a whole lot easier to me!

Interspersed throughout the narrative, you will find other explanations and many forms. I encourage you to complete the forms and questionnaires that are applicable to your situation. These are tools that I use in my certified public accountant (CPA) practice with clients every day. My sincere wish is that you will have the same good results our clients have experienced. Above all, I wish you success and happiness in your business ventures, and, in fact, in all of life's adventures.

Meet Ted and Ellen: What Went Wrong?

"What went wrong?" was the first thing that Ellen, my old college pal, said to me when we met to catch up one day.

"We planned everything—good education, good career—and we're making more money than we ever thought we would," she continued. "Yet we live hand-to-mouth. They are talking about downsizing where Ted works, and I worry that we'd be out in the street if that happened to him." She was obviously upset.

"Ellen, the one thing I know is that you are not alone!" I replied, reflecting on my experience with clients in my tax practice.

When Did the Dream Die?

Years earlier, I had met Ted and Ellen while we were attending college. They were looking forward to building their life together—a nice house in the suburbs with the two children they planned. And back then, even though it was barely two decades ago, we all knew the surest route to success was the tried-and-true formula—get a good job, save to buy your first home, start your family, and live happily ever after.

Ted and Ellen were hardworking and achieved their success—new home and family—faster than most. And then one day I ran into them again. The first thing I noticed was how tired they both were. Ellen hadn't been able to be the stay-at-home mom that she wanted to be and was exhausted from juggling the demands of a typical eight-to-five job with the demands of caring for their eight-year-old son, Josh, and three-year-old daughter, Sarah.

Ted worked days at a job for the state, traditionally a safe, secure job with good benefits. The benefits, though, were quickly being taken away. He was worried about how much longer he would have that job and had started a computer consulting business on the side. He spent his evenings and weekends locked away from his family in a corner of the family room working on his computer.

Both Ted and Ellen felt guilty about the time they spent away from their children and they worried about money for their future (would there be money for the children's braces, education, and so forth?), and about their own personal future (would there be anything left for them when they were ready to retire?).

We met as friends, but it soon became apparent that I could help them in a professional manner.

I had established my career as a tax advisor and strategist for the wealthy, and as a result had learned many of the loopholes the wealthy used. The simple fact is that the wealthy approach their tax and financial planning in a radically different way than what we have been taught.

Ted and Ellen were happy to discuss their financial plans with me. Together, we created a strategy that reduced their income tax and used the money they previously paid to the government to build wealth, tax-free, for their future. That means that much of the money they used to spend on taxes is now being used to build their future.

Using the same process we still employ today at my CPA firm of (1) assessing, (2) team building, (3) evaluating, (4) implementing, and (5) reassessing, they learned how to jump-start their wealth.

In a series of conversations, they learned the basics of devising a tax plan, and then, together, we built a customized tax strategy, using the approach of the wealthy.

PART I

The Five STEPS to Financial Freedom

Chapter 1

STARTING POINT— UNDERSTANDING YOUR FINANCIAL STORY

Five STEPS to Financial Freedom through Loopholes

S uccess leaves a trail. One of the easiest ways to have your own success is to follow where others have gone before. We all have different goals and come from different circumstances, but there are five basic steps that will ensure the best possible results for everyone, no matter where you are now. These five STEPS are:

S   Starting point.
T   Team.
E   Evaluation strategy.
P   Plan and path.
S   Starting point (reevaluation).

S Is for Starting Point

First, you need to know where you are. It's like having to get on the scales before you start a new diet—you might not want to really know what the numbers say, but you do need to know your starting point.

That's just how it is for your financial plan. Your best results will

> Remember: The members of your team will *help* you or *harm* you as you follow your own financial dream.

come when you can take a realistic look at where you are financially—without excuses, blame, or justifications. Find out where you are, so you can plot an accurate course to where you want to be!

T Is for Team

After you have a good idea of where you are, you will need to start to think about the members you need for your financial team. Most likely, the main members of your team initially will be advisors, educators, and mentors. But your team can also include customers, clients, vendors, business alliances, and friends, among others. You can make conscious choices about the members of your team. You can learn how to evaluate what you need and how these people will fit into your plan. Finally, you can recognize the hidden influences they have on decisions you have made and will make in the future.

E Is for Evaluation/Strategy

After you know where you are and begin to assemble your team, it is time to call on your advisors to help you evaluate your situation and design a personalized strategy for you to achieve your goals. No one team member—your tax strategist, bookkeeper, legal counsel, or financial planner—will make all of the decisions. It is through the cooperative work of your whole team that you will receive the best advice and plan creation.

P Is for Plan and Path

After S, T, and E, you now need to move forward on the path and implement the strategy designed. This can be the hardest part as you move into previously unknown financial waters. You will want to make sure that the team you have in place has experience in the necessary areas

---

Five Steps to Financial Freedom!

S is for starting point—Understand your financial story.

T is for team—Build a team that supports your goals.

E is for evaluation—With your team, construct a tax loopholes strategy.

P is for path—Create an action plan to implement your tax loopholes strategy.

S is for starting point—Look at your new financial statements. What worked? What didn't work?

---

and can give you good advice based on their own personal education, experience, and special skills.

S Is for Starting Point (Reevaluation)

You've taken the first four steps and now you need to again evaluate where you are. Just like a rocket going to the moon needs continual calculations to keep it on its path, you must constantly evaluate where you are and where you are going to ensure that you reach your goals.

By taking the time to thoughtfully consider where you are and where you've come from, you put yourself in a position to achieve the optimum results.

These five STEPS to financial freedom can start you and your family on the path to financial freedom *today*.

Where Are You Now?

Why is it so hard for many people to look at their financial information?

In school, you received a report card to tell your parents and institutions of higher learning how well you did. In life, your financial statements are the report cards that tell investors and financiers how well you are doing. The financial statement, unlike the report cards of old, is something you volunteer to get. And, most people choose to just not look at the data. Sometimes the truth is just too painful.

Traditional education has a part to play here. People are taught more about the technical aspects of their chosen field than they are taught about the practical aspects of running a business in that field. Doctors are taught medical techniques, but are not taught how to run a business so they can grow wealthy without having to give up all their free time. An architect is taught design, but is never told how to set up a profitable architecture firm.

How to Find Out Where You Are

Your financial statements tell a story. And your financial statements are often the best crystal ball when it comes to predicting what your future is going to be.

First, understand what a financial statement is. No, we're not going to turn you into an accountant, but there are basics of how financial statements work that you need to learn so you can immediately spot the financial story of every statement. Can you imagine being able to look at a financial statement and instantly know what the future of that company is going to be? Even better, imagine looking at your own monthly financial statements to identify what is working, so you can do more of it, and what isn't working, so you can change it! How could that change your life?

Second, utilize the simplified forms in this book so you can start to see where your money is going and identify the cash flow patterns in your own life.

Finally (my favorite step), design your ideal financial statement. How much cash do you want flowing into your pocket each month? How much money do you need in order to create the dreams of you and your family? Put your goals in writing with financial statements and they become a measurable tool that you can use to guide your investment and business decisions. But if you never write them down, they will never happen.

Jean's Great Deal

I received a call some time ago from a client of mine. She was a highly educated medical doctor with a flourishing practice. But if she didn't work, she didn't get paid. She wanted to make her money work for her, instead of always having to work for her money.

That meant her goal was to build assets. I was happy to hear that she had bought her first piece of rental property. She was proud that she had found the ideal property and had diligently filled out the cash-on-cash analysis forms I had provided her. The cash-on-cash analysis form is an excellent way to evaluate a potential investment. (The cash-on-cash ratio tells you what the annual return is on the cash invested. It is one of the best tools for comparing real estate investments with other forms of investments.) You can see a copy of this form in Appendix D.

We set a time to meet the following day, and when I arrived Jean immediately showed me the sheet listing the projected rental income, with the property mortgage payment, property tax expense, insurance expense, and repairs and maintenance allowance deducted. She had left the cash-on-cash calculation blank, though. She had trouble with that calculation and, after looking at her numbers, I knew why.

The problem was that the cash-on-cash ratio tells you the rate of return for your investment, and in her case, there was no return! The property expenses exceeded the income. I gently pointed that out to her, and she responded, "That's great! I can write the expenses off on my taxes!"

I then spent the rest of our appointment explaining that tax write-off schemes give you back only cents on the dollar. She was not getting return for her money. Plus, she was one of those higher-income taxpayers who couldn't fully use real estate loopholes.

By the end of the appointment, Jean had decided to sell the property and take a capital loss that would hit her once, instead of the continued drain of a tax write-off.

Jean took that lesson to heart and learned from it. She analyzed a property before she bought it. She always knew her exit strategy in

(Continued)

Jean's Great Deal (Continued)

advance. Then, she found out how to take advantage of the real estate loopholes that she could not take before.

In Jean's case, she worked 50+ hours a week in her medical practice when I first met her. Her new real estate investments created cash flow that helped her reduce the number of hours she spent in her practice. That meant that she could now put more hours into real estate investing. One of the benefits of real estate investments is that the real estate loopholes generally give you more deductions than you receive in cash flow. The best write-off of all is depreciation, which you can maximize to create paper losses. However, if your income is more than $150,000 per year, you cannot use those paper losses as deductions against your other income to reduce your taxes. That's the spot Jean had been in.

Jean was now spending more time in real estate activities than she did as a medical doctor. That meant that she could now take advantage of the loopholes available to a real estate professional. If you spend more time in real estate activities than you do in your regular job and the number of hours in real estate exceeds 750 hours in a year, you can fully write off your real estate paper losses against other income—no matter how much money you make and no matter how much your paper losses are. Of course, Jean kept good records to document her real estate professional status, so she had no worries from an IRS audit.

Where is she now? Jean works one or two days per week in her medical practice and leases out the excess office space to another doctor who also pays a portion of the support staff expenses so she has passive income from her medical practice. The rest of her time is spent looking for more real estate deals. She has holdings in two states and even internationally. All of it puts money in her pocket each and every month. She pays less tax . . . and makes more money!

To paraphrase a popular saying:

If you think getting a financial education is expensive . . .
try ignorance.

Know Where Your Money Goes

As can be seen in the story about Jean, I do not advise my clients to create additional expenses just for the tax write-off. Instead, I advise them to first look at where they already spend money. They usually will look at the past three months' spending and take an average of their expenses to use as the monthly numbers. This can be a painful experience, as some of my clients have to come face-to-face for the first time with where their money really goes. Don't cheat yourself! Do this exercise accurately and with as much detail as you can. The more care you take, the better the results.

Your business must track income and expenses so your CPA can accurately prepare your tax return. But what do you do about your personal expenses? Our clients find more tax deductions and have better financial planning tools when they track their personal expenses as well as their business expenses. You can do this by using a bookkeeper or through a personal money-management software program.

I have discovered that clients who do not accurately track their personal expenses *always* and *without exception* shortchange themselves. They can't substantiate the deductions they can take and they simply don't remember many of them.

Take advantage of every deduction by knowing where *all* your money goes. See Chapter 3 for a form you can use to determine where you spend your income.

Financial Statements Made Easy

There are three financial statements that every business should use. Each of these serves a different purpose. Unfortunately, many people stop at one or maybe two statements when they look at a business.

Don't skip this section even if you don't have a business. A household is really a business. You want to know how your assets and liabilities look (balance sheet), how much income and expenses you have (income statement), and which way your cash is flowing (statement of cash flows).

Follow along on Figure 1.1 as we consider the elements of financial statements.

FIGURE 1.1   Financial Statements Made Easy

Financial Statements Made Easy

Personal
Financial Statement

INCOME STATEMENT

INCOME
Earned
Portfolio
Passive
EXPENSES
Tax
House
Car
Meals
Other

What's Left ⎯⎯⎯

BALANCE SHEET

ASSETS	**LIABILITIES**
Cash	Home Mortgage
Pension	Auto Payable
?	Credit Card
	Other
	EQUITY
	Net Worth

STATEMENT OF CASH FLOWS

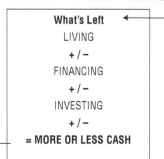

What's Left ◄⎯⎯
LIVING
+ / −
FINANCING
+ / −
INVESTING
+ / −
= MORE OR LESS CASH

Business
Financial Statement

INCOME STATEMENT

INCOME
Earned
Portfolio
Passive
EXPENSES
Home Office
Business Car
Business Meals
Other
Tax
What's Left ⎯⎯⎯

BALANCE SHEET

ASSETS	**LIABILITIES**
Cash	Liabilities of
Inventory	the Company
Accounts	
Receivable	
Real Estate	
Intellectual	**EQUITY**
Property	Net Worth

STATEMENT OF CASH FLOWS

What's Left ◄⎯⎯
OPERATIONS
+ / −
FINANCING
+ / −
INVESTING
+ / −
= MORE OR LESS CASH

Income Statement

In some cases when reviewing an investment you might be presented with an income statement only. The income statement is only one part of the financial statements. You *must* see all statements in order to get a full sense of the investment potential. The income statement is a great place to start, though!

The income statement shows the income and expense items for a specific period of time, whereas the balance sheet is a snapshot as of a certain date. The first thing to note on the income statement is the time period. Is it for a month, a year, or some other period? The income statement tells you the income that came in and the expenses that went out during this particular time.

Types of Income

Since the 1986 Tax Reform Act, the IRS has defined three different "buckets" of income. These three different buckets are taxed differently. There are also restrictions on losses and expenses that are incurred within those three categories. For example, in general, the amount of passive loss that you can take against earned income is limited.

The three types of income are: (1) earned, (2) portfolio, and (3) passive.

Earned income is the money you work for. It includes the wages from a job (even if the employer is your own company), net income from your sole proprietorship (not incorporated business), and income from your active involvement in a partnership.

Portfolio income is the money your money makes for you. This includes interest, dividends, and capital gains. There are both short-term and long-term capital gains, but both refer to the gain that your money makes for you. Short-term means you held the asset for less than one year. Long-term means you've held it longer.

Passive income is the income your investments make for you. The most common source of passive income is from real estate investments.

Earned income is the highest-taxed income there is. In 2004, the highest federal tax rate for earned income was 35 percent. But add in payroll taxes (or self-employment taxes, if you're in the wrong business structure) and you are looking at a tax rate of more than 40 percent!

Now, contrast that with the tax rate for portfolio income. Interest

---

Three Types of Income with Three Types of Taxes

Earned income: You work for the money—35 percent tax rate.

Portfolio income: Your money works for you—generally 15 percent tax rate.

Passive income: Your investments work for you—as low as 0 percent tax rate.

---

and short-term capital gains are taxed at the earned income tax rate, but without self-employment or payroll tax. The current highest federal tax rate for the majority of portfolio income—dividends and long-term capital gains—is 15 percent.

Passive income is the best kind of all! If you take advantage of all the real estate loopholes, such as maximizing depreciation, you can pay at 0 percent tax rate.

Where does your income currently come from? Which tax rate are you paying at? If you're like most Americans, most of your income is coming from earned income. That means you work hard for the money and you pay the highest possible tax rate.

Losses

Since 1986, U.S. tax laws have stated that losses can be claimed only against income in the same category. For example, passive losses can generally be used only against passive income. Investment expenses, such as for margin interest or investment education, can go only against portfolio income. Of course, this is a simplified version of a more complicated piece of tax law. For example, you are allowed up to $25,000 in real estate losses against other forms of income as long as your income does not exceed $100,000 per year. If your income is over $150,000 and unless you can qualify as a real estate professional, you will not be able to deduct your real estate losses against other income. The allowable real estate loss phases out when your income reaches an amount between $100,000 and $150,000.

Tax-Deferred and Tax-Free Income

As mentioned, the three types of taxable income are earned, portfolio, and passive. However, there are also two other types of incomes that you *don't* currently pay tax on. Tax-deferred tax means "tax later," while tax-free means "tax never." Sometimes, if you've set up your strategy right, tax-deferred can mean tax never. But remember, there is generally a day of tax reckoning on tax-deferred income.

Two common types of tax-deferred income are (1) like-kind exchange and (2) 401(k) plans.

Like-Kind Exchange

A like-kind exchange allows you to exchange one investment for another investment, under certain circumstances. There are like-kind provisions for life insurance policies, cars, equipment, and real estate. The real estate like-kind exchange, also known as a 1031 exchange or a Starker exchange, is probably the most common.

The like-kind exchange is described in Section 1031 of the Internal Revenue Code and is further defined in a court ruling, *Starker v. Commissioner*—hence the other names. This is a specific exchange of real estate that has been held for business or investment. You cannot do a Section 1031 like-kind exchange on your personal residence or on non-real estate items. A like-kind exchange allows you to sell a piece of property that is highly appreciated and roll over the gain into another piece of property. You don't pay tax on the sale now.

The second piece of property merely has to be another piece of investment real estate property. It does not need to be exactly the same kind of property. For example, you could exchange a single-family residential rental for a piece of commercial land. Or you could exchange an apartment building for a shopping center.

There are some rules for the like-kind exchange that must be closely followed. We strongly recommend that you have an exchange accommodator help you with the details of the exchange. An exchange accommodator is someone who comes from a specialized profession that only handles property exchanges. Neither your accountant nor your lawyer can fill this position for you. In general, you must declare three possible choices for the exchange within 45 days and you must close on the replacement property within 180 days. You need to invest all of the cash from the sale into the next property, and the next property must be purchased for at least as much as the sale price of the first property.

Recent tax law has given us a few more opportunities. For example, there is a method of holding title to property called "tenants-in-common" in which there is more than one owner. While you can't exchange an investment property for an interest in a partnership even if the partnership owns real estate, you can exchange an investment property for a group ownership property if the property is held as tenants-in-common.

Like-Kind Exchange Example

You have a rental property that you have owned for a number of years. You originally purchased it for $100,000 and you have accumulated depreciation of $40,000. That means your basis in the property is now $60,000 ($100,000 minus $40,000). You are offered $200,000 for the house and decide to sell. After the mortgage on the property of $55,000 and the cost of sale of $15,000 are paid, you would have net cash of $130,000. However, you would have tax due on the $125,000 gain on the property. And the $40,000 of recaptured depreciation is taxed at a higher rate. You decide to defer these taxes by making a like-kind exchange.

Cash Received

Sale price	$200,000
Cost of sale	(15,000)
Mortgage	(55,000)
Cash received	$130,000

Gain on Property

Sale price	$200,000
Cost of sale	(15,000)
Basis in property	(60,000)
Gain on property	$125,000

The new property would receive the rollover basis from the old property. If you buy a property for $200,000, your same basis will roll over. Depending on how the cost of sale is paid (through proceeds or through an additional deposit by the seller or the buyer), the cost of sale may additionally adjust the basis.

401(k) Plans

Another form of tax-deferred income is a 401(k) plan. (Most forms of pension plans are tax-deferred.) A deduction is made currently from your income for the contribution and then later you pay tax. That's what tax-deferred means—tax later.

I like the like-kind exchange plan for tax deferral in the right circumstances, but I'm not such a fan of the 401(k) plan. Here are the three reasons why I hesitate before recommending such a strategy for wealth building.

1. A 401(k) plan generally assumes that the values of the underlying mutual funds will go up. Well, we all know these funds don't always go up. In fact, the stock market moves up, it moves down, and it moves sideways. If you're a day trader, watching your stocks on a minute-by-minute basis, then you know you can make money, in fact a lot of money, when the stock market moves down. But most people in 401(k) plans are stuck with watching their funds *lose* money as they spiral down.

2. The typical reason given for using a pension plan is that you're going to make less money in the future. Well, the average American *is* likely to be making considerably less money in the future. I like to say that there are three financial plans that you can have for your future: a plan to be poor, a plan to be middle-class, or a plan to be rich. If you are looking at receiving less money in the future, you have a plan to be poor. My clients have a plan to be rich. So, an automatic deferral of income might not be the smartest thing. In fact, by the time we're done with all of the loopholes we discuss in this book you might be like my clients and find that you can pay a whole lot less tax right now. It doesn't make sense to defer income to the future when we don't know for sure what the tax loopholes will be.

3. The biggest reason of all to *not* use a 401(k) plan is that a 401(k) plan turns portfolio income into earned income. That means you are turning money taxed at 15 percent into money taxed at 35 percent. Here's how this works. If your 401(k) plan makes money, it will generally make money because of capital gains. That's because your mutual funds have gone up in value. Capital gains are taxed at a maximum rate of 15 percent. But, because the funds were held inside a pension plan, your tax rate may be as high as 35 percent or more when you take the money out!

You have more than doubled your tax rate. There is one way that this plan makes sense, however: If you plan to be poor you won't have the high tax rate. My guess, though, is if you're reading this book you have a plan to be rich! In that case, why double your tax rate?

Just to be fair, there are two reasons that a 401(k) plan might make sense.

1. If your employer is matching the funds you put in your plan, take the money! That's especially true if you can control where the money is invested.

2. If you're young enough, it doesn't matter if the tax rate is more than double when the money comes out. The tax deferral aspect allows your plan to continually reinvest money while the plan grows without paying tax. If you're 25 years old, deferring the tax on the principal amount within the plan means that you have more money working for you. However, if you are 50, you can't catch up and overcome the disadvantage of the rate.

How can you find out what is the right plan for you? Ask your CPA or financial planner. If they answer without doing a calculation or asking your age, say "thank you" and ask someone else. If you want to be average, get average advice. The rich get advice that is different.

Expenses on the Income Statement

If you are an employee without a business (even a part-time or weekends-only business), then your biggest and first expense is taxes. You pay for your expenses with after-tax money. It's possible to find some itemized deductions such as mortgage interest, property tax, charitable deductions, and the like. In fact, my web site, www.taxloopholes.com, lists the most common itemized deductions with loopholes hints to utilize those each year during tax season. As your income climbs, however, your itemized deductions phase out. (You take them but later have to add them back.) You'll also see that you lose the ability to benefit from exemptions for yourself, your spouse, and your dependents. And, the scariest news of all, the Alternative Minimum Tax (AMT) will begin to affect millions more Americans as incomes rise with inflation. Itemized deductions will be the main reason most people become affected by this alternative form of tax. Mortgage interest and state taxes are not fully deductible when calculating AMT.

The fact remains that if you're an employee, your first and greatest expense will be taxes.

If you have a business, or investments that you run like a business, you can take your legitimate tax deductions before you pay tax. That equals less tax, meaning more money in your pocket!

Balance Sheet

The balance sheet is a financial snapshot. It shows the assets, liabilities, and equity (net worth) of a person or a company at a given point in time. The equity is the value of the assets minus liabilities.

When we talk about the average 50-year-old American having a net worth of less than zero, that means that their liabilities (the amount they owe) are more than their assets (the value of what they own).

There are a number of problems for most individuals when they are preparing their own balance sheets (personal financial statements).

- They use overinflated values for assets. The asset value should be what you think you can sell it for if you had to sell it quickly.
- Most assets are illiquid. Cash is king. You can get to your cash quickly, and if there is a downturn in the economy you'll be fine. An investment in a business might actually be worth a great deal of money, but you have to find a buyer or bring in a cash partner to get to it.
- They think only of the asset value ("My house is worth $200,000!"), but they have forgotten the payments that are due, the cost to sell it, and the time it would take to do so.
- Most people have a net worth built entirely on personal assets. They proudly list their art collections, jewelry, automobiles, gun collections, and the like. Those might be nice collectible items, but they don't put any money in your pocket.
- Many people don't understand the difference between a debt that makes you money (good debt) and a debt that costs you money (bad debt). Good debt buys you an appreciating asset that creates cash flow. You can never get enough of that type of debt—it's called financial leverage. Bad debt buys you a depreciating asset. You continue paying long after the luster is gone.

Five Common Wealth-Building Mistakes

1. Overstating the value of assets.
2. Building assets with little liquidity.
3. Focusing on the asset and forgetting the underlying liability.
4. Building assets that are nothing more than materialistic possessions.
5. Failing to understand the difference between good debt and bad debt.

Take a look at your own assets and liabilities. Have you made any of these five common mistakes?

Statement of Cash Flows

The third type of financial statement is a statement of cash flows. These are not commonly prepared for small businesses, which I think is a real mistake as they are an excellent indicator of the strength of the business. Even worse, they are almost never prepared for an individual. A company could be making income (shown through the income statement) and yet go broke. And an individual could have money in an account and still be on the way to financial ruin. Here's an example of how a business could have a strong income statement and a solid balance sheet and go out of business.

The statement of cash flows is different from the other two statements—the balance sheet and the income statement—as the statement of cash flows starts with the net income and then adjusts from there. In Figure 1.1, look at how "What's Left" flows through to the top line of the statement of cash flows. The amount is then adjusted by cash that is provided (or taken by) operations, cash that is provided by (or taken by) financing, and cash that is provided by (or taken by) investing.

In Odetta's case, the operations section was taking all of her income. A statement of cash flows would show that the cash flow at the end was negative. That's a danger sign!

It's also a danger sign to see cash flow provided by extensive financ-

---

Success Almost Kills Business

Odetta's small retail store was growing at a phenomenal rate. She had clearly found a niche in the market with her customized aromatherapy business. She couldn't keep up with the demand for her customized formulas and so hired an assistant. Of course, the assistant now took more of her time during the training period but Odetta realized that was just part of the growing pains. She also had to keep ordering more and more essential oils to broaden her inventory. Odetta didn't have time to study her financial statements but had confidence in her accountant, who kept showing her an income statement as proof of the buckets of money she was making. Odetta kept going like that until one day she had a huge tax bill for her highly profitable business and no money to pay it. If she made so much money, where was it?

The problem was that Odetta had spent her cash flow building her inventory. The inventory was not a deduction, so she had a huge profit, but no cash. If Odetta had received, and reviewed, a statement of cash flows on a regular basis she would have been forewarned so she could have better controlled her cash depletion.

---

ing. That means you have some cash, but you're getting it by borrowing. Think of your home as a company. If you were an investor, would you invest money in your company?

Following is a line-by-line analysis you might want to use when you're looking at a financial statement from a company.

Account	Analysis Point
Net Income	Income as shown from the income statement.
Cash Flow from Operations	Changes will be made to the net income based on operations items. This would include adding back the depreciation, amortization, adjusting for increases/decreases in accounts

Cash Flow from Operations
(*Continued*)

payable and receivable. If this number is negative—a cash flow *to* operations—this isn't necessarily a bad thing. But you will want to note where the cash is coming from to fund the operations drain. Also, note *why* the operations are causing a drain in cash. Is this going to continue? Are there enough resources to continue funding?

One of the accounting scandals of 2001 had a large corporation capitalizing (treating as assets) items that should have been expensed. A review of the cash flow from operations would have shown a buildup in assets. If someone had questioned what those assets were and whether they really helped the business, the entire scandal might have been disclosed before so many people were financially impacted.

Cash Flow from Financing

This is a good indication of what is going on with the company. Is it building up debt to pay for operations? That might work as a short-term strategy, but at some point the operations need to provide enough positive cash flow to cover all expenses.

Cash Flow from Investing

Is the company buying or selling assets? This section generally will be utilized as the company matures. Watch for the company selling its investments. What has happened that it now needs cash? Or is it just selling because it is a smart time to take profits?

Real-Life Financial
Statement Assessment

Remember Ted and Ellen? Roughly my age, they had taken the employee route instead of the business building and real estate investing route that I had. The first step for them, determining their starting point, was the hardest one. They had never had to fully create, and then analyze, their financial statements. They had to learn a new language (the language of financial statements) and then face the hard truth of what the numbers told them.

In their case, they had some cash and personal assets such as nice cars, a residence, and furniture, and they had a great deal of bad debt. Their income was entirely earned income, so they paid the highest rate of tax. Their taxes were paid first and then their money to live on came out of what was left. Their statement of cash flows review was very simple. Their net income, what little there was of it, had no impact from operations (no business) or investments (no investments) but was increased by all of the financing they did. That meant they created cash for their living expenses based on credit card purchases.

As hard as it was for them to get through the first step, the creation of their own financial statements, it took even more strength to look at the analysis and result of what they had created. They had that courage, and that's what made all the difference in their lives and in the lives of their family.

Chapter 2

TEAM—BUILDING A TEAM THAT SUPPORTS YOU

Who Is on Your Team?

It was time for my second meeting with Ted and Ellen. In our first meeting, we had assessed their current financial status, set their goals, and created their personalized strategy to achieve their goals. And, right on cue, Ted had a concern.

"I was talking to my neighbor, who has a Harvard MBA, and I told him that we were probably going to do a corporation for my and Ellen's business. He said we shouldn't do that. I'm worried about what he said—after all, he's a Harvard MBA," Ted said at the beginning of our meeting.

"And," added Ellen, "I talked to my friend who is a stockbroker and she said that my new business wasn't a good idea. She said that I'd never make any money at it."

I paused a minute before I replied. I had heard these and other concerns so many times before. The issue was always centered on whom my client chose to take advice from.

"I'm glad that you are excited enough about your plans to talk to others about them. And you've found out one of the frequent consequences of doing that. People will often try to dissuade you. Actually, you've had it pretty easy. I've heard a lot worse!"

Crabs in a Box

There is a story I like to tell from my own experience growing up in Oregon called the "crabs in a box" story. One of our weekend activities would be to go to the Oregon coastline and go crabbing for Dungeness crabs.

There are specially designed crab traps that you bait and throw into the ocean from the docks. The traps lure the crabs through a funnel-like opening that lets them in but doesn't let them out. Meanwhile, you just wait on the dock, usually drinking coffee to keep warm against the cold Oregon rain. After a while, you pull up the crab trap to see your catch. You carefully pick up the crabs while watching out for those big front claws and, after measuring and checking the gender of the crabs, keep the legal ones. And this is where it gets interesting. As long as you have more than one crab, you can put them in a very shallow box. I've seen them kept in a box that is barely five inches high. You see, even though the crabs could easily climb out and escape back to the icy cold sea, they don't. That is because as soon as one starts to explore the route of freedom, the other crabs in the box pull it back in.

Many of our friends and advisors are like those crabs. They know where they are and it's familiar, even if it is just a box, and they're all in it together. They pull others back into the box because they don't want them to leave. Part of the desire to pull the others back is because they are afraid for them. And part of the desire is that they don't want to see the other guy succeed, because it would mean that they would have to change themselves also—it would be a challenge to their own complacency.

This is a common viewpoint in the human race. In fact, Australians have a saying about the "tall poppy." It is practically their moral responsibility to cut a friend down to size if the person starts rising above their present circumstances. In other words, they cut down the tall poppy.

Point of View

There are two main reasons why you might receive opposition as you bring about changes in your life. First, your friends or advisors can only see things from their own point of view. Second, change may be challenging to them and their own circumstances. You changing and growing may force them to confront things about their own situation that they do not want to look at.

Assume that you traveled from a small village to the top of a hill. From that vantage point, you can see the shining city that lies on the other side of the hill. The shining city can't be seen from the village, so when you travel back to the village, the people who live there tell you the shining city couldn't possibly exist. You saw it but only because you had first changed your point of view.

That's what happens to many people when they decide to make big changes in their lives. Perhaps they have talked to advisors who had different outlooks or maybe they have attended a seminar that opened up a range of possibilities to them. They then go back to their prior situation. They have seen what is possible and are excited about it. But people around them didn't have the opportunity to see the possibilities. They warn them that they can't achieve what they want, that it's impossible, that they won't succeed, or maybe even that it's illegal.

I am still amazed that when I make changes in my business life, I find myself going through the same cycle. Some people tell me I shouldn't make the changes, or that I cannot. I understand what is happening, and, just like my clients, I get feelings of self-doubt—am I doing the right thing?

If I step back for a moment, I recognize what is happening by the type of comments I hear from these people. They will say things such as "You didn't used to do it that way," "No one else does it like that," or "You will lose all your clients (friends)." You may have heard similar comments.

When You Hear "You Can't Do That!"

One way I respond to hearing negative comments regarding changes I am making is to go through the following mental review:

First, what has been the speaker's experience? People will speak from the point of view of their own experiences. If they have never had a successful business, or had a business that failed, they may feel that *you*

> Free advice may be the most expensive advice you ever get.

can't have a successful business. They will be telling you that *you* can't succeed, but the truth is that they don't think that *they* could succeed.

Second, what is their comment really saying? For example: "You didn't used to do it that way" could mean that they are afraid of change. Or "No one else does it like that" could mean that they are afraid to be different. Or "You will lose all your clients (friends)" could mean that they are afraid to change themselves because *they* might experience those losses. Or it could mean that they are afraid that your relationship with them will change.

If you hear critical comments from friends or advisors, keep them in perspective, and in this case, look at *their* perspective. Do they know all the facts regarding your personal circumstances? Many times friends who *think* they know all about you in actuality do not. If they don't know all the facts, can they really advise you?

Do You Really Need a Team?

Can you do your own accounting and tax planning? Absolutely. In fact, in the beginning you may want to take care of the bookkeeping yourself, provided you are able to keep good records.

If you don't work directly with a personal advisor, make sure you do have access to an expert to check in with. For example, you might want to have an accountant or full charge bookkeeper review your accounting at year-end.

Particularly if you are just beginning in your business, the tax strategy of selecting the right business structure and finding your own hidden business deductions might also be something you can do yourself. Again, though, we recommend that you have an expert with whom you can discuss the implications. Attend seminars, read books, listen to tapes, and attend classes to get the information you need to create a basic plan. We offer a special on-line mentorship for beginning businesses and real estate investors that provides virtual classes and gives you the ability to ask us about specific items related to tax strategies and asset protection for an entire year. A program like that might be the best solution to keep costs down in the beginning.

> The three most expensive words in the English language are "Do it yourself."—Tom Wheelwright, managing partner, DKAdvisors

Doing it yourself might make sense for you in the beginning with your new business, but it generally isn't advisable as a long-range strategy. As your business and investments grow, you will likely find that the most expensive person in your business is you! If you have the need to control all of the business, then everything will need to go through you. You become the bottleneck in the growth of your business. If you want to grow, you need a team that supports your goals!

Who's on Your Team Now?

List the people you spend the most time with—your family, friends, co-workers, and so on. Try to list at least five people. Now, next to each person's name, write the experience this person has had in what you want to achieve. For example, if you want to achieve financial freedom by successfully investing in real estate that provides cash flow, you must determine what experience this person has in real estate. Do they personally have real estate that provides good cash flow? Have they achieved, or advised others who have achieved, financial freedom? Do they have the business and financial success that you want?

After you prepare the list, look at it with a critical eye. Are these people the advisors you need for the next step on your personal path to financial freedom? Do they have the needed experience to support your decisions and critically analyze them?

Five People with Whom I Spend the Most Time

Name	Business Experience
_____	_____
_____	_____
_____	_____
_____	_____
_____	_____

Who Do You Want on Your Team?

Different goals mean different team members. First, determine the type of people you need on your team. For example, your business may need the following specialties:

Insurance Specialists

General insurance.
Life insurance.
Health insurance.
Disability insurance.
Errors and omissions insurance.
Liability insurance.
Umbrella insurance.

Accounting Specialists

Tax strategist (for your personalized loopholes strategy).
Bookkeeper.
Accounts payable clerk.
Accounts receivable clerk.
Payroll clerk.
Accountant.
Certified public accountant.
Cost accountant.
Auditor.

Corporation Specialists

Corporate administration.
Corporate setup.

Legal Specialists

Transactional (contracts) attorney.
Intellectual property attorney.
Real estate attorney.

Financial Specialists

Banker.

Financial consultant.

Leasing company representative.

Credit advisor.

Investment advisor.

Hard money lender.

You might choose to fill some of those roles yourself in the beginning. But make sure you carefully record the functions that you perform and create step-by-step systems as you go. At some point, you'll want to turn over the work to someone else. Make sure your replacement fully understands what you have done and the outcomes you want to achieve.

How Do You Find the Right Advisors?

I am asked some version of this question almost daily. Here are some ideas to get you started.

- Check with local licensing boards (bar association for lawyers, state board for accountants, and so forth).
- Ask other business owners.
- Look for articles in the newspaper written by professionals and contact the authors.
- Once you find one professional you like, such as a lawyer, ask that individual for the names of a good insurance agent and any other professionals you're looking for.
- Seek out people who have achieved success and ask them for recommendations for advisors.

One more hint: Think outside the box!

When I'm asked, "How can I find a CPA who thinks like you in my hometown?," I always answer, "Why do you need to work with a CPA in your hometown?" In today's age of e-mail, phone, and fax, we work with clients all over the country. If you can widen the horizons of your possible candidates, you will find the experienced advisors to partner with you on your road to financial success.

Evaluating Your Advisors

Once you have your list of potential advisors pulled together, it is vital that you assess their ability and interest in working with you. Complete an Advisor Checklist for each potential advisor for your team. (See Figure 2.1.)

Take the time to go through this checklist with each potential team member. The checklist will walk you through determining each person's experience in the area of the goals you seek. Most people use only one question—whether the person has the requisite credentials—to determine if the advisor is right for them. But your advisors are subject to the same issue of point of view discussed earlier in the chapter. The most effective team for you will be one that includes advisors who have the correct skills, credentials, and personal experience to help you achieve your goals.

And once you have your group of advisors, it doesn't stop there. The only way to get different results is to do things differently. Your new advisors, if they themselves are financially successful, will be able to give you guidance in new ways of doing things. You will get the best results when you thoughtfully consider and act on the advice you receive from well-chosen advisors.

Building Your Team

You've identified who is on your team now; you've found new team members, assessed their abilities, and kept the ones who can help you reach your dreams. Now what? It's only the beginning. Now you need to get the results you want from your team.

The best results come from building strong relationships with your experts so you all work at the highest level and with the greatest commitment.

Most of my experience in this area has come from being someone else's team member in helping them achieve their goals of more wealth,

FIGURE 2.1 Advisor Checklist

Advisor Checklist

For each advisor you add to your team, ask the following questions. You might want to complete a form for each member of the team. When you complete the checklist you are making a conscious decision about each member. The more you are conscious and focused on what you want, the more easily and quickly you will get what you want.

1. What role will this advisor perform as part of your team?

Experience
2. How much experience does this advisor have in delivering the specific results you are seeking?
3. What experience does he/she have with the specific issues you will have?
4. What is the average income and business experience of his/her clientele? (Is this where you want to be?)

Personal Viewpoint
5. Does this advisor personally have experience in your proposed outcome?
6. Is he/she at an income/wealth level that is similar to where you want to be?

Education
7. Does this advisor have the educational requirements for the role?
8. Does he/she have the necessary professional credentials for this role?

Compensation
9. How is this advisor compensated? (flat fee, product sale, hourly)
10. Does he/she have a vested interest in helping you achieve your desired outcome?

Responsibility
11. Does this advisor assume any responsibility?
    (The highest degree of responsibility will come from the person who signs the income tax return or gives you an opinion letter regarding a plan. These people put their credentials on the line.)

Client Contact
12. How does this advisor maintain contact with clients, and how often? (proactive, reactive)
13. Will this response time work for you?
14. Is this someone you feel you can trust and be honest with?

Your Needs
15. What can this advisor do to help you meet your goals?
16. Are you looking for someone you can model?
17. Do you expect to be educated by this advisor?
18. If yes to #16 or #17, how would this advisor do this?

Advisor Organization
19. Does the advisor have an organization that supports achieving your goals or is he/she working alone?

less tax, and reduced risk from frivolous lawsuits. In fact, I've been doing it now for more than 25 years. From that perspective, I've seen what works, and what doesn't work, when you're working with professional consultants.

There are five things you can do to help your professional deliver huge results for you.

1. Establish trust.
2. Learn your advisor's language.
3. Give your advisors all the information they need.
4. Ask only powerful questions.
5. Quickly make corrections if something goes wrong.

Establish Trust

Failure to trust your advisors can be a big stumbling block to some people. It might mean that you don't trust the other person to have your best interests at heart, or it could be that you don't trust them to do the job right.

I remember a story I once heard from another entrepreneur. His company could land two large projects if the presentations were good enough. This would make a significant financial difference to this company. However, the owner could not completely oversee preparation of the presentation while still maintaining his daily workload. For the first time, he had to rely on someone other than himself. He left one person in charge of the final run-through so that he could attend a seminar. But his head wasn't in the seminar. Everyone knew that his thoughts were still back at the office. The person he left in charge had been with the company for a while and was talented, reliable, and competent. But this was the biggest deal he'd ever seen. And it wasn't just one deal—it was two.

As the owner continued to worry about his office and the unknown status of the projects, someone finally said to him, "You haven't really turned the project over unless you can allow them to fail."

For those of us who value perfection that might be the hardest statement you've ever had to read. Can you trust your team members enough to let go of a project and allow it to fail?

Now, here's the good news. If you've done your homework with first testing the point of view and experience of your advisors, you don't have to be able to let your project fail. You have to be able to let it succeed! And you have to be able to let the project succeed far better under their guidance than it would have under your guidance. The question isn't whether you are prepared for failure. It's whether you are prepared for success.

When people tell me that they can't trust others, what they are really saying is that they can't trust themselves.

If you want good advisors, you'll have to let them do their jobs. A quality team member who is used to working with successful people is used to being trusted. Frankly, they won't tolerate anything less. The best advisors want you to win; that's how they win, too!

Learn Your Advisor's Language

Does it seem like lawyers and accountants have their own language? Well, we do!

If you want the best results from your advisors, learn to speak the language that they do. At my firm, we generally schedule appointments with our clients in half-hour or one-hour blocks. The strategy results for the clients differ largely based on their knowledge. I could spend an entire hour talking about the basics of business structures . . . or we could talk strategies using business structures that put money in the client's pocket immediately. The difference between the two results—gaining education at a high per hour price or implementing loopholes strategies that produce immediate results—is due to the knowledge and ability of the clients to understand the strategies.

Clients ask me whether they should purchase and listen to tax education products if they're planning on asking me the questions in our next appointment anyway. I always tell them to listen to the tapes or read the books. If my client already has the basic foundation, then we can immediately begin discussing the fun things!

You alone are responsible for your own financial well-being. And no one will ever care about your business as much as you do. You must understand the basics of financial literacy if you want to communicate effectively with your advisors. The more you understand the big picture of your finances, the more success you will have.

In fact, after you understand how your personal financial statement works, you will begin to see that you can read other people's stories by reading their personal financial statements as well. You can see in a moment what their future will be—riches or bankruptcy. You will also be able to tell the financial story behind a business or investment you are thinking of making. You will be able to tell where the problems are and assess whether it is realistic for you to think that you can correct those problems to create wealth. Plus, you can see how that financial statement will blend with your own and how it will impact it either positively or negatively. That knowledge all starts with you learning the financial language of accountants.

Give Your Advisors All the Information They Need

Your advisors should ask you more questions than you ask. That's the sign of a good advisor—knowing the questions to ask. They should ask you what your goals are and when you want to achieve them. Additionally, they will need to see your current financial statements and additional backup information as they request.

It might seem like they are asking the same question multiple times. Be patient. Give them the information they need! The better they understand where you are now and where you are going, the better their advice will be.

My husband and I are very active real estate investors. We generally buy one property per month. That means we have a very active file with our mortgage broker. And occasionally it seems like he requests information on properties that he already has. But we always get the information to him within an hour of his request. That's because the easier we make his job, the better our results will be.

Give your advisors all the information they need and want!

Ask Only Powerful Questions

One of the best questions I was ever asked at a seminar prompted this whole section. I was in Los Angeles when a young new entrepreneur asked me if there was something I could see immediately that told me whether a person was going to achieve his or her goals of wealth. In a flash, I knew there *was* something different that I could tell within 5 minutes of meeting a person.

It had to do with the quality of the questions they asked. A powerful question is one that starts with "How can I . . ." and clearly defines what the outcome is. For example, "How can I protect from frivolous lawsuits my three residential rental properties located in California with a combined net worth of $600,000?" is a very powerful question. Since it might be a little too long, it would be equally effective to first state the facts: "I own three residential rental properties in California with a combined net worth of $600,000. How can I protect them from frivolous lawsuits?" You've now given your tax strategist or lawyer the opportunity to explore the issues related to (1) the state in which the properties are located, (2) the large amount of equity in the properties, (3) the risk associated with three properties, and (4) the income tax, estate planning, and asset protection issues of the property.

Contrast this with a limiting question such as "How do I put my property in a limited liability company (LLC)?" or "How do I change the title on a property in order to put it in a limited partnership (LP)?" I can answer those questions, and do regularly. The problem is the person asking the question might have just read an answer into my response that would be very dangerous for the questioner. Maybe they shouldn't put their property into an LLC. I can tell them how to change the title on the property, but doing so might void their title insurance, create gift or estate problems, and/or trigger the due on sale clause on their mortgage on the property. The problem with these types of questions is that they presume a solution and the asker is merely asking for procedure.

One of the keys is learning whom to ask and how to ask. If you want to know procedures of bookkeeping, ask a bookkeeper. If you want to know how to transfer a title, ask a title company or legal representative. If you want a strategy that minimizes taxes and protects assets, ask a tax strategist.

There is also the issue of confidentiality to consider when you discuss your financial, business, and tax strategies. Most people are aware of attorney-client privilege. But few are aware of the related privilege that CPAs can have on tax-related matters. There are some important distinctions, though. In the case of CPAs, the privilege extends only to tax-related matters and varies from state to state. Talk to your CPA to find out what the state law is in your area. One solution that many people use is to have their attorney hire the CPA. In this way, the communication and work with their CPA falls within the attorney-client privilege. No one else has the right to call your strategy confidential or privileged because they can be subpoenaed. I have seen and heard other people (corporate setup specialists, for example) call their services confidential, but the plain fact is that

---

Best Results Come from Powerful Questions

- Don't ask limiting questions.
- Ask the right person the right question.
- Protect the confidentiality of your financial matters.
- Don't ask what-if questions.
- Your advisor should ask more questions than you do.

---

confidentiality won't stand up to a court challenge unless they are CPAs (in some states), attorneys, or CPAs who have been hired by attorneys.

Consider the relevance of your questions. The most exhausting questions, which have absolutely no point, are the what-if questions asked by people who have no real experience and often don't understand the terminology.

A good advisor has had personal success and so knows intimately what works and what doesn't work. Spending your time and your advisor's time on what-if situations that are unlikely to come to fruition is a waste of time. Make the best use of your time and resources by being focused on what you want and by considering the likely challenges you will face. Once you have addressed those and have a plan on how to move forward with confidence, let the what-if scenarios go.

The best advisors know what they need to know. As mentioned before, they should ask you more questions than you ask them. If you've properly assessed the quality of your advisors before you began working with them, now is the time to sit back and listen so you can take advantage of their knowledge to help you grow your wealth and take you on the path to your dreams.

Quickly Make Corrections If Something Goes Wrong

Life is what happens when you're making other plans, so the saying goes. Things often don't turn out as you anticipated. Sometimes that is because you made mistakes or wrong assumptions and sometimes it is just life happening that gets in the way. The way you live your life, the extent to which you enjoy it, and the success you have will be all about how you handle those unintended results that come up. There are three basic ways all of us can handle them: blame, justify, or take responsibility.

Blame

You can always spot the person who avoids responsibility by assigning blame. They have a lot of "story" around why something didn't happen as they wanted, and it's always someone else's fault. I bet you, like me, have heard the same story many times: "I'd be rich, if it weren't for my wife. She won't let me invest in anything." Or "My husband just doesn't have any insight into these things. He'd never understand." People who deal with unintended results by laying blame can't ever get beyond what stopped them from getting the result they wanted. In fact, they can't ever get the lesson and see what they could do differently.

In every case, the person who makes these kinds of statements will ultimately blame team members for their personal financial failure. You see the same thing with people who become rich and then suddenly have nothing. Very few of them ever say they didn't plan well or that they selected poor advisors; instead they are the first to blame their advisors for their loss of fortune. Those same people, if they ever get their wealth back, will lose it again because they haven't examined themselves.

My experience has taught me to be careful around people who deal in blame. If they deal from this mode, they are simply not going to grow beyond it. Another reason, and a more practical one, is that I know that no matter what we do or how well we do it, there will always be unintended results. That's how life works. I personally don't like being near someone who practices blame when there are unintended results—I might get caught in the crossfire! This is not a productive behavior to practice or to receive! Most good advisors simply refuse to take this kind of person on as a client.

By the way, there may be times when you have a situation that clearly is a result of someone else's obvious actions against you. In that case, there is blame if you want to assess it. But instead, is there a way to look at the lesson in this so that you can be sure you don't repeat it? Maybe you didn't select the best advisor. How can you make sure you do next time? Maybe there were some circumstances that occurred that you hadn't planned for. How can you plan for them next time? It is from the things that don't work that we learn the most.

Justify

I recently heard someone justify why he wasn't rich. I was at a seminar and the person next to me muttered his own justification under his breath, when the room was challenged to explore why they didn't have the financial freedom they wanted. My neighbor's response to the challenge was, "I could be rich, except I decided to take a more spiritual path." In other words, he used a spiritual viewpoint as an excuse for not being wealthy. His comment also contained an unspoken criticism of anyone who was rich—he believed they couldn't be spiritual at the same time. The next time you hear someone say something as a justification for why they can't have something you think is possible, listen to what they are really saying. Chances are there is a statement within it—a kernel—that isn't true, and that is the part that is so grating. In fact, I know very spiritual people who are wealthy. I have a friend who has made a good living out of being what he calls a "social entrepreneur." He's touched a lot of lives positively with his for-profit business in a way that no nonprofit business had been able to.

Everyone has different goals and priorities, and that's one of the things that make life so interesting. It's okay to choose different goals than someone else, but don't lie to yourself in the process.

Another example of justification I heard one time was "I would be rich except that I don't have the education that is needed." In some cases, people might use justifying as a way to stop themselves without even knowing they do so. The person who justifies will, like the person who blames, not be able to learn from their unintended results. But in the case of the justifiers, they don't even get in the game, and they use justifying as their excuse for not doing so.

I don't see people who justify in my practice, because they haven't yet reached the point where they want to move forward.

Take Responsibility

The final behavioral type comes from the kind of person we all like to emulate. In my opinion, they are the true heroes of humankind. These are the people who step up and take responsibility. This doesn't mean that they blame themselves (that would just be blame directed at themselves instead of others). No, it means they recognize that something didn't work and they keep going. They are like Thomas Edison, who said, when asked if he was discouraged by his failures, that he was not. In fact, he said he had not failed, he had just discovered numerous ways that something didn't work. If he had indulged in blame or justification, he would never have gone on to make the inventions he did.

Where Is Your Advisor Leading You?

A few years ago a new client named Jeff come in to see me. As Jeff explained his goals, the story of why he had left his previous CPA came out.

His former CPA was a great guy and a good friend. It was always fun to go visit him. How many people can say that about their CPAs? As Jeff walked into his former CPA's office for what would turn out to be his last appointment, though, the CPA exclaimed, "Jeff, I am always so glad to see you. Do you know that you are the richest person I know?"

Suddenly Jeff realized why the advice that he had been receiving was contrary to the loopholes strategies he had read about. His advisor was giving him the same advice he gave his other clients, who wanted to have a middle-class existence. That advice was not the advice that Jeff wanted. He learned, in that moment, that the advice you get from your advisors is colored by their experience and point of view.

Now, two years later, Jeff's business has expanded to three states and he has plans to bring in investors to build it even further. He has invested in real estate that provides positive cash flow. Even better, although his business has grown, his taxes are less.

The client who regularly takes responsibility for his or her own actions is a joy and an inspiration to be around. I look forward to those appointments and they get my full attention because I am inspired, energized, and enthused by being around these people. I know that they get the same results from everyone else around them, because they have the tangible results of their improvement in all aspects of their lives. This is the best way to build a team to support you!

The team you build consciously and thoughtfully can be the most important asset you have. Make the most of this asset you build to grow your financial future!

Chapter 3

EVALUATION— CONSTRUCTING A TAX LOOPHOLES STRATEGY

How Do You Get What You Want?

After you know what you really want, the next step is figuring how to get there. The third step on your way to financial freedom is evaluating your situation and developing a strategy to get you moving on the path to your goals.

What are your financial goals? Our clients have had goals such as:

- Providing a safe cushion for my family.
- Increasing my passive income by $10,000 all the way to $100,000 per month.
- Reducing my tax liability by 30 to 50 percent.
- Protecting my assets.
- Retiring in five years with a net income of $50,000 to $1 million per year.

Make sure your advisors know your goals before you start creating a plan. Don't assume that they know what you want.

And, hopefully, you've also asked your advisors what plan they will use to evaluate where you are. If they don't have a systematic approach to reviewing your data, you will likely have a very customized approach.

This means the process will be more expensive and the results will be untested. And, that means more cost and more risk.

If you're ready to move forward on your own tax-advantaged wealth-building plan, start with an evaluation of where you are and what goals you have. Figure 3.1 is a copy of the First Step Financial Profile that we use in working with clients. Reference the information we receive as you follow along with the evaluation for Ted and Ellen. How does your information compare? What are your goals? Make sure your advisor understands and supports those goals for you. Otherwise, the strategy you receive won't help you achieve what you want.

Evaluating Where You Are

I like to use the Jump Start! method to evaluate current financial strategies. This method looks at the three major components for tax-advantaged wealth building:

1. Business.
2. Real estate.
3. Home.

There are seven steps in a comprehensive Jump Start! plan that are demonstrated in Figure 3.2.

The plan begins with a business. Not everyone wants to have a business, and it is possible to build wealth without owning a business. However, if you want to maximize tax loopholes and your own wealth potential, consider starting a business. That's where the loopholes are!

Under the business component, there are three specific steps. Step 1 identifies the loopholes available for the income that flows into the business. Step 2 identifies the loopholes of tax-free benefits for you that are a deduction for the business. Step 3 is to pay your taxes! But you'll pay your taxes using every legal method to first reduce the amount you pay and then defer the payment as long as possible.

We will now focus our attention on real estate loopholes. Step 4 identifies the ways you can invest money from your business into real estate to provide the best possible advantage. Step 5 utilizes the tremendous real estate loopholes to take money out of your real estate tax-free!

FIGURE 3.1   First Step Financial Profile

First Step Financial Profile

Businesses and Real Estate Investment Profile

Describe your businesses, real estate investments, stocks, bonds, mutual funds, and all liquid assets such as checking, savings, and money market accounts. As with all parts of this document, it is vital that each section is accurate and complete for best results.

List business and investment names	Specify ownership (LLC, S-corp, etc.)	What kind of business is this?	Date started or purchased?	Who specifically owns the business/ investments? List percentage owned by you, spouse/others	Taxable Income Last Year	Projected Taxable Income This Year

Rate the following items, indicating their importance to you.

Rate each area on a scale from 1 to 5 (5 being the most important):

____ Protect my assets   ____ Maintain safe, secure investments

____ Minimize taxes   ____ Build a real estate portfolio

____ Implement wealth velocity strategies   ____ Provide future benefits to family

State your specific financial goals and objectives:

_____

_____

_____

_____

_____

_____

(Continued)

FIGURE 3.1 *(Continued)*

With regard to achieving your goals and objectives, indicate the time frame in which you would like to take action:

❏ 0–3 months—Establish tax strategies

❏ 3–6 months—Take significant action

❏ Next 12 months—Implement plans

❏ Next 5 years—Expand wealth plans

Your Priorities

On a scale of 1 to 20 (1 being most important), rank the following according to their importance to you:

____ Expand and grow my business by (Date) _____

____ Develop investment strategies by (Date) _____

____ Invest in real estate by (Date) _____

____ Invest in stocks, bonds and mutual funds by (Date) _____

____ Increase my cash flow by (Date) _____

____ Create $__/month in passive income by (Date) _____

____ Get more organized financially by (Date) _____

____ Set goals and achieve them by (Date) _____

____ Reduce and eliminate bad debt by (Date) _____

____ Cut my tax bill by (Date) _____

____ Create an exit strategy for my business by (Date) _____

____ Acquire or sell a business by (Date) _____

____ Improve my asset protection plan by (Date) _____

____ Update my estate plan by (Date) _____

____ Pay for my children's education by (Date) _____

____ Retire by (Date) _____

____ Develop personal financial planning strategies by (Date) _____

____ Establish a better financial team by (Date) _____

____ Other _____

____ Other _____

FIGURE 3.1   *(Continued)*

What Do You Want?

What are your dreams and goals? Tell us about your specific short- and long-term dreams and goals; include "Achieve by" date.

1. _____   Achieve by: _____

2. _____   Achieve by: _____

3. _____   Achieve by: _____

4. _____   Achieve by: _____

5. _____   Achieve by: _____

6. _____   Achieve by: _____

7. _____   Achieve by: _____

8. _____   Achieve by: _____

9. _____   Achieve by: _____

10. _____   Achieve by: _____

Specific Questions

Please list your specific tax, business, and financial management questions or concerns.

1. _____

2. _____

3. _____

4. _____

5. _____

6. _____

7. _____

8. _____

9. _____

10. _____

(Continued)

FIGURE 3.1   *(Continued)*

How Do You Spend Your Personal Income?

Instructions: For each of the following items, enter the *average amount* you pay per month. These are expenses you currently *do not deduct* in a business. Do not include business expenses.

Note: You can substitute your personal expense list from a software package, if applicable.

	$ Amount		$ Amount
Auto and Truck Expenses		**Personal Health Expenses**	
Child Care Expenses		Dental Work	
		Glasses/Exam	
Education Expenses		Health Club	
Books & Tapes		Hearing Aids	
Dues and Subscriptions		Massage	
Seminars		Medical Co-Payments	
Travel		Medical Insurance	
		Prescriptions	
Entertainment Expenses		Therapy	
Travel			
Vacations		**Home Office Expenses**	
Equipment Expenses			
Computer			
Computer Software			

Your Current Real Estate Portfolio
Complete the following for current real estate you own. Include your personal residence.

Property	State	Purpose (e.g., future development, rental, vacation, home)	Fair Market Value	Mortgage

FIGURE 3.2   Jump Start! Your Wealth

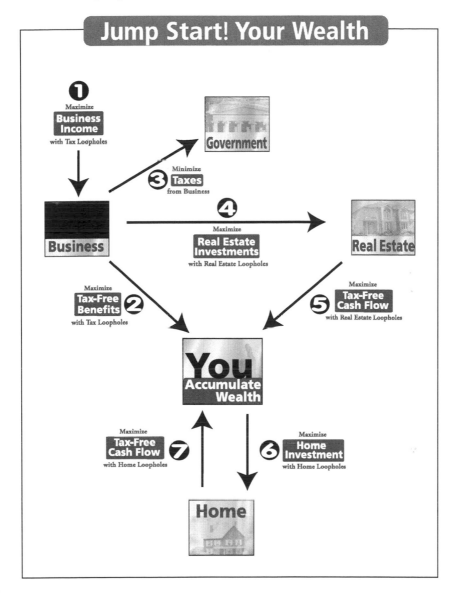

Everyone needs a place to live. And now there's a way to make your house pay you, instead of the other way around. That's what Steps 6 and 7 deal with—the home loopholes. Step 6 strategies maximize home loopholes to buy the property in the smartest way. Step 7 then examines the advantages of home loopholes to put money in your pocket.

When we conduct the strategy evaluation, we want to look at each area of the seven steps of loopholes to make sure you're maximizing all of them. Later in the book, we walk through each part of this, step by step, so you can create your own Jump Start! plan.

In the next few pages, we review the process that we used to first evaluate and then determine a strategy for Ted and Ellen. The review has been formatted in terms of the Jump Start! method.

Evaluation for Ted and Ellen

Ted and Ellen first needed to set their goals and then needed to look at where they spent their money to determine potential tax loopholes. After they completed the First Step Financial Profile we fully understood what their goals were and where their money went. It's important to complete this first assessment before you begin to create a strategy. First, know where you are; then, figure out where you want to be; and finally, create the strategy that gets you there!

Ted had already begun a small consulting business part-time. Ellen was considering starting a business and then investing in real estate.

One of the most important goals for them was to grow their passive income. They felt owning real estate and growing a business would accomplish this. They identified the amount of passive income that they wanted and worked on the business strategy to help them accomplish their goals.

I was happy to hear that they had included starting a business in their plans. Government incentives to promote public policy are written for business owners and investors. Any other so-called loopholes phase out as income increases or are completely negated by the Alternative Minimum Tax.

Step 1—Creating Income

Step 1 reviews the tax loopholes involved in how Ted makes money in his business and how Ellen plans to make money in her new business venture.

As a computer consultant, Ted makes a monthly income in excess of all of the deductions that we anticipate taking. Currently, he is taxed as sole proprietorship. If you haven't selected a business structure, the IRS selects one for you—the sole proprietorship. If you have a partner, the default business structure is that of a general partnership. In both cases, the taxable income will be reported on your personal tax return and you will have to pay self-employment tax in the amount of 15.3 percent.

In Ted's case, his business structure (or actually lack of a business structure) meant he paid an extra $3,000 per year in self-employment tax. That was our first order of business: get the right business structure to reduce taxes. In Ted's case, we set up an S corporation so that the income would flow through directly to him. He took part of the income out in the form of salary, on which he then paid payroll taxes, and the rest in the form of a distribution. The distribution would not be subject to payroll taxes, only income tax.

Ellen was just beginning to explore possible business choices. She tried a number of things but ultimately ended up running an eBay business after she cleaned out their garage and put the items up for sale on eBay. It worked! She then helped her mother clean out her house and put the items up for sale on eBay, and she and her mother split the proceeds. Ellen then searched out other sources for products to sell on the Internet and found a retail business down the street from her house that was interested in selling its discontinued household products. She worked out a great deal for buying the products on consignment and started selling. Ellen's first question regarding business income was whether she even had a real business!

We reviewed the nine factors used by the IRS to determine if a business is legitimate and decided that once she made the connection with the retailer, she had made the commitment to have a business and began running the business like a real business. The nine criteria that the IRS uses for determining a real business are:

1. Do you carry on the activity in a businesslike manner?

2. Do the time and effort you put into the activity indicate you intend to make it profitable?

3. Do you depend on income from the activity for your livelihood?

4. Are your losses due to circumstances beyond your control (or are they normal in the start-up phase of your type of business)?

5. Do you change your methods of operation in an attempt to improve profitability?

6. Do you, or your advisors, have the knowledge needed to carry on the activity as a successful business?

7. Were you successful in making a profit in similar activities in the past?

8. Does the activity make a profit in some years? (How much profit it makes is also considered.)

9. Can you expect to make a future profit from the appreciation of the assets used in the activity?

Ellen was able to prove that she was serious about her business, and although there was a business loss in the beginning, she was confident that she would soon turn it around to create a profit.

We decided to set up an S corporation for Ellen's new venture. This allowed her losses to flow through to their personal tax return where they were able to offset some of Ted's income.

Tax savings total from Step 1 loopholes: $1,500.

Step 2—Hidden Business Deduction

We next determined the hidden business deductions for both Ted's and Ellen's businesses. To do this, we reviewed the "How Do You Spend Your Personal Income?" portion of their First Step Financial Profile. A copy of this form is more fully discussed at Chapter 9 as part of the Jump Start! Your Wealth method.

We reviewed the general business deductions to make sure Ted and Ellen took advantage of standard deductions such as inventory items sold, computer, software, advertising, and contractors. We also looked at the items that they currently paid for with after-tax money. In other words, as employees, they made their money, paid their taxes, and then paid all their expenses with what was left. But, as business owners, they would make the money, pay the business expenses, and then pay tax on what is left. The difference is that the business owner will pay much less tax.

In the case of Ted and Ellen, we discovered another $10,000 in expenses in the form of business use of an automobile; meals out; educational expenses such as books, tapes, and subscriptions; employing a child in the business; and travel. Their current tax rate is approximately

30 percent, so the extra deductions saved them $3,000. If they had formed a C corporation for Ted's business, we would have been able to take a few more additional tax-free benefits as well. However, the S corporation was a better choice for Ted because it allowed him to reduce his payroll taxes.

Tax savings total from Step 2 loopholes: $3,000.

Step 3—Pay Your Taxes!

We now looked at some smart strategies for paying Ted and Ellen's taxes. One strategy for paying your taxes is to use a business structure that has a different year-end than you personally do. In other words, you would use a C corporation with a year-end date of anything other than December 31. In the case of Ted and Ellen, this won't work because they both will form S corporations. The S corporations generally must have a December 31 year-end.

However, we were able to project a total annual tax savings of $4,500 immediately from Steps 1 and 2. As they grow their businesses, we'll be able to take advantage of even more loopholes. Meanwhile, they know that they will be able to have an additional $4,500. They could wait until they file their tax return and get the refund from the IRS. But that's the equivalent of giving the government an interest-free loan. That's not good business! So, instead, we had Ted and Ellen change their withholding certificates at work so that they had $4,500 less withheld from their checks. If they had been currently paying estimated tax payments, we would have reduced those amounts instead. Generally, I don't recommend that you use estimated tax payments as a way to pay additional taxes if you can instead have the additional amounts withheld directly from paychecks. If you use the estimated tax payment method, your quarterly payments will be tracked and if you underpay one quarter, you face interest penalties per quarter. On the other hand, if you use payroll withholding, there is no underpayment penalty as long as you meet the minimum requirements. In most cases, the minimum tax payment requirements are 90 percent of the current year's tax or 100 percent of the prior year's tax.

Total savings from Step 3 loophole: $225 (based on an assumed return of 10 percent on $4,500, earned equally throughout the year).

Step 4—Invest in Real Estate

Ted and Ellen needed some of the income they earned from their businesses, so they weren't fully able to take advantage of this strategy. For now, they made the decision to begin looking for a single-family property that they could rent out. This would start them on the road to creating passive income from real estate rentals.

We discussed the different ways you could make money from real estate. Some examples of that are: commercial rental properties, multifamily residential rental properties, fix-up properties (later put up for sale), development, raw land held for appreciation, and the like. They wanted property that required a lower down payment to begin and offered good tax benefits and depreciation. The single-family residence was the best fit for their plan.

One of the traps for new investors is the excitement they feel when they see all the real estate possibilities. The problem isn't lack of opportunities. The risk is actually choking on opportunities. The fix-up properties (also known as "flips") weren't a good solution because they would require much more hands-on work; in addition, after the property was sold, they would have to start over. They would miss out on the tax benefits of long-term ownership.

Raw land would not give them depreciation deductions. Property development was outside of their core competencies, and the down payment requirement for a multifamily or commercial property was more then they could currently handle.

Step 5—Tax-Free Money from Real Estate

Ted and Ellen weren't ready for this step yet. Once they had purchased their first property we would then be looking for all the techniques to ways that real estate creates value.

Immediate cash would come from received cash flow (excess of rental income over expenses) from the property. The cash flow would then be offset by the phantom depreciation deduction. We love depreciation! It's a tax benefit that the government gives you that you don't have to pay tax for. Even better, there are loopholes available that allow you maximize this loophole so you won't have to pay tax even if you have huge cash flow. More on that in the Jump Start! section (Part II).

Ted and Ellen planned to buy property in an area that has had historically high appreciation. While the past is never a guaranteed indicator of the future, it does provide evidence of a trend. If an area has experienced high appreciation in the past and nothing significant has changed in the market, then the chances are values will increase in the future.

The appreciation that Ted and Ellen expected from their property can be accessed in a number of ways: (1) They can sell the property and take out the gains. Disadvantages are: They will pay tax. They lose their cash flow. (2) They can sell the property and exchange the property into a separate property. Advantage: They will be able to defer the current taxes. Disadvantage: They will ultimately have reduced depreciation as the depreciable basis of the first property rolls into the second. (3) They can keep the first property and borrow out the equity through either a new loan or a second mortgage. Advantages: They've still got the property. The cash they've received is tax-free.

These are all strategies that Ted and Ellen would be able to start utilizing as soon as they began to invest in real estate.

Step 6—Buy a Home

Ted and Ellen already owned a home. They had purchased their home, though, thinking that was the way to wealth. Actually, buying a home isn't a real loophole. In fact, a home, when you buy it wrong, becomes a big liability. It will take money out of your pocket every month for an uncertain theoretical return.

Since Ted and Ellen already owned a home and weren't willing to move, we looked for ways they could protect what they already had.

Ted and Ellen lived in California. The equity (fair market value less current debt) on their house was currently $150,000. If they were ever sued and lost the lawsuit, all of that equity would be gone. There are three methods for protecting the equity in your home: (1) homestead exemption, (2) limited liability company (LLC), and (3) debt.

The homestead exemption protects a fixed amount of equity for the homeowner. The amount of the homestead exemption varies by state. For example, Florida has unlimited homestead exemption. So does Texas. Unfortunately, California protects only $75,000 of the homeowner's equity. That meant that Ted and Ellen had a lot at risk.

The second option was an LLC. The IRS now allows you as a homeowner to form a single-member LLC to hold your personal residence. This will give your equity protection. Unfortunately, having an LLC in California is expensive. Ted and Ellen learned that it would cost them $800 per year to have this additional protection.

The third option is the one they decided to explore. Debt, when it's used the right way, not only makes you money, but also protects your assets. Ted and Ellen decided to investigate refinancing their house because the interest rates were currently lower than their existing mortgage rate. They were going to ask for a "cash-out refinance." That meant that they would pull out additional money from their house and, at the same time, reduce their equity to the amount protected by the homestead exemption.

Ted and Ellen now had the money to invest in their real estate. That started Steps 4 and 5 working in full force!

Step 7—Home Loopholes

Ted currently ran his computer consulting business out of a spare bedroom in their house. He had heard that it was an IRS red flag to take a home office deduction, so he hadn't been taking advantage of this very legal home loophole.

We reviewed the current rules for the home office and discovered that there was no problem at all taking advantage of the home office for Ted. In order to have a legitimate home office, you must prove two things:

1. You have a space in your home that is used exclusively for business.
2. You regularly perform some kind of business activity in that space.

"Exclusively" means just that. You can't use a corner of the dining room table or the kitchen counter. It needs to be a spot that is used only for business.

Once you have established a legitimate home office expense, you can then take a deduction for a pro rata portion of the home-related expenses such as mortgage interest, property tax, insurance, utilities, maintenance, and the like. The proration is determined by dividing the square footage of the business use by the total square footage. You can also depreciate a pro rata portion of the home.

The second tax myth that Ted and Ellen had heard was that you shouldn't take the home office deduction because it would put the future tax-free gain in jeopardy when you sold your house.

The home office deduction will not reduce the $500,000 (for married filing jointly) capital gains exclusion. The IRS tells us that if the home office is part of the same "dwelling unit" as the home, then there is no need to attribute part of the gain to the business for the sale of the principal residence. If you have taken a depreciation deduction for that part of the home, then you will need to recapture the depreciation upon sale. But that's it! You do not need to pay capital gains tax on the sale.

Ted used a room that was 200 square feet. The total area of the house was 2,000 square feet, so he was using 10 percent of the home for business. That meant that 10 percent of their home-related costs were now a deduction against Ted's income. The home office deduction can't create a loss, but it can be used to offset income. Because Ellen's business wasn't yet making a profit, it didn't make sense to attribute any of the office space to Ellen's business. The home office expense would all be used against Ted's business.

Total savings from Step 7 loophole: $1,500.

Immediately after the evaluation and strategy, Ted and Ellen saw how they could put a total of $6,225 in their pocket—every single year! They also discovered more than $70,000 in cash that could be used to invest in property. Assuming a very conservative cash-on-cash return of 10 percent, that meant they would create another $7,000 in income. Of course, there would be extra mortgage every month, but Ted and Ellen's payments went up only an extra $2,000 per year because they were able to get a better mortgage rate. They soon had an additional $13,000 per year available.

And they looked forward to their ongoing evaluation and strategy preparation so that they could continually refine their plan to include Steps 4 and 5 to maximize their real estate investing as well.

What's next? They now need to put it all in place.

Chapter 4

PATH—CREATING AN ACTION PLAN

The best plans in the world don't mean a thing if you never implement them. If you truly trust your team, have provided all of the necessary information to them, and have jointly created a strategy that leads to what you really want, it's now time to take a deep breath and just do it!

There are a number of schools of thought on how to implement. Some people like to just jump in, feeling that in the chaos something good will happen. That's one strategy, and who knows, you just might get lucky enough to actually create what you want out of it. Other people get themselves psyched up with numerous positive affirmations. That's a great strategy if your goal is to get yourself psyched up. But you're going to need to take action if you really want anything to happen.

The method we recommend involves looking at what you want to create, just like we did with Ted and Ellen, and then creating a step-by-step strategy on how you can achieve that.

Action

This next step might seem the most uncertain for you, as you start putting your plan into action. Ted and Ellen already had begun their business and investment plans. They needed to get the correct business structures in place to take advantage of what they had. Your personal action steps might be entirely different. You might need to take action to investigate and start a business. You might need to get more education about the types of investments you need to make. Your advisors will be the ones to help you decide what your own personal action steps should be. Do not assume that because the next step for Ted and Ellen was to form various business structures that you should do the same.

Implementing Ted and Ellen's Tax Plan

Ted and Ellen both needed to form new business structures. The basic steps they used follow.

Ted and Ellen's Action Items

Incorporate Ted's Business

1. File appropriate paperwork with state agency.
2. After receipt of approval, apply for employer identification number (EIN) from the IRS (Form SS-4).
3. Apply for local licensing—business permit, sales tax permit, whatever else is required.
4. Apply for S corporation status from the IRS (Form 2553). (*Note:* Ted and Ellen live in a community property state, so, although Ted solely owned this company, Ellen also needed to sign off on the S corporation form.)
5. Hold first stockholders meeting to elect board of directors.
6. Hold first board of directors meeting.
7. Prepare organizational minutes.
8. Issue stock certificates.
9. Open checking account with stockholder loan.
10. Apply for credit card.
11. Set up accounting information.
12. Start filing system.
13. Purchase assets at fair market value from old sole proprietorship.
14. Notify customers of business structure change.

Incorporate Ellen's Business

1. File appropriate paperwork with state agency.
2. After receipt of approval, apply for employer identification number (EIN) from the IRS (Form SS-4).
3. Apply for local licensing—business permit, sales tax permit, whatever else is required.
4. Apply for S corporation status from the IRS (Form 2553). (*Note:* Ted and Ellen live in a community property state, so, although Ellen will solely own this company, Ted will also need to sign off on the S corporation form.)
5. Hold first stockholders meeting to elect board of directors.
6. Hold first board of directors meeting.
7. Prepare organizational minutes.
8. Issue stock certificates.
9. Open checking account with stockholder loan.
10. Set up accounting information.
11. Start filing system.

Ted and Ellen are not beginning the real estate company immediately, and so are not spending the money to set up the business at this time.

It's hard to know what to do first when you're just starting your business and investing career. When should you implement all of the steps you've envisioned for your future? Generally, I recommend that you are certain that you will begin a business, not just have an idea you might, before you form a business structure. The same is true for business structures for your investments. Make sure you're truly going to have the investments before you start the business structures. Otherwise, you can end up with having spent considerable time and energy setting up the structures and not even needing them. Even worse, if you set up a corporation and then later discover you won't need it, you will have to form a plan of liquidation with the IRS and file dissolution papers with your state governing agency. The moral is: Be certain of your business before you form the structures.

Recordkeeping Requirements

Both Ted and Ellen had to begin thinking about the accounting and filing system requirements for their businesses. The best time to start these systems is right away! I've found that if my clients wait until year-end to figure out what their income and expenses for their business actually are they've lost the ability to plan. They're also going to pay a great deal more for the bookkeeping at a time when bookkeepers and accountants are too busy with tax clients for this type of work. Plus, chances are you'll forget about some expenses or lose some of the necessary documentation. The answer to all of those problems is to start immediately with your bookkeeping requirements.

What to Keep and Why

Businesses and real estate have some very real requirements for records. If you're planning to be a serious business owner and real estate investor, then plan on keeping track of records as you go. If you don't have good records, you might be unable to prove your deductions and then lose them in a subsequent audit or, if you are sued, be unable to prove that you really are running the investments like a business. Either way you lose! Good records can protect you against those problems.

There are three types of record systems that we recommend: (1) temporary files, (2) permanent files, and (3) financial statement files. A discussion of each of these types follows.

Temporary Files

There will be income items and expenses for your business or for the properties you own every year. For ease of use with your accounting system, keep the backup copies in alphabetical files that are "closed" each year after your tax return is prepared. Remember that each company will need its own set of files. For example, Ted's company will need a set of temporary files and Ellen's company will need a separate set of temporary files. When they begin their real estate investing, that real estate investment company will need its own set of separate temporary files.

As you pay an invoice, we recommend that you note on your copy the following information:

Date paid.
Check number.
Amount paid.

We have a rubber stamp that is used to stamp each invoice that has these three items, each followed by a line. This prompts the accounts payable clerk to complete each line. The invoice copy is then filed alphabetically by the vendor name.

If you don't have a large number of invoices each year, you might just want to create file folders with "A–C", "D–F," and so on. In this way, you can quickly find your reference information and not have to set up a lot of files as you go.

Be careful of expenses that end up being capitalized. These are expenses that actually represent improvements to the property or are assets to your business. For example, a room addition would be an improvement that would be capitalized. Invoices representing additions to basis (capitalized expenses) need to be filed with the permanent files. Another example would be an asset that you buy for your business that has use beyond one year, such as a computer. The invoice representing the purchase of your computer, your business automobile, furniture, fixtures, equipment, and the like will all be filed with the permanent files.

At the end of the year, begin a new set of file folders and start filing current invoices in those folders. There will likely be two sets of files—the past year (for the tax return that hasn't yet been filed) and the current year—at certain times of the year. Make sure you have room in a filing cabinet for those files.

After the tax return is filed, take the invoices, complete with their file folders, and store them in a separate box. We typically recommend that you retain these records for five years. However, you may want to keep them for 10 years in case there is ever a lawsuit. Clearly label the box with the year so you know when you can shred the documents.

Permanent Files

The permanent files are files that you will keep active long past the tax year. These are items related to ongoing issues such as the assets of the company, basis for the property and underlying notes, as well as information related to the business structures.

The basis files will include documents such as the closing statements upon the sale of the property, any previous property owned (such as a Section 1031 like-kind exchange that was performed) that affects the basis, invoices and contracts for improvements made to the property, as well as any sales documents for portions of the property. These should be filed under the property name.

You will also want to keep files related to any agreements (e.g., insurance policies, government notices, contracts, employee agreements, rental agreements, and management agreements) in the permanent files.

Keep at least one file on each asset.

If you have sold a property or assets and continue to receive payments, keep records of all contracts with the rest of the files in the permanent files for as long as you have transactions related to the agreement.

When you have sold an asset or property and are completely paid in full, transfer all of the files related to the asset or property to the temporary files. At the end of the tax year, these files will become part of the records kept at year-end.

You will also need to keep permanent files for the business structure. For example, if you have a limited liability company (LLC), you will need to keep the documents related to the setup plus your annual minutes. It is important that you keep all business structure paperwork handy. If you are ever sued, that's the first thing you'll need to produce. Failure to produce the necessary documentation might mean that you haven't run the business in a businesslike manner, which could put all of your other assets at risk.

Financial Statement Files

Most business owners and investors use a software program to track their income and expenses. We use Intuit's QuickBooks Pro (available at www.intuit.com for approximately $300) with many of our clients. This program allows our clients to securely send their accounting data via the Internet. We then can look at the financial information at the same time that the client does. That's how we work with clients efficiently and accurately at long distances. In fact, we find that we work *better* with clients who are not in our geographic area because it provides the incentive for all of us to be more efficient.

First of all, consider your computer system files. Consult with your computer support expert's advice for backups in your particular case. We generally follow the grandfather-father-son system of backups. In other words, we have three backup tapes that are recycled through the series, so that we always have three days of backup available. We do a weekly backup as well that is taken and stored off-site.

Additionally, we recommend that you print the following reports after you have entered the year-end adjusting journal entries (AJEs) provided by your accountant:

Working trial balance as of the year-end.
Balance sheet as of the year-end.
Income statement for the year just ended.
General ledger, with all details.
Payroll records, full details for all employees.
Bank statement reconcilement.
Accounts receivable and accounts payable ledgers, if used.

Keep those reports with the other temporary files at year-end. If you are audited for that year, the IRS auditor will ask to see copies of all of these financial reports. So, it is important you keep clean copies of these, without any notes written on them that you wouldn't want prying eyes to see.

Implementing Your Tax Plan

The foregoing discussion is just a general guideline. Every type of business, set of circumstances, and business locale requires different steps. This is where you will need to rely on the experience of your advisors to follow the appropriate steps.

Chapter 5

STARTING POINT— WHAT WORKED, WHAT DIDN'T WORK

How Did You Do?

The first edition of *Loopholes of the Rich* talked about the importance of reevaluating your strategy and your action steps. Since that time, I have seen, again and again, how the frequency and quality of the reevaluation after action is taken as the most critical factor in determining how quickly success is achieved.

Some people are reluctant to commit to regular reevaluation appointments with their team. And that makes sense, because, frankly, using advisors costs money. In the beginning, it might be more feasible to check in with your advisors on a quarterly basis. The biggest results, though, are going to happen when you can make quick corrections. I have clients who insist on twice-monthly meetings now. They've seen the results of what can happen when you watch what's working, and what's not, with an eye to making corrections that translate to financial freedom.

Jason's Unintended Results

Jason had a retail business that was moving into the Internet world. He knew that if he could get the marketing and fulfillment components figured out his possible customer base would increase by millions. But it was a brand-new arena so he just couldn't predict the results.

He was too busy at first to meet with us on a regular basis, so the first year of operations provided a big, unpleasant tax surprise when we met in March. He had pretty much vanished during the last part of the previous year, so we hadn't had a chance to do any year-end planning. We were now just beginning to determine what the results really were.

He figured that because he didn't have much money in the account right now that he wouldn't have much of a tax consequence. Boy, was he wrong! In fact, after we completed the accounting for the year, we discovered that he owed more than $57,000 in taxes. That was more money than he currently had in the bank. He had made some big financial decisions without taking into account the tax consequences. And now those consequences were right in his face. For example, he had used cash to build up inventory. The inventory wasn't a current deduction. In fact, he had just exchanged one asset (cash) for another asset (inventory). If he'd met with us earlier, we could have discussed the ramifications of some of his big equipment purchases. He could have paid for them with financing at good rates and still taken the full deduction. That was one way that he could have taken a deduction without using cash. He also had missed out on the big Section 179 deduction available to him. The Section 179 deduction would have allowed him to take a full deduction for the purchase of equipment. Instead, he had depreciated it over seven years.

The point now was to maximize the deductions that we could do after the year had already ended. There weren't many, but the effort also gave us the opportunity to plan for more deductions in the future. Even more importantly, we started planning long-range strategies such as buying real estate properties. The real estate properties became another source of cash flow for Jason. It was also a

(Continued)

Jason's Unintended Results (*Continued*)

way for him to grow his wealth. And, because his wife was able to qualify as a real estate professional, we could actually create paper losses in the real estate business that offset business income.

We knew we would reduce his taxes and grow his wealth with this plan. There was also a very unexpected result: Because we now met on a consistent monthly basis, Jason became very comfortable with his tax loopholes strategy. He used to say, "Why make more money? The government is just going to tax it." But that all changed as he saw he could actually make more money and pay less tax than he had before.

Two years later, the gross income in his business had doubled. The Internet strategy had worked. It wasn't easy; there were a lot of false starts, but because he had frequent meetings to review the financial statements of his business he knew instantly when something wasn't working. He started meeting with us to save taxes, which he did, but he also got the unintended result of a lot more income as his business grew.

We have found that many of our clients double or triple their gross incomes within three years of starting on a monthly program. Does it work? Yes, but it means that you must commit to regularly reading the results and making the changes that are required.

Reevaluate

After you have gone through the first four steps of STEPS (starting point, team, evaluation/strategy, plan and path), it is necessary to give the process a little time and then look at what has happened.

Do another assessment. Where are you now? What does your personal financial statement look like after a period of time (generally a month) has gone by? What does your business financial statement look like? Where do you need to improve? How does this financial statement compare with the previous one? Are you moving toward your goal? Ask yourself all these questions and give yourself honest answers.

After you have looked at where you are, decide what changes you need to make to your business strategy. You will likely have found things that worked and a lot of things that didn't work. Is your plan still on track to help you meet your goals? What new action steps do you need to take?

Then, look at your team: How does each member help or hurt you as you move toward your goal? Have your needs changed? Are your advisors fulfilling what you need? Do you need additional or different advisors?

The reevaluation can be the most enlightening exercise or the most demoralizing—it depends completely on how you view the process. As you evaluate each step, look at what got in your way. You might want to start keeping track of the things that go wrong. You especially want to note when something seems to bother you a lot.

Awareness

The first step toward change is awareness. I can listen to a person's conversation and in a matter of minutes assess whether he or she is on the path to wealth. You will hear patterns emerge as a person talks. These patterns generally represent the blocks that the person has throughout his or her entire financial life. The tendency is to blame others for these problems. But the fact is that the one constant in all of this is ourselves. If we keep getting employees that we can't work with, why do we keep hiring them? If we can't seem to find a market that wants to buy our product, why are we not hearing what the market really wants?

The problem is never really about money. It's really about us.

What Stops You

After working with literally thousands of clients, I have discovered that there are some similar blocks that many possess. Review the list and see if any of them ring true for you.

- **Lack of education.** Signs: "I never seem to find the good deals." "There aren't any good deals." "I don't know where to start." "I just need more money and everything will be okay." "I don't care what the numbers say, this is a good deal."

- **Lack of control.** Signs: "I don't need to do a financial statement; let me just explain it all to you." "I don't have time for all of this." "I don't know how much money I've spent. That's up to the bookkeeper."
- **Too much control (lack of trust).** Signs: "No one else can do this as well as I can." "I don't want to spend the money on advisors." "I can just read a book and understand all this." "Bookkeeping (legal, accounting, tax preparation, etc.) isn't rocket science."
- **Fear of loss.** Signs: "I don't want the IRS showing up and arresting me." "My friends think I'm crazy for doing this." "Someone is going to sue me; I just know it."

Any of these blocks can stop you. And at one time or another, one of these, or something like it, has probably been true for all of us.

How to Find Your Blocks

The easiest way to identify your blocks is to go through the reevaluation process periodically (I recommend monthly), looking at all aspects of STEPS (starting point, team, evaluation/strategy, and plan and path). Write down everything that didn't work and then look back at the previous month. What patterns do you see emerging? What do those blocks mean? Can you get more education to help you make better decisions? Is fear immobilizing you? How real is that fear, and what can you do to change it?

One of the most common fears is the fear of the IRS. Chapters 17 and 18 specifically address how to reduce the risk both *of* IRS audit and *from* IRS audit.

Not Much Progress

"I feel like we didn't make much progress at all," said Ted at the end of the process. "Our businesses didn't make much money and our personal financial statements are actually worse because we spent so much money getting our businesses set up."

"It seems to me that the decrease is all due to money you invested in yourself and in your businesses," I replied. "At this point, I think we all agree that the plan is just beginning to work and there aren't many changes that need to be made. I do want to finish by talking about your concern about the money you have invested in your education and in your businesses to make sure you have the right structure and advisors in place. I believe that kind of investment actually brings you the highest possible kind of reward. We call it the Small Change Principle."

Little Changes Make Big Differences

For many people who are just starting out in their businesses, personal spending is typically less than usual. As a result, finding the hidden business deductions will be less important. They might find that they save only $1,000 per year or less. (The average tax saved for clients of our firm is $80,000 per year and the average taxable income for our clients is $350,000 per year.)

Some people are disappointed to see only small savings, but the fact is that small changes you make now can give big results in the future. That is because of the magic of compounding—the Small Change Principle.

For example, $1,000 saved each year for 20 years at a very conservative rate of return of 10 percent will give you $63,000! As you weigh the pros and cons of taking advantage of the ideas in this book, don't think of the benefit you get now of $1,000; think of that pot at the end of the rainbow—$63,000.

You can also see the Small Change Principle in nonmonetary ways. Little changes you make in your knowledge and habits can make large changes over time. The overwhelming factor in both cases is the element of time. I have found that people overestimate what they can do in a year and underestimate what they can accomplish in 20 years. When you take the long-range plan on goals, you have time on your side. I don't know about you, but I'm looking for anything that makes it easier. And this is one plan that works.

There is a two-edged sword, though. If you are doing things wrong, it will also multiply over time and with volume. Even if you're starting small, it is very important that you get on the right path. Time will make it easier.

Positive Steps

My husband and I do the following exercise on a daily basis (well, not exactly faithfully, but certainly whenever we find ourselves overwhelmed or feel that we aren't making forward progress).

For each day, either at the end of the day or at the beginning of the next, write down five things that you did that worked ("wins"). (See Figure 5.1.) Don't go on to the next step until you have written down five things. Now next to each one of those items, say why that was important. After that is complete, write down what you want to do next to continue the progress for each of the five things.

If possible, find someone to share these wins with on a daily basis. This can be anyone—your spouse, your friend, your child. In fact, if you have a child who is discouraged in school, this exercise has a proven track record of changing that discouragement into confidence. Give it a try!

Why This Works

I believe that the best decisions are made from a feeling of strength and confidence. The worst of mankind's behavior comes out when someone

FIGURE 5.1 Positive Steps

Positive Steps Date: _____		
What Worked Today? (Wins)	Why Was That Important?	What's Next
1.		
2.		
3.		
4.		
5.		

feels beaten down and fearful. When there is hope, the best of mankind's behavior shines through.

You are making significant changes in the way you approach your finances and your business. You are changing the way you do things and the people you choose to advise you. And, subtly, surely, you are changing the way you think. That can be unsettling! Give yourself a break, and a pat on the back, by committing to perform this exercise for a month.

PART II

Jump Start!
Your Wealth

Chapter 6

JUMP START! PRINCIPLES FOR TAX-ADVANTAGED WEALTH BUILDING

Jump Start! Your Wealth

In Part I, we discussed the five STEPS related to how you can create a financial plan that changes your future. Let's look now at a comprehensive plan that explains how the rich really do legally make more money and pay less tax. I call it the Jump Start! method because following this plan with the five STEPS method can increase your wealth, no matter where you are.

Is this the only way to get rich? Of course not. You can get rich by being lucky. It's a case of being in the right place at the right time. You might walk into a Las Vegas casino and bet everything on "seven" and have it come up. Or you could buy a lottery ticket and hit it big. You hear those stories every month.

You could also get rich by inheriting money or by marrying money. We're not going to be helping you create either of those plans. But if you do happen to inherit money or marry money, the Jump Start! plan can increase it even more.

So, if you are looking for a plan that has more certainty, read on. It will require a change on your part. I've found that every single self-improvement plan requires change. We don't want you to have to do it alone; that's why we first covered so much information about how to find a good team member who supports your goals.

This method works because we are purposely identifying where the loopholes exist and then changing the situation so you can utilize those loopholes yourself. Remember that the government gave us tax incentives to promote certain actions. But, it's up to us to do those activities so we get the loopholes advantage.

It's more than just spotting the loopholes, though; it's also a matter of maximizing the loopholes by maximizing three principles of wealth building:

1. Leverage.
2. Velocity.
3. Cash flow.

Leverage of Money

Leverage is simply the ability to do more with less. Leverage of money means that you could either take your $100,000 and buy a building for $100,000 or take your $100,000 and buy a building for $1,000,000 while getting a loan for the other 90 percent or $900,000.

Now, let's assume that you have a choice of buying these two buildings in an area that you are confident will have an appreciation of 5 percent. Of course, no one can guarantee that kind of results. But we do know that the average property appreciation in the United States is over 6 percent, so 5 percent is actually conservative. At any rate, let's continue the example. The $100,000 building will go up in value 5 percent for a total value of $105,000. Congratulations, your $100,000 investment has just made a 5 percent return—the difference between the $105,000 value and the $100,000 original purchase price.

Now let's look at the million-dollar property. The property went up in value 5 percent as well. That means it is now worth $1,050,000. This time, I can really say "Congratulations!" Your $100,000 investment earned a 50 percent return or $50,000, which is the difference between the $1,050,000 and the $1,000,000 original purchase price.

Leverage of Time

Leverage of time, like leverage of money, means that you are able to do more with less. You can have the leverage of time through the use of systems and other people's time. Consider what happens in your regular day. How many of those things are you really good at . . . and how many things are you barely competent at?

Take a minute and write down at least 12 things that you do on a regular basis. On a piece of paper write these four categories:

1. Energy.
2. Excellent.
3. Competent.
4. Incompetent.

Energy describes the things you do that you do really well. You are better at these things than anyone you've ever seen and you get tremendous energy when you do these things. *Excellent* describes the tasks that you also do really well, but if you spend all day doing them, you get tired; you don't get any energy from doing those tasks. *Competent* describes the items that you are barely good at. If you work really hard at these tasks and study new training, you would end up being fairly capable. *Incompetent* describes the things that you don't do well and you'll never do well.

I get energy from creating tax strategies, writing, and speaking. Those are the items I put in the "energy" category. I am a skilled typist, but I don't get any energy from it. That's something that would go in the "excellent" category. I'm competent at filing. If I studied it, I'd still be competent. And I'm definitely incompetent at fixing the copier machine; it's best for everyone involved if I stay away from anything mechanical. Those are examples of things that I would have on my list.

Now go through and assign a percentage next to each general category to determine how much time you spend in that area. For example, you might have:

Energy   10%
Excellent   25%
Competent   50%
Incompetent   15%

Your numbers are probably much like those shown. Now consider how much money you currently make from the return of merely 10 percent of your time spent in things you do really well and that energize you. What would happen if you spent *all* of your time on the things that energize you? Would you make more money? Would you grow your wealth? Would you be happier? That's the return that a good system can give you—ultimate leverage on your time as well.

To develop those systems, first start with the items that you show in the "incompetent" area. What can you do immediately to get those items off your task list? In the other areas, you need to create systems to use to hand off the tasks. But, in the case of "incompetent," you probably don't want to teach anyone your system for doing that task!

When it comes to tasks that you rank as "competent" and "excellent," chances are you are able to produce some respectable results. In these cases, you have valuable information that you need to quickly, efficiently, and accurately communicate to the people who will take over the tasks. That's the beauty of systems. I also recommend that you have your replacements complete this exercise as well. You want to turn over work that you are merely competent at to people who get energy from it. That's when you'll see the best results!

The method we use to quickly develop systems is to assemble the following items:

Pad of "sticky" notes.
Large piece of paper.
Pen.

Now, as fast as you can think of them, write on each sticky note a separate step in the task that you want to create a system for. For example, one of the early systems I created was a system to prepare tax returns so that we had consistent tax loophole implementation. Obviously, I couldn't personally prepare all of the returns, but I wanted the results to be exactly the same as if I had.

So, I sat down and wrote each step of the tax return preparation process. One sticky note might be to reconcile prior year carryforward numbers on the current year to assure that the program had properly carried these items forward. Another item was to check the financial statements of the client to make sure he or she had properly accounted for all expense items. I used a lot of sticky notes that weekend as I started the documentation of this system, but the key was I had the beginning of the system I needed.

The next step is to assemble those notes in the proper order. Assign a person to each step of the task. You may find, at least initially, that you will still need to do parts of the process. But make sure you don't find yourself doing each step again. It could be that you don't yet know the person who will do the work. That's okay; just write a description of the traits and skills that person will have.

Now calculate how much time you will free up by removing those tasks from your life. Will you find another 10 hours per month? Or, perhaps, you'll find even more. What would your life be like if you could spend those 10 hours on activities that you are really good at? In fact, these are activities that you could be the best in the world at and they give you tremendous energy. How much money would your company make now? Compare that increase with the investment cost of hiring a person to do portions of the system that you don't do well.

That's the secret of true leverage—using other people's time in ways that increase your time and wealth and make them happy for the experience.

Velocity

Basically, velocity is a measurement of how fast something goes. Economists use the term *velocity of money* to define the rate at which money circulates in our economy. Investors use this measurement to determine how robust an economy is.

It's really only in recent times that politicians have attempted to control a country's economy by controlling velocity. Velocity is very much an offshoot of capitalism. It's said that to predict the future you first must understand the past. Since the term *velocity* is so new in our economic times, it's an interesting exercise to look at why this concept even became important to economists in the first place.

Economies grow and they shrink. That's called the boom and bust cycle of a country, a civilization, or even of a global economy. As an economy grows and demand for a product or service grows, new suppliers or providers will enter the marketplace. That adds more capacity. At the same time, the original suppliers often innovate to produce more products and services in a faster way. There's even more capacity.

If supply starts outpacing demand, then prices go down. That's the typical supply and demand cycle. It's also the beginning roots of the boom and bust of an economy.

Initially, early business trade was conducted using gold or other precious metals. This became impractical as trade extended to foreign lands. The next step was letters of credit, which then led to banking. The banks, now extended to global economies, looked for ways to tame the business cycle. They wanted to cool down the overheated booms and heat up the cooling busts.

As time went on and bank panics occurred, the concept of central banking gave governments and economists the hope that the business cycle could be smoothed. Manipulation of the velocity of money became a core tool in their arsenal. Increase the growth of the economy—increase the velocity. Slow an economy down—decrease the velocity.

Just like a bank is not merely a building with money in it, your own wealth is more than just the paper and coins in your pocket. Velocity is really the mobilization of your money. It's the speed at which your money moves. The higher the velocity, the higher the pace and the faster your personal economy grows. Is there more risk? Absolutely! As your business and investments grow, it's necessary to take your personal financial literacy up a notch as well. It's also necessary to access the full level of your advisor's abilities. If you're moving too fast for your advisor's abilities, make necessary changes.

The good news is that you can control the velocity. If you're not comfortable with the speed at which your personal wealth is growing,

---

Increase the Velocity of Your Money

- Look for untapped cash reserves such as cash values in life insurance policies and excess balances in bank accounts, and put this money to work for you.
- Access the equity in your real estate with lines of credit or by refinancing. Invest the extra cash created in new investments.
- Eliminate bad debt.
- Increase good debt.
- Monitor all assets on a regular basis. Reduce underperforming assets.
- Increase your time leverage by the use of systems in your business and investments.
- Exploit every legal tax loophole available.

---

make the changes necessary to increase or decrease the leveraging of your money and time.

Just like the central bank can control the economy by adjusting velocity, you can control your own economy by adjusting your own velocity.

Taxes are often called a drag on the economy. Consider this: If you have $100 to spend in an economy, you will create $100 worth of income for someone else. Theoretically, they then have $100 to spend with someone else to create more income. In its purest sense, we could take this example out so that the same $100 bill could create hundreds of thousands of dollars in commerce.

But, what if people have to pay 50 percent tax on every dollar they make? You spend your $100 with someone else and they pay taxes on half. That means they have $50 to invest with someone else, who then has to pay 50 percent tax. It doesn't take long to reduce that $100 bill to just pennies. Taxes drag down the potential of the money—they reduce velocity by taking away the power of the money.

A tax loopholes strategy will provide the best defense against drags on the velocity of your money. Take full advantage of all of the seven Jump Start! steps to fully use the tax loopholes available to you.

Cash Flow

It's often said that "cash is king." And cash flow is how you get the cash. My business partner, Tom, likes to say the key to business is to "Think big and act small." Most of us have big dreams and, once we understand we can really have what we want, we're ready to start acting like we already have it. Often, though, there is a lag between our dream and the reality. That difference generally translates to cash.

The number one reason that businesses fail is due to lack of proper capitalization. If a new business makes a mistake, can it survive the mistake? That's why small businesses fold when big businesses survive even though they might provide inferior products and services. The big business has the cash reserves and the equity positions to weather the storms. The small business often does not.

There are things that you can do right away to improve your cash flow. If you have a business, accelerate the velocity at which your business cycle works. Collect on receivables faster. Give discounts for cash. And, on the other hand, use good debt in your business. Apply for credit from suppliers.

Look for ways to maximize both the short-range and long-range income from your business moves. It's great to have plans that provide for tomorrow, but how will you pay the bills due tomorrow?

Weigh the cash consequences of every change in your business. Watch your current business statistics closely. Which are the most important stats for your particular business?

As an example, we watch the growth of our database and click-throughs from the free e-mail newsletters that we send out. If I write about a hot new tax strategy and provide more information at our web site, how many people actually go to the web site and read the rest of the free information? If nobody cares, either I've written poor copy or it was something that no one cared about. Those are important statistics to monitor. What are the stats for your business? Is it lead conversion from prospects? Maybe it's dollars per customer visit. Or it could be profit per employee. Establish the stats so you can monitor the progress of your business as changes in your business, industry, and the economy occur.

I rarely advise any client to invest in real estate that produces a negative cash flow. It is possible to find properties that provide positive cash flow returns. You might need to look outside your geographic area or you might need to look for types of properties that are different than you first anticipated or you might even need to buy a property that is in much worse shape than you had anticipated, but you can find the properties.

I have a friend who is a very successful investor in San Francisco. The San Francisco market has very high prices and rent controls. Yet he makes cash flow returns on every single one of his properties. How does he do it? He looks for problems. He doesn't want a property that has one problem; he wants a property that has three or more problems. That's where the deals are! As long as he knows that he can fix the problems and he has the resources and time to fix them, he will make money on the deal. He was able to buy the property at a great price because he was the only one negotiating for the property. One of my favorite stories he tells is when he found a property at a great price in the East Bay area. He told a lady about this great property and she reacted with complete fear. "They shoot people in that area," she said.

"Maybe," he replied, "but they don't shoot landlords."

If you can look beyond what you are used to looking at and look for uncommon solutions, you can find real estate properties that will provide cash flow in any area of the country.

The Seven Steps of Jump Start!

You can choose to do any or all of the following Jump Start! steps. The more fully you participate in as many of the steps as possible, the more positive your results will be.

1. Create a business. Make sure it's in the proper business structure and that you have anticipated: (1) at least one clear exit strategy, (2) sources of funding for the business, (3) how to take money out of the business, and (4) a strategy to run the business in a way that reduces risk for you. Sometimes starting a business is as simple as changing your employment status from an employee to an independent contractor.

2. Discover your hidden business deductions. It can be a major eye-opener when the first-time business owner discovers all the things that are now tax-deductible. These are the things you used to spend personal money on. The difference is that they are now deductible. Discover and properly document those expenses. This is how your business can give you money tax-free.

3. Pay your taxes. Use proper planning to prepay just enough in taxes at the latest possible time. In this way, you can get 0 percent loans from the government on your tax money. When you have multiple businesses in the right structures, you can often select when you pay taxes and defer payment to a far distant time.

4. What's left goes into real estate. You might not be able to hit the ideal investment strategy of having all leftover business cash go into real estate. But the more you can put into real estate, without needing to draw anything out for personal living expenses, the faster your income will grow. Make sure your real estate investment is done using the proper leverage with the optimum structures.

5. Real estate income comes out tax-free. A good real estate investment will create positive cash flow for you. If you have made a good deal, you'll have positive cash flow from the first day. And if you have a good tax plan, you'll pay *zero taxes* on that cash flow.

6. Buy a house the right way. You need a place to live, and let's face it, that's not an asset that will put money in your pocket. In fact, your home quite likely will be one of the biggest expenses you'll have. Look for good deals in neighborhoods that are appreciating and make the best deal possible on financing. Make sure you have a contingency plan in case the value drops and your other income goes down. And, above all, use the homestead laws and/or proper business structures to protect your investment.

7. Make your home give you money. The biggest gift that Congress has ever given us is available *only* for homeowners. The one requirement is that you have to sell your home. You can also take the money out, tax free, from your home to invest in other businesses or real estate properties. It's a gift—take advantage of all that the IRS allows.

The Results?

You now have the three most powerful engines to build your wealth—your home, your real estate, and your business. Instead of you working for your money, you now have your money working for you in multiple places. You are no longer at the whim of an employer or a 401(k) plan for your financial freedom. You control it with a plan that grows wealth in all of the ways you could possibly want!

Chapter 7

CREATING INCOME WITH LESS TAX

Create a Business

As a CPA, I see numerous financial statements and tax returns of other people. One advantage I have is I get to see what is real and what isn't. Some people say they have a lot of money and they really do. Some people say they have a lot of money and you see them suddenly booted out of the house they never really owned and having their cars repossessed. And I also get to see the financial statements of people worth millions, even billions, of dollars who never tell anyone how much money they have. I get to see the truth.

Business owners have the best ability to create cash and wealth out of an idea. And they have many tax loopholes available for them. Employees, no matter how much money they make, have very limited tax-planning opportunities. And taxes are the number one expense for most Americans. In fact, as employees' income increases, they lose the ability to write off deductions such as mortgage interest, property tax, charitable donations, and the like. And if they make enough money, they also lose the exemptions for their donations and for themselves.

Even more, business owners can actually control when they pay their taxes and how much they pay in taxes. When you have a business, it is also possible to take deductions for items that were previously personal expenses. We call those the hidden business deductions.

81

The Problem Is Your Paycheck!

Have you ever heard people complain that if they just made a little bit more money, everything would be okay? When I hear that complaint from someone, I always reply, "The problem *is* your paycheck, but not in the way you think it is."

The answer isn't to change the amount of money you *make*. Change the *way* you make your money first and then you can change the amount of money you *keep*. It's not how much money you make that counts, it's how much money you keep.

Earn-Tax-Spend Syndrome

How did we ever get into this tax mess, anyway? Most people don't realize how new the current concept of taxation by the federal government actually is. In fact, it wasn't until 1943 that the government began requiring employers to withhold taxes from employees. In less than 60 years, the middle class has become conditioned to having the government get their cut first.

Ask a group of people how much they make, and most will automatically reply with the net amount of their check. The net amount is the amount that is left after the government takes out its share. That is the amount of the paycheck that you bring home.

From your share, you then have to pay all of your expenses. So, even though you make a good salary, the real answer is how much you keep after the government is finished and you pay your expenses. If you're like most Americans, you might end up keeping a little, if anything.

But a business, when set up the correct way, can reverse this process. By identifying and documenting your business deductions you can control the amount of money you spend on taxes. Remember, that's one of the largest expenses the average American has.

If you're an employee, you follow the Earn-Tax-Spend Syndrome of the average taxpayer. However, if you follow the Business Owner's System to Wealth you have the Earn-Spend-Tax loophole strategy. (See Figure 7.1.)

FIGURE 7.1 Earn-Tax-Spend versus Earn-Spend-Tax

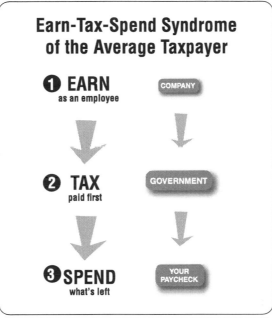

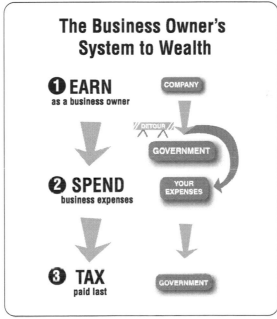

What Is a Business?

There are many opportunities in today's world for starting a business part-time while you keep a day job. In fact, it's best that you continue with your current day job until your business can support you.

In Ted's case, he clearly had created a position for himself as a self-employed person. This was a good starting point for him to begin tax planning as a business owner. You might want to consider what skills you have that can be turned into a business. As more and more businesses downsize, there are a great many start-up businesses formed by downsized employees doing consulting to the very companies that had laid them off as employees.

Other possibilities include network marketing and purchasing a franchise. The benefit of starting this way is that the systems are already in place for your business. The key ingredient that you add in either case is that you follow a program. Generally that means you can just start off selling. Everything else that goes into a business (administration, fulfillment, customer service, accounting, and the like) is outlined in the program provided by the network marketing company or the franchiser. You just follow their system.

Still others become involved in real estate investing or stock trading.

Lately, the growing phenomenon of eBay selling has created a brand-new way to start a business. You might start a business just by cleaning out your garage and posting the items for sale on eBay the way Ellen did.

Hobby versus Business

You undoubtedly have heard that you should "do what you love and the money will follow." That is true as long as that thing you love is run like a business. Otherwise, you run the risk of being considered a sham business under the IRS's hobby loss rules.

If the IRS considers your business a hobby, you can deduct expenses only up to the amount of income for that venture. That means that you cannot take advantage of many of the special business deductions for start-ups. This ruling is especially detrimental in the beginning stages of a business, when most have expenses that exceed their incomes. In this case, the business loss is not deductible.

Rules for Having a Business

There is a general rule of thumb that you might have heard that states that a business is not a hobby if there is income in three out of five years (three out of seven in the case of certain agricultural activities). Clearly, if you have net income (after all expenses are deducted) that income is taxable, so the question of whether the business is a hobby is not valid. The three years out of five rule (or three years out of seven) is not hard-and-fast, though. In some cases, businesses have been disallowed during the loss years even when there was profit in other years. Additionally, in some cases, businesses have been allowed as losses even when there is a loss year after year.

The key deciding factors actually have to do with whether the business is run like a business. No one factor alone is controlling; all factors are taken into account.

You will find the Nine Steps to Business form in Figure 7.2. Complete this form to make sure your business meets the necessary criteria.

When Is a Business not a Business?

Why does the IRS go to so much trouble to make sure you have a business? The reason is because some people have taken advantage of the system that allows you to take business losses against other earned income. And so, in an effort to correct this situation, the pendulum has swung the other way. Instead of only having to prove you have expenses, you also have to prove that you really have a business when you have losses.

There are some industries that are particularly vulnerable to questions by the IRS. These businesses fall into two general categories: (1) businesses that could have a hobby aspect, such as animal breeding or craft-type industries, and (2) businesses that have the potential for personal use write-offs with no real business purpose. This second category, "sham businesses," is particularly vulnerable to unfavorable court rulings. In fact, home-based sham businesses are on the IRS's dirty dozen list of potential scams that it is auditing. Avoid the risk of having your business declared a hobby or, worse yet, a sham, by making sure your business really is a business.

FIGURE 7.2 Nine Steps to Business

Nine Steps to Business
Instructions
> Fill in the name of your company.
> Fill in the type of business. You can use the IRS business type listing in Appendix C as a reference. Your accountant will use this listing to determine the business type when filing your tax return.
> Answer the questions with yes or no. Every "no" answer weakens your position as a business.
> Review this form with your tax advisor.

Name of Company _____

Type of Business _____

Businesslike Manner
1. Do you have a separate bank account for your business?   YES / NO
2. Do you (or your CPA) keep accounting records for your business?   YES / NO
3. Do you keep copies of receipts in a filing system?   YES / NO
4. Do you make an effort to collect accounts receivable?   YES / NO
5. Do you review profit and loss statements regularly?   YES / NO

Time and Effort
6. Do you keep track of time spent in your business activity?   YES / NO
7. Do you keep track of business appointments in a scheduler or diary?   YES / NO
8. Do you have notes of conversations you have had with consultants or experts to enhance your business?   YES / NO
9. Do you keep evidence from business seminars you have attended?   YES / NO

Depend on Income
10. Will you need the income from your business to sustain your lifestyle? YES / NO
11. Do you intend to replace your current job with this business?   YES / NO

Reasonable Losses
If you have losses, do you have documentation that:
12. They are normal for the type of business you are in at the beginning? YES / NO
13. That others have experienced the same kind of downturn?   YES / NO

Effort to Make Money
If you have losses, do you have evidence that:
14. You have made changes to try to improve the business?   YES / NO
15. You have investigated ways to make your business profitable?   YES / NO
16. You have consulted with experienced business owners or other advisors regarding your business?   YES / NO

FIGURE 7.2 (*Continued*)

Experienced Advisors
17. Have you identified the advisors you need for your business?   YES / NO
18. Do your advisors have the business experience needed to give you good advice? YES / NO

Your Experience
19. Have you been successful in this kind of business before?   YES / NO
20. Have you been successful in a similar business?   YES / NO

Past Profit
21. Has the business been profitable in previous years?   YES / NO
22. If so, has the profit been enough to make it sensible to continue?   YES / NO

Asset Appreciation
23. Is the business building assets that will have future appreciation?   YES / NO

Scoring the Test
For each of the nine sectors, rate how strong your case is as to business purpose on a scale of 1 to 5, with 5 being strongest. For the weakest elements, what can you do to strengthen your point?

Businesslike Manner	1	2	3	4	5
Time and Effort	1	2	3	4	5
Depend on Income	1	2	3	4	5
Reasonable Losses	1	2	3	4	5
Effort to Make Money	1	2	3	4	5
Experienced Advisors	1	2	3	4	5
Your Experience	1	2	3	4	5
Past Profit	1	2	3	4	5
Asset Appreciation	1	2	3	4	5

What can you do to improve your position?

_____

_____

_____

_____

_____

Employee or Independent Contractor?

More and more people are leaving their middle management jobs and becoming independent contractors in the same field. But what does it really mean to be an independent contractor? Who gets to decide if you are a legitimate independent contractor or really are just an employee in disguise? And which is better?

If you're an employee, you will pay more tax. And your employer will pay more tax.

The better way for the smart employee and employer is to legitimately set up independent contractor status. If you're the business owner paying the independent contractor, you no longer will be responsible for withholding taxes and making Medicare or Social Security contributions. Your work space requirements may go down, along with your equipment costs. Work hours lost due to sickness or accidents can be reduced.

If you're the new independent contractor, you can now take advantage of tax loopholes and home loopholes that you never could take before.

Twenty IRS Factors for Independent Contractor Freedom

First, here is what the IRS says about the independent contractor issue:

> It does not matter that a written agreement may take a position with regard to any factors or state that certain factors do not apply, if the facts indicate otherwise. If an employer treats an employee as an independent contractor and the relief provisions discussed earlier do not apply, the person responsible for the collection and payment of withholding taxes may be held personally liable for an amount equal to the taxes that should have been withheld.

So, making sure that you properly structure your business work requirements is the first step. Fortunately, the IRS has provided with some guidelines on how to do just that.

The IRS looks at 20 key factors to determine whether a person is an independent contractor or an employee. Each guideline has been numbered and is followed by the TaxLoopholes response in italics directed to the employer of an independent contractor. If you're the employee, help your employer prove the independent contractor status.

1. Instructions. An employee must comply with instructions about when, where, and how to work. Even if no instructions are given, the control factor is present if the employer has the right to control how the work results are achieved.

TaxLoopholes response: You can control the work product standard, but not the way in which the work is performed. Give your independent contractors a goal and a time frame to complete that goal, and that's it. Don't tell your independent contractor when, where, or how to work.

2. Training. An employee may be trained to perform services in a particular manner. Independent contractors ordinarily use their own methods and receive no training from the purchasers of their services.

TaxLoopholes response: Don't hire novices whom you will have to train. You can make this a condition of your independent contractor service agreement so that if someone claims to be qualified to perform a task and is not, you can void the contract. Remember, a good independent contractor shouldn't need much, if any, training.

3. Integration. An employee's services are usually integrated into the business operations because the services are important to the success or continuation of the business. This shows that the employee is subject to direction and control.

TaxLoopholes response: Don't integrate your independent contractors' positions or services. Don't include the description of contracted services in your company's personnel manual and don't give your independent contractors any responsibility for supervising or overseeing in any way your regular employees.

4. Services rendered personally. An employee renders services personally. This shows that the employer is interested in the methods as well as the results.

TaxLoopholes response: This one is a bit tougher. Usually your independent contractor will be performing the services personally. Try to mitigate this point by making sure your independent contractor operates through a properly formed legal entity. Bear in mind also that this may not be, on its own, enough to satisfy the IRS. So, make sure that you meet as many of the other factors as possible.

5. Hiring assistants. An employee works for an employer who hires, supervises, and pays workers. An independent contractor can hire, supervise, and pay assistants under a contract that requires him or her to provide materials and labor and to be responsible only for the result.

TaxLoopholes response: This factor goes hand in hand with Factor 4. Besides making sure that you contract only with independent contractors who work through properly formed legal entities, make sure that you contract for the entity to provide the service, and not for a particular person connected to that entity. This works especially well when your independent contractor company has more than one individual providing services through it.

6. Continuing relationship. An employee generally has a continuing relationship with an employer. A continuing relationship may exist even if work is performed at recurring although irregular intervals.

TaxLoopholes response: Make sure that you enter into separate contracts with your independent contractors for specific tasks. A long-term "anything required" contract is a surefire way to draw IRS attention. If your independent contractor is performing a repetitive task, keep your contract lengths short (i.e., require a new contract to be signed every three months).

7. Set hours of work. An employee may be required to work or be available full-time. An independent contractor generally can set his or her work hours.

TaxLoopholes response: Review Factor 1, and make sure that you allow your independent contractors the ability to perform the work as and when that person sees fit. Provide only a project to be done and a deadline for completion.

8. Full-time required. An employee may be required to work or be available full-time. This indicates control by the employer. An independent contractor can work when and for whom he or she chooses.

TaxLoopholes response: Again, it comes back to Factor 1, and the element of control you have over how an independent contractor spends his or her time.

If at all possible, you want to make sure your independent contractor doesn't work for you exclusively, and has enough time to work for others. Remember the old saying, "It's nice to share."

9. Work done on premises. An employee usually works on the premises of an employer, or works on a route or at a location designated by an employer.

TaxLoopholes response: Make sure your agreement clearly spells out the ability (or requirement) for your independent contractor to work off-site, at his or her own premises, wherever possible. Obviously this won't work all of the time—an independent contractor who provides equipment maintenance service will be coming to your business premises—but you can offset the issue here by not making any mention in your independent contractor service agreement of where that independent contractor is to provide the services.

10. Order or sequence set. An employee may be required to perform services in the order or sequence set by an employer. This shows that the employee is subject to direction and control.

TaxLoopholes response: This comes back to Factor 1 again—do not state the sequence for a task to be performed. Set out only the goal and the deadline, and allow your independent contractor to take care of all of the details in between.

11. Reports. An employee may be required to submit reports to an employer. This shows that the employer maintains control.

TaxLoopholes response: If reports are necessary, make sure these are not required in the contract itself, but merely a courtesy provided by the independent contractor for informational reasons.

12. Payments. An employee is generally paid by the hour, week, or month. An independent contractor is usually paid by the job or on a straight commission.

TaxLoopholes response: Make sure that your independent contractor service agreement specifies either a set amount to be paid for the project to be done or an hourly rate to be paid for that particular project. Try to avoid an open-ended contract term combined with an hourly rate, as that begins to look more like an employment agreement than an independent contractor service agreement.

13. Expenses. An employer generally pays an employee's business and travel expenses. This shows that the employee is subject to regulation and control.

TaxLoopholes response: Do not pay for anything other than the contracted-for amount whenever possible. If you must agree to reimburse expenses, then make sure they are paid by the independent contractor first, documented, and then subsequently reimbursed by you. Remember that your independent contractors can take advantage of tax loopholes to write off expenses incurred during the course of carrying out the services they have contracted with you to perform.

14. Tools and materials. An employer normally furnishes an employee with significant tools, materials, and other equipment.

TaxLoopholes response: Make sure your independent contractor supplies his or her own tools and equipment wherever possible. For example, a bookkeeper could use his or her own computer to maintain your company's books, or a cleaning service could provide their own cleaning tools, transportation, and supplies. Again, by providing his or her own tools, equipment, and supplies, an independent contractor can take advantage of the great tax loopholes available to small business owners to reduce the taxes he or she pays.

15. Investment. An independent contractor has a significant investment in the facilities he or she uses in performing services for someone else.

TaxLoopholes response: An independent contractor who operates out of a home office or separate premises offers a great way for you to meet this guideline. Operating from a proper home office or separate premises helps you to solidify your assertion that this individual (or, preferably, legal entity) is a true independent contractor. And if your independent contractor operates out of a home office, your independent contractor is also able to take advantage of the tax loopholes available to deduct home office expenses.

16. Profit or loss. An independent contractor can make a profit or suffer a loss.

TaxLoopholes response: You are not responsible for ensuring your independent contractor is able to make a profit on the contracted work performed for you. Your only relationship is that of employer and independent contractor. Do not guarantee a profit under any circumstances.

17. Works for more than one person or firm. An independent contractor is generally free to provide his or her services to two or more unrelated persons or firms at the same time.

TaxLoopholes response: It is to your advantage as an employer for your independent contractors to work for several other clients (and most independent contractors will agree!). Remember, the more time an independent contractor spends working only for you, the more likely the IRS is to consider that individual an employee. If the work your independent contractor will be doing is sensitive and requires you to disclose confidential information, use nondisclosure and confidentiality agreements to ensure your secrets stay secret (and to provide you with a legal way to recover damages if your secrets are revealed to others). Or make sure your independent contractor service agreement has a section that deals with confidentiality and allows you to collect damages from an independent contractor who breaches those sections.

18. Offers service to the general public. An independent contractor makes his or her services available to the general public.

TaxLoopholes response: Again, as with Factor 17, don't restrict your independent contractor's ability to work for other clients—even your competitors. Instead, use nondisclosure and confidentiality language in your independent contractor service agreements or even use separate nondisclosure and confidentiality agreements to maintain secrecy. Alternatively, depending on the service to be provided, consider asking your independent contractor to make a determination as to whether a conflict of interest exists before signing a contract. Or ask your own attorney for a legal opinion if you are truly concerned.

19. Right to fire. An employer can fire an employee. An independent contractor cannot be fired so long as he or she produces a result that meets the specifications of the contract.

TaxLoopholes response: This doesn't mean you can't contract to receive an acceptable result—you can, and should! You can also set out the grounds for early termination of your independent contractor service agreement. The difference here is that you are setting out the ways in which you can cancel a contract for nonperformance of its terms by an independent contractor, and not by firing an employee.

20. Right to quit. An employee can quit his or her job at any time without incurring liability. An independent contractor usually agrees to complete a specific job and is responsible for its satisfactory completion, or is legally obligated to make good for failure to complete it.

TaxLoopholes response: Just as you can't void an independent contractor service agreement without proper reason or notice, so, too, your independent contractor can't unilaterally walk away from the service agreement. A good independent contractor will request terms upon which he or she may withdraw from the contract, and this is not unreasonable (depending on the specific terms!). Make sure your independent contractor service agreement sets out specific terms under which either of you may withdraw from the agreement.

Independent Contractor Summary

With careful structuring, both your business and your independent contractor's business can benefit and take advantage of tax loopholes. Make sure you have this structure in place before any work is done. If necessary, talk to your attorney. There is also a way to ask the IRS to make a formal determination, but this can be tricky. If the IRS rules that the relationship is that of employer/employee, it is too late for you to make any changes!

There is one additional warning: If you've previously been an employee, the job function needs to change in order to change to independent contractor status. Otherwise, you'll run the risk of the IRS questioning why the change of status was made.

Three Types of Income for a Business

We earlier discussed the three types of income: earned, portfolio, and passive. Of these, earned income has the highest tax rate. And the employee with earned income not only pays the highest tax rate but also has the lowest number of loopholes available.

A business can also have three types of income. In this case, it depends on the nature of the business services. If the business works for the money, the income is earned. If the business's money earns the money, such as interest, dividends, and capital gains, the income is portfolio. And if the business owns an investment that creates cash flow, the income is considered passive.

One loophole strategy is to change the type of income your business receives. Change the earned income into portfolio or passive income.

One of my favorite ways to do this is to buy a building that your business rents. You own the building (held in a limited liability company or a limited partnership) so the business pays you rent for use of the building. This reduces the earned income of the business and becomes passive income for the LLC or LP.

You now have a business that is both creating income and increasing worth, plus you have a building that is creating tax-free cash flow and growing in value due to appreciation. You have just increased the velocity of your tax-advantaged wealth-building plan.

This strategy can also create real estate passive income that you can use to offset other real estate passive losses. If you have income over $150,000 and neither you nor your spouse can qualify as a real estate professional, you cannot take advantage of the paper real estate losses against your earned income. But you can first use your business to change earned income into passive income (through a building rental) and then offset that passive income against passive loss.

If you want to use this last tax loophole tip, remember to charge your business the highest amount you can reasonably charge for the rent. The more you reduce your earned income and increase your passive income, the lower your taxes will be.

Chapter 8

USING BUSINESS STRUCTURES TO CREATE LEGAL TAX LOOPHOLES

Basics of Business Structures

A good business structure will reduce taxes and reduce risk from frivolous lawsuits. A bad business structure increases your risk, costs you excess tax, and takes up too much time.

Limited Liability Company

The Limited Liability Company (LLC) is a popular business struc-ture these days. The LLC is not consistently applied in all states. We strongly recommend that you check out the state laws in your area first.

The LLC itself is not a taxing structure. There is no such thing as an "LLC Tax Return." The LLC can elect to be taxed as any other structure. If no such election is made, a single-member LLC will be taxed as a sole proprietorship and a multiowner LLC will be taxed as a general partnership.

Sole Proprietorship

The sole proprietorship is a bad business structure. It puts everything you own at risk and subjects you to an excess tax of 15.3 percent—self-employment tax—on all net income.

The sole proprietorship is reported on Schedule C of a regular tax return. All of the income is taxable at the individual owner's personal rate.

When Would You Use a Sole Proprietorship?

I don't think you should ever use a sole proprietorship. This is a business structure that is formed by default. If you have a business and don't form a structure, you are a sole proprietorship.

Limited Partnership

A limited partnership (LP) is a good business structure.

A limited partnership has a minimum of two partners—one or more general partners and one or more limited partners. The general partner is responsible for all actions of the partnership and has full liability. The limited partners' risk is limited to the amount of their investment. In other words, if a limited partner invested $10,000, the most she could lose would be $10,000.

A limited partnership is a flow-through taxable income. One potential drawback is that the individual partners can have taxable income if the partnership makes money, even if there is no distribution of cash to the partners. This is called "phantom income," which means that if you are a limited partner, with no control, you may be required to pay tax on income that flows through to you on paper from the partnership even when there is no cash to accompany it. In other words, the partnership has income, and as a partner, you pay tax on your portion of the income. But as a limited partner, you can't control the distributions of cash. So it's possible to have tax and no cash as a limited partner.

The general partner is required to pay self-employment tax on earned income, in addition to the regular federal and state income taxes. A good strategy is to have the general partner position be held by an S corporation or C corporation if the partnership will have earned income. If the limited partnership is being used to hold real estate, the general partnership interest could be held by an S corporation, C corporation, or LLC.

Limited partnership warning: Carefully read any partnership agreements to ensure that distributions are required to cover a portion of attributed partnership income.

When Would You Use a Limited Partnership?

The limited partnership is a great entity to use to hold long-term real estate investments in states where the LLC (limited liability company) structure isn't advisable. For example, California has a high annual cost for the LLC. The LP might be a better choice in California.

The limited partnership structure is also used in estate planning. The limited power that limited partners have translates to below fair market value. That means that gifts can be maximized through the use of a limited partnership.

General Partnership

A general partnership is a bad business structure. The general partnership is a default structure that is used when two or more people enter into a joint venture project without a clear business structure.

All general partners of a general partnership will be subject to self-employment tax. Plus each partner is exposed to full liability for acts of any of the other partners as well as risks associated with the business itself.

When Would You Use a General Partnership?

Never use a general partnership.

S Corporation

An S corporation is a good business structure. It is a regular corporation in which you have made a special election with the IRS to be taxed as an S corporation. There are some further restrictions as to the number of shareholders and types of shareholders that are allowed. Plus, you have a restricted time period in which you can adopt the S corporation status.

The S corporation provides liability protection to the shareholders against acts of the business. In other words, if something happens within the business, the shareholders' other assets are safe. It does not protect the business against liability.

Income from the S corporation flows through to the shareholders and is taxed at the individuals' rate. Income from an S corporation is never subject to self-employment tax.

When Would You Use an S Corporation?

An S corporation is an excellent structure to use for a small business that has a loss or has income that doesn't exceed $30,000 to $50,000. It is also good for professionals who are stuck with the qualified personal service (QPS) designation. If you are stuck with QPS designation, you'll pay extra taxes if you operate as a C corporation. So, the S corporation status makes sense for the QPS designated owners.

C Corporation

The C corporation is a good business structure. It is also very unique. It is the only structure that is taxed on its own tax rate schedule. In other words, you can take advantage of the graduated tax rate tables that are available to individuals and to corporations. Plus, a C corporation allows you to provide the greatest number of deductible employee benefits tax-free.

When Would You Use a C Corporation?

In general, I recommend a C corporation to a fairly sophisticated business owner who anticipates income in excess of $50,000 (after salary and benefits to the owner), has other significant personal income, and/or plans to make a public offering of the company.

C corporation warning: More than any other, this is one business structure where you definitely need to have a well-thought-out plan first. Don't rely on free advice from your friends and other nonprofessional advisors. There are many benefits available, as long as the proper elections are made initially.

Requirements of Business Structures

A business structure becomes a separate entity. It helps to view this as a legal person that requires certain things to stay alive (legal). It's not enough to just form a business structure; you also must maintain that structure. A poorly set up structure or a poorly maintained structure will not give you the asset and income tax protection you want. Before you start your company, make sure you understand the rules of what it takes to keep the company legal. (See Figures 8.1 and 8.2.)

Protecting Your Business Structure

One purpose of the business structure is that you want to separate the business from you personally. The risk is that a court may decide that you have operated your business as an "alter ego." In other words, it might decide that there wasn't a separate business that gave you protection from potential lawsuits. To make sure your assets are protected from risk, always do the following for your corporation:

- Open separate bank account(s) in the name of the business.
- Do not commingle personal and business income or expenses.
- Sign all documents with your title in the structure (president, manager, etc.).
- All advertising, stationery, signs and the like should reflect the legal business name (include "Inc." or "LLC").
- Draw up employment contracts between the owner-employers and the business.
- All key decisions should be approved in the minutes of the operations, such as:

  Proceedings of annual meetings of directors and shareholders.
  Issuance of stock to new or existing shareholders.
  Purchase of real property.
  Approval of a long-term lease.
  Authorization of a significant loan amount or substantial line of credit.
  Adoption of a stock option or retirement plan.
  Important federal or state tax elections.
  Other important decisions that have been made by your board of directors or shareholders.

These are the requirements to maintain a corporation, but we also recommend that you follow the same rules for all business structures. If the

FIGURE 8.1 Checklist for C or S Corporation

Preincorporation Checklist for C or S Corporation

1. Name of Entity: _____

2. Alternative Name(s):_____
   (In many states, corporate names using financial words such as "Mortgage" or "Trust," or professional designations such as "Engineers" require advance approval.)

3. Business Address:_____
   (Try to avoid using your home address.)

4. Registered Address: _____
   (This should be the same as your resident agent's address.)

5. Type of Entity (profit or nonprofit):_____
   (A nonprofit corporation is formed for charitable, educational, religious, and other not-for-profit activities. Federal approval of such status must be granted by the IRS. No stock may be issued.)

6. C Corporation or S Corporation? _____
   (C corporations are used by companies anticipating growth, non-U.S. shareholders, corporate shareholders, and a possible public listing. S corporations may have a maximum of 75 shareholders, and all shareholders must be U.S. residents. Shareholders of an S corporation have profits and losses included directly on their personal income tax returns like a partnership.)

7. In what state will you be forming your company?_____

8. Will you be registering in any other states, and if so, which ones?

   _____
   (If your company will own property in another state, conduct business, or pay wages to employees who live in another state and perform company work in that state (in many cases this includes you), you will need to register your entity in that other state as well.)

9. What will your business do? _____
   (Basic, one-line summary)

10. How many directors will you first appoint? _____
    (Most states require a minimum of one director, who is named in the Articles of Incorporation. You can always add more later—check your bylaws for details.)

11. Must the directors also be shareholders? _____
    (You may choose. Usually there is no requirement that directors also be shareholders.)

12. Provide the names and addresses of all directors: _____

    _____

(Continued)

FIGURE 8.1   *(Continued)*

13. Provide the names and addresses of all officers:
    (You must appoint a president, secretary, and treasurer. Nevada allows this to be one person, who may or may not also be a director.)

    President _____

    Secretary _____

    Treasurer _____

14. Number of Authorized Shares and Par Value:
    (Check your state's rules about whether the number of shares you authorize will impact your filing fee or any franchise fees. Unless you are planning on taking your company public or selling shares to third-party investors to raise capital, you probably don't need more than about 10,000 common shares. If you want different classes of shares (i.e., nonvoting shares, preferential profit distributions, etc.), then talk to your attorney before proceeding. Par value is a concept used in many states to assign a lowest possible value to shares. In many cases your incorporation fee will be based on this value, so try to keep it as low as possible ($0.001 per share is a common choice).)

15. Provide the names and addresses of initial shareholders, number of shares being issued, and consideration being paid.
    (Consideration for shares may be cash, assets, or services.)

Name and Address	Number of Shares	Consideration Paid
_____	_____	_____
_____	_____	_____
_____	_____	_____
_____	_____	_____

16. What is the fiscal year-end for your corporation? _____
    (C corporations may choose any month, but S corporations must select December 31.)

17. Name and Address of Resident Agent: _____

    _____

18. Name and Address of Incorporator (if different from resident agent):

    _____

FIGURE 8.2 Checklist for Limited Liability Company or Limited Partnership

Preformation Checklist for Limited Liability Company or Limited Partnership

1. Name of Entity: _____

2. Alternative Name(s): _____
   (In many states, LLC or LP names using financial words such as "Mortgage" or "Trust," or professional organizations such as "Engineers" require advance approval.)

3. Business Address: _____
   (Try to avoid using your home address.)

4. Registered Address: _____
   (This should be the same as your resident agent's address.)

5. Are you forming an LLC or an LP? _____

6. In what state will you be forming your LLC or LP? _____

7. Will you be registering in any other states, and if so, which ones? _____
   (If your LLC/LP will own property in another state, conduct business, or pay wages to employees who live in another state and perform company work in that state (in many cases this includes you), you will need to register your entity in that other state as well).

8. What will your business do?_____
   (Basic, one-line summary)

9. Duration of existence:_____
   (This is an old concept. Most states allow LLCs to have perpetual existence. LPs normally have a 99-year life span.)

IF YOU ARE FORMING A LIMITED PARTNERSHIP, SKIP SECTIONS 10 AND 11 AND GO TO QUESTION 12.

10. If you are forming an LLC, will your LLC be managed by all of its members, by a committee of members, or by a separate manager or managers, who may or may not be members of the LLC? _____

11. Names, addresses, and percentage of ownership holdings of all members and manager(s):
    (You may list all of your members, or just your manager(s), if you are a manager-managed LLC. A manager may be a corporate entity.)

Manager ❑ Member ❑	Manager ❑ Member ❑	Manager ❑ Member ❑
Ownership Percentage ___%	Ownership Percentage ___%	Ownership Percentage ___%

(Continued)

FIGURE 8.2   *(Continued)*

IF YOU ARE FORMING A LIMITED LIABILITY COMPANY, SKIP SECTIONS 12, 13, AND 14 AND GO TO QUESTION 15.

12. If you are forming a Limited Partnership, what is the name and address of the General Partner?
(May be an individual, individuals, or a corporate entity)

_____

_____

13. Will the general partner have an ownership interest in the limited partnership? If so, how much, or what percentage?_____
(Consult with your CPA or tax advisor on this issue.)

14. Names, addresses, and percentage of ownership holdings of all limited partners:_____
(Use a separate sheet if necessary.)

_____

Ownership Percentage ___%	Ownership Percentage ___%	Ownership Percentage ___%

15. What is the fiscal year end for the entity?_____
(You must select December 31st to receive flow-through taxation benefits.)

16. Name and Address of Resident Agent: _____

_____

_____

17. Name and Address of Organizer (if different from resident agent):_____
(For limited partnerships, the incorporator will be the same as the general partner.)

_____

_____

IRS ever audits you, one of the first things required will be proof that you ran your business in a businesslike fashion. Prove it with great records and documentation.

Why is all this necessary? If you do not follow good business practices, you must be prepared to stand personally liable for all debts and liabilities of the corporation, plus you might sacrifice all tax benefits that you planned on receiving from your corporation. Those seem like pretty good reasons to keep the necessary documentation!

Losing Everything

Early in my career, I met with a new client who had just finally completed paying off a devastating judgment. Prior to becoming my client, he had operated a large strip mall under a corporation. However, he ran the corporation very loosely. He received Social Security checks and deposited those into the corporate account. At the end of the year, his prior tax preparer would credit those checks into a loan that the corporation owed to him.

Then, tragedy struck. Someone slipped on uneven pavement in the parking lot and was seriously injured. A lawsuit ensued. My new client had had liability insurance that capped at a certain level. The person was willing to settle for that amount until his attorney discovered that my client had been depositing his personal Social Security checks into the business. It didn't matter that at year-end the accountant had made the proper adjustments; the fact was that these were personal income items that had been deposited directly into the business.

As a result, he was found to have commingled funds. The court awarded a judgment against all of my new client's personal assets. He lost practically everything!

Tax Tail Wagging the Economic Dog

There must be a business purpose to your business structure. Once you understand how business structures can actually utilize tax loopholes, it's tempting to create a whole series of business structures to change earned income into passive income and maximize the use of the C corporation graduated tax structures. But the tax courts are onto that trick! They have used the expression "tax tail wagging the economic dog" to describe the type of sham business that is set up only for tax purposes.

You are allowed, in fact encouraged, to take advantage of the most optimum tax structures and tax planning. But there must also be a business purpose, and that business purpose can't be merely to pay less tax.

Business Structure Considerations

View all of the necessary factors when you design your own business structures. (See Figure 8.3.) Seek good advisors who are experienced in a wide range of structures to help you make your choice. These first steps may seem time-consuming, but the extra time planning the right strategy will reward you in reaching your goals faster and with more ease.

There are three primary areas to consider:

1. Tax planning.
2. Funding sources and exit strategies.
3. Asset protection.

Tax Planning

The focus of tax planning should start with you. How will the income from your business and investments impact the total amount of tax you pay? To start planning for the best tax plan for your business income, start by assessing your current taxable income, the type of this current income, the future projections of that income, what hidden business deductions you have now, your family situation, and your personal short-term and long-term financial goals. It really is all about you at this point. You are

FIGURE 8.3 The 16 Factors for Business Structure Setup

The 16 Factors for Business Structure Setup

Where Are You?

1. Your current taxable income:
   Marginal Tax Rate _____

2. Source of your current income and future projections of that income:

   % Earned Income ____   % Passive Income ____   % Portfolio Income ____

   Unused Passive Losses (annually) _____

   Unused Investment Expenses (annually) _____

3. Hidden business deductions:

   Amount of additional business deductions after review of Chapter 9

   _____

   _____

   _____

   Total   _____

   Potential C corporation benefits (stated as annual total):

   Health Insurance   _____

   Disability Insurance   _____

   Annual Medical Checkup   _____

   Personal Liability Insurance   _____

   Free Housing/Meals   _____

   Uniforms and Small Tools   _____

   Medical Reimbursement   _____

   Recreation/Health Facility   _____

   Tuition Reimbursement   _____

   Child Care   _____

   Cost of $50,000 Term Insurance   _____

   Total   _____

(Continued)

FIGURE 8.3 *(Continued)*

4. Dependents who can be employed (other entities):

   Name, Age, Job Description, Annual Salary

   _____

   _____

   _____

5. Short-term financial goals:

   _____

   _____

   _____

6. Long-term financial goals:

   _____

   _____

   _____

Recap

1. Taxable income   _____

   Less   3. Total hidden business deductions   (_____)

           4. Dependent salary   (_____)

New Taxable Total   _____

New Marginal Tax Rate   _____

Total Possible Corporate Benefits   _____

Reviewing 1 through 6 above, how important is:
(1 = least, 5 = most)

Reducing personal taxable income	1	2	3	4	5
Changing character of income	1	2	3	4	5
Investment of income for growth	1	2	3	4	5
Investment of income for cash flow	1	2	3	4	5

FIGURE 8.3 *(Continued)*

Business

7. Current business and projection of income of that business:

   Current Taxable Business Income (subtract hidden business deductions from total)

   _____

   Projected Taxable Business Income for:

   One year from now   _____

   Two years from now   _____

   Three years from now   _____

8. Probability of projected business income:

   _____

9. Type of business:

   _____

10. Plan for proceeds from business and from saved taxes:

    _____

11. Plans for business continuation—exit strategies:

    What is your exit strategy for the business?

    _____

12. Funding needs for the business:

    Amount needed for funding and growth—when needed

    _____

Reviewing 7 through 12 above, how important is:
(1 = least, 5 = most)

Current importance of business income not adding to personal	1	2	3	4	5
Future importance of business income not adding to personal	1	2	3	4	5
Likelihood of investors	1	2	3	4	5
Necessity of personal funding	1	2	3	4	5
Level of cash influx needed	1	2	3	4	5
Likelihood of sale of assets to business	1	2	3	4	5
Likelihood of sale of stock of business	1	2	3	4	5
Likelihood of public offering	1	2	3	4	5
Real estate ownership in business	Yes – 1			No – 2	
Unresolved personal service issue	Yes – 1			No – 2	
Unresolved personal holding company	Yes – 1			No – 2	

(Continued)

FIGURE 8.3   *(Continued)*

Asset Protection

13. Your likely exposure to risk from personal acts:
     Publicly visible _____
     High risk   _____

14. Your risk tolerance:
     Your level of risk tolerance   1   2   3   4   5
       (see Figure 8.5)

15. Exposure to risk from the business:
     How high is the exposure to risk from your business? _____

16. Your net worth and projections of net worth:
     What is your current net worth level? _____
     Do you anticipate it significantly increasing? _____

Reviewing 13 through 16 above, how important is:
(1 = least, 5 = most)

Level of risk from your personal acts	1	2	3	4	5
Your risk tolerance	1	2	3	4	5
Level of risk from business acts	1	2	3	4	5
Level of net worth	1	2	3	4	5

unique, and the cookie-cutter approach of our mass-produced economy is not likely to give you the best result for your personal situation.

The purpose of these steps is to first identify how much your taxable income really is, after taking advantage of hidden business deductions and making use of extra entities such as your children or dependent parents. I have found that many new clients have great tax-saving potential without needing to make dramatic changes to their business structure. We first look for the simplest solutions to reducing your taxes by answering these questions.

The next step is to examine the type of income that you have. As we have seen, the concept of the three character types of income comes directly from the Internal Revenue Code. It has been especially important since the 1986 Tax Reform Act. Since that time, we have not been able to take advantage of losses or expenses in one area against income of a different type. For example, you cannot deduct investment expenses (portfolio) against earned income.

Finally, we look at your short-term and long-term financial goals. Many of our clients have a primary goal of creating passive income. This goal can be best achieved by proper business structure setup.

Funding Sources and Exit Strategies

Most business owners are painfully aware of the need to find money for the business's operation at the start-up stage. Funding sources are also an important issue as you go through growth spurts in your business. How will you fund your company's start and growth? You may wish to set it up to allow outside investors or to receive funding from the investments and businesses you already have. The structure you choose for your business can make obtaining money easy . . . or hard.

As your business grows and becomes successful, your next question about money will be about how you will get the money out. What is your exit strategy from the business? There are many different answers to that question. Some of my clients have a goal of setting up the business to create a passive flow of income for them in the future. They plan to use it as a source of personal income with little or no involvement by them. Or they may want to take the company public, sell off a part to outside investors, merge with a larger company, or sell the company as its value increases. Some clients want to build a business that will provide for the family for many future generations—truly creating a family business.

Asset Protection

The United States is the most litigious nation in the world. Most people today are waking up to the need to provide protection for the assets they have worked so hard to build. The business assets need to be protected from acts of the individual owner, and the owner wants to be protected from acts attributed to the business. I have found that most clients have very different points of view regarding the risk that they are willing to tolerate. That is a very personal decision and there are no right or wrong answers. The best answer is simply what is the most comfortable for the owner. Additionally, there are some types of professions, and types of people, that are viewed as more wealthy by the public. Some people are more visible and in the public eye. You might have noticed that fact yourself if you peruse the *Forbes* list of the richest people. Some of the names you will recognize immediately, and there will likely be some of whom you have never heard. The more visible you are, the more risk you run of a lawsuit.

Which Business Structure Is Right for You?

Choosing a business structure is a critical step in your TaxLoopholes strategy. There are a number of factors to consider.

Current Taxable Income

A good tax plan must take into account current taxable income, from all sources, and its proper characterization. What tax bracket are you in now? Your tax bracket is defined as the marginal rate you pay on the next dollar that is earned.

Tax planning note: If personal income is high and is likely to continue at the same rate,

- If the business has income, consider using a C corporation to contain income at the corporate level and pay tax at its own rate.
- If the business has initial losses, consider a flow-through entity such as an S corporation to flow the losses through to your personal return so they can be used to offset other income.

If personal income is at a lower rate now (10 percent to 15 percent marginal tax rate) or if your personal income is expected to decrease to a lower tax rate,

- If the business has low income, an S corporation will flow the income through to you personally. This may be the easiest solution.
- If the business has initial losses, these would be lost to you personally due to your own personally low taxable income. If, however, you expect significantly more income in your future business, you can consider forming a C corporation. The C corporation could then carry forward the initial losses to future years.

Source of Current Income and Future Projections of That Income

Where does your personal income come from now? Is it earned, passive, portfolio, or a combination of all three? Are there any passive losses or portfolio expenses that currently are not being allowed against other income? What are your future projections for the income of each category?

After you have reviewed the type of income and losses that you have, determine what changes you might want to make to the character of the income.

Tax planning note: If your current income is all earned with no passive or portfolio losses or income, invest the proceeds from your business to create streams of passive and portfolio income.

If instead you have current income and passive or portfolio losses, it becomes more important to establish sources of those types of income to offset the underused losses. If your past passive losses are due to real estate, you or your spouse may also be able to qualify as a real estate professional to take advantage of those losses.

A good tax plan should both take into account your immediate needs and allow for flexibility for your future needs. Assess your needs to change the character of the income. How will you do that, if you need to?

Do you anticipate any changes in your income? For example, some clients start thinking about tax planning as they are preparing to leave their full-time employment to pursue their existing business full-time. How will that affect the amount and type of income you receive?

Hidden Business Deductions

Identify your hidden business deductions as well as your business deductions from Appendix B. The purpose of this exercise is to determine what your actual taxable income will be. You may find that you can reduce your personal income tax liability merely by documenting and tracking the expenses you already have.

There are also deductions that are allowable only for C corporations. What benefits can you take if you form a C corporation? What is the total of those benefits? We don't recommend that you form a C corporation *only* because you will be able to deduct these expenses, but it is an important factor to consider.

Dependents Who Can Be Employed (Other Entities)

Sometimes the simplest tax plan for using additional tax rates can be employing (and documenting) by paying your children. My experience has been that most children of entrepreneurs already do help their parents. It often is just a case of paying them as employees, which can greatly reduce the tax you pay, rather than giving your children nondeductible allowances. Make sure you have written job descriptions, pay a reasonable amount for the work performed, and keep time cards. My clients have employed their children as webmasters. Often children have as good or better skills than many computer experts who charge a lot of money for the same service. Why not pay your child, deduct the payment, and reinforce a skill set for them?

Also remember that as your children become employees, they will also be able to take advantage of the pension plans that are available to any employee. For example, if you pay your child $6,000 in salary, you can also set up a SIMPLE (savings incentive match plan for employees) pension plan in the amount of $6,000. If you are in a 35 percent tax bracket and pay your child $6,000, with $6,000 going into a SIMPLE pension plan, you will save $4,200 in taxes and your child will pay only $100—for a net savings of $4,100. This is done easily and relatively inexpensively without the need of any new elaborate tax structures.

Short-Term/Long-Term Financial Goals

What are the current financial goals for all sources of income you receive? How much is the income likely to be next year and in 10 years?

Current Business and Projection of Income from That Business

What type of business do you have or propose to have? What is the current income? Is it portfolio, passive, or earned income? Are you currently subject to self-employment tax? Do you project losses in the business? Would these losses be useful in offsetting other current income you have? Does the business provide tax credits? Will these be more useful for you or for the business?

At this step, compare the income you make from your business and its impact on your personal return. For example:

- **High personal income, high business income.** The best structure, based on this consideration alone, could be a C corporation that allows you to pay tax using a separate tax rate structure. You may also look for ways to form additional C corporations, being careful to avoid the controlled group status (discussed in Chapter 15). In this way, you can take advantage of multiple tax rates for each entity. It is also true that at the high income level, the tax-free benefits available only through a C corporation become especially important.

- **High personal income, initial business losses.** The best structure, based on this part of the analysis alone, could be an S corporation, which will allow the initial business losses to flow directly to your personal return, reducing the tax you pay at your personal level.

Probability of Projected Business Income

How much income will your business make? This may be the toughest question for you to objectively answer. But it is crucially important. You need to assess the probability of your business income projections. I recommend that clients do a worst-case, medium-case, and best-case projection of income. Then assess a reasonable probability to the outcome. Typically, when you examine in this much detail the potential pitfalls of your business, you will actually achieve much higher and better results. You have looked at the potential problems square on and many times that alone is your best defense against them. If you aren't sure of the probability, talk to experts in your field and have them assess your probability. We all have great expectations in the beginning of any venture, or else we wouldn't even attempt it. But the fact is that most businesses fail in the first three years of the venture. So, what is the realistic projection for your business?

Type of Business

What type of business will you have? There are some types of business that can be problematic if performed within a C corporation structure. Specifically, these are qualified personal service corporations, real estate investments, and investment companies.

If you have a concern that the income might make your corporation a qualified personal service corporation, you may decide to form an S corporation instead of a C corporation. If you provide services in the fields of architecture, engineering, health, law, accounting, actuarial sciences, the performing arts, or consulting, make sure you look at the personal service issue in the C corporation section (Chapter 15).

You might also have a concern that the income would be considered from a personal holding company. Typically the income that comes from a personal holding company, such as interest and dividends, can be attributed to appreciating assets. I never recommend that any potentially appreciating asset be put inside of either a C corporation or an S corporation. If you have, or plan to have, appreciating assets such as stocks or real estate, the best structure might be a limited partnership with a corporation as the general partner.

Plan for Proceeds from Business and from Saved Taxes

What do you intend to do with the proceeds of your business? This can be an important element of your tax plan. It is much easier to take money out of an S corporation or partnership, for example, than a C corporation. The ease of distribution from these flow-through entities needs to be weighed against potential savings from the C corporation. With all elements of a tax plan, you should determine your path using a cost/benefit analysis. Does the potential benefit of tax savings outweigh the potential cost of the business structure?

Exit Strategies for Your Business

Start with the end in mind. What is the exit strategy for your business? Chances are you will either (1) close the company, (2) sell the company, or (3) turn it into a long-term family operation. Each of these options has a number of considerations when you are looking at the best type of structure.

If you are running a business to create cash flow for other interests and plan to then close down the initial business at some point, the C corporation will be a harder structure for you to implement. Suddenly closing down the C corporation can result in double taxation through liquidating dividends. Closing out a C corporation takes a long-term strategy that gradually siphons out the assets over time. If you don't want to commit to that type of wind-down, don't start a C corporation if the plan is to close it down in the future.

If your plan is to turn your business into a long-term family operation, how do you anticipate transferring ownership to your family members? If the transfer will be done by means of a gift, then make sure you take into account gift tax and estate tax considerations. If you plan to sell ownership in the company, the next few subsections will be applicable.

When you plan for your business, this is one case where you truly begin with the end in mind. What do you want from the business? Do you want it to continue for your family to run someday? Are you looking for a short-term business to build other assets and then close the business? Do you want to sell the business? If you do sell, what would the likely value be? Would you sell stock through an initial public offering (IPO), to a competitor, to a larger company, or to others? What would they be looking for? Or do you want to set up a true business that gives you cash flow for an extended period with little or no involvement by you?

Selling a Business—Asset Sale versus Sale of Stock

The issue of how you will sell or distribute assets is primarily an issue within an S corporation or a C corporation. Partnerships can distribute assets at "basis." In other words, they can transfer out to partners (in partnerships) at the amount shown on the books, so there is no tax impact.

If your plan includes the sale of your business, consider how that sale will occur. Will you sell the assets of the business (most likely) or sell or merge stock into a larger company? In general, small companies that are purchased by someone wanting to run your company as it has been will want to buy the assets of the company. Larger companies are more likely to want to buy the stock, or to exchange some of their stock for yours.

If you have a C corporation and sell the stock, there can be great benefits through the 50 percent capital gain exclusion (discussed in the next subsection), and also the possibility of double taxation through liquidating dividends. The first is a good thing! The second is something you will need to plan to avoid. In Chapter 16, we will discuss advanced strategies for the C corporation.

Small Business Capital Gain Exclusion—Selling Stock

A shareholder can exclude up to 50 percent of income from the gain or exchange of qualified small business stock—referred to as Section 1202 stock—that has been held for more than five years. The excluded gain is limited to the greater of $10 million or 10 times the taxpayer's basis in stock. Stock must be issued after August 10, 1993, and have been acquired at original issue in exchange for money, property, or services. The corporation must have at least 80 percent of its assets used in a qualified field. Businesses related to health, law, engineering, architecture, farming, insurance, financing, and hospitality are specifically excluded from the list of qualified fields.

Loss on Sale—Section 1244

What if the business doesn't turn out to be everything you want? If you have a corporation (either S corporation or C corporation), the amount of basis in stock that you have is now considered worthless. Normally, you are limited to $3,000 per year in capital losses that exceed capital gains. There is a way around this trap, if you plan ahead. If the business qualifies as a Section 1244 company, then you could take the loss against ordinary income. Well-drafted corporate documents should include a statement that the company is intended to be a Code Section 1244 company. To qualify, the company must have received less than $1 million in capital contributions.

In other words, a few simple lines in the initial documents or in your minutes will allow you to take up to $75,000 per year in current year losses against other income in case your business venture fails.

Combine Sections 1202 and 1244

The best plan for a business that is anticipated to be held for more than five years and then sold through a stock sale for a high price would be to set it up as a Section 1202 and 1244 qualified company. Then, if your plan succeeds, you will be able to legally avoid a tremendous amount of tax. And if your plan does not succeed, you will be able to take a substantial loss at that point against your current income. Note that a Section 1202 company must be a C corporation.

Initial Public Offering

Perhaps your plan is to take your company public in an IPO. There are many different strategies you might choose. In general, only a C corporation can be taken public by selling stock to the outside public. There are three ways to do this: (1) by selling the stock to accredited investors; (2) by selling shares in your company on U.S. stock exchanges; or (3) by selling shares in your company on another country's stock exchange. There are separate requirements for each of these options. Therefore, much fore-

---

Key: To receive the small business capital gain exclusion, you must hold the stock five years or more; gain is limited by the greater of 10 times your basis or $10 million, and the company must have been engaged in a qualified field.

thought, along with specialists advising you, would be a recommended course of action.

One plan is to begin a company using an S corporation. Generally, a company will lose money in the first few years of existence. An S corporation allows you to take that loss against other income on your tax return. When the company begins to make money, or if you plan to take the company public, you can either change the status to a C corporation or dissolve the S corporation and begin a new C corporation.

Sometimes companies will buy an existing C corporation to merge their company into, in order to immediately begin trading stock.

Set your goals, so you know where you are going! As you can see, there are many ways to accomplish the goals you have.

Employee Stock Ownership Plan

Another exit strategy can be to set up an employee stock ownership plan (ESOP), so that your employees buy the company from you. If this is your plan, you will again be selling stock, not assets, and most likely the employees will receive a loan from a financing institution in order to purchase the business. You will most likely want to have your business in the form of a C corporation.

Plan for Funding

How will you fund the company? Initially, you will likely be putting your own money into the company. This can be done in one of two ways: (1) capital contribution or (2) loan to the company. Additionally, you may have some resources (such as equipment and furniture) that you contribute to the company initially. These resources, the cash, and other assets, all need to be repaid in some form back to you by the corporation.

In general, most people try to contribute as little as possible in the form of capital contributions (i.e., stock), and maximize the amount of loans in the corporation. This way, there is a note payable booked on the corporation's records for the shareholder. The note can pay interest—creating portfolio income—to the recipient. It is a deduction for the corporation. This is one way that a corporation can change the character of income: by changing the earned income into portfolio income.

The IRS has challenged the undercapitalization of companies where the amount paid for stock is not reasonable for the company. The exact amount that is paid for the stock is something that you will need to discuss with your own advisor. You will want to consider what the worth of the company is. If you have a business that is providing income streams with little or no work from you, then it might be worth as much as 10 times the projected net income. On the other hand, if it is a risky beginning venture, the value might be simply cents per share, like a penny stock. Part of the assessment process in determining how much the capital stock you own is worth is trying to determine a reasonable value for it initially.

In some cases, you may not want to set up the majority of your funding in the form of a note payable. If you determine that you might want to exercise the small business exclusion under Section 1202 (see earlier in this chapter), for example, you would want to have a higher value in the common stock.

Potential Corporate Pitfall—Taxable Start-Up

Frequently, when you first begin your new corporation, you will find that you "contribute" time and property (furniture, computer equipment, and such) into the new venture. This reality of business could end up creating additional tax if you put your time and property into the new corporation unwittingly.

When there is an exchange for value going into a corporation (either S corporation or C corporation), you could run the risk of taxable gain without even knowing it. If you exchange services for stock, for example, and you have already set a value on the stock, then the stock received for services is taxable income to you! In other words, if you sold 1,000 shares of stock for $10,000 and then exchanged your services for an equal amount—1,000 shares—you have had $10,000 in attributed income. At this point, you have shares in a brand-new start-up company that has no ability to pay but at the same time you have $10,000 you must pay personal income tax on! This can be a "buyer beware" if you put a company together and exchange your sweat equity for ownership.

There is some relief from this tax consequence, though, when property is contributed to a corporation. There are four methods available for transferring property to a corporation. These are:

1. Completely tax-free exchange. If you meet the requirements of this code section, you will be able to transfer property to a corporation solely in exchange for the stock of that corporation.

2. Partially tax-free transaction. In this case, you transfer property in exchange for the stock plus you receive other property.

3. Sales exchange. In this case, you sell the property to the corporation in a transaction completely independent of the actual formation of the corporation.

4. Lease. You would still have ownership of the property and would lease it to the corporation.

Corporate Solution to a Taxable Start-Up

The IRS provides a solution to this potential taxable situation if you can meet the requirements of Section 351. This section provides that no gain or loss is recognized on the transfer of property by one or more persons to a corporation in exchange solely for stock in such corporation if, immediately after the exchange, the transferors control the corporation.

"Property" is defined as real and personal property and includes cash, stocks and bonds, accounts receivable, installment obligations, treasury stock, leasehold improvements, patents, trade secrets, and know-how.

A corporation is considered "controlled" when the persons transferring property to the corporation own at least 80 percent of the voting power of all voting stock and 80 percent of the shares of all other classes immediately after the exchange is completed.

The exceptions of Section 351 are possible to be met, if properly addressed. Figure 8.4 provides a quick checklist for determining if the major requirements have been met. This checklist is designed to just let you know if you are in the correct ballpark for passing the test. It should not be viewed as a substitute for good tax strategy advice.

Stock Valuation

There are two different considerations in determining how much you want to have in stock. These are determined based on your exit strategy. As noted earlier, there can be a significant reduction (50 percent!) in capital gains tax due upon sale in the case of small business stock sales. These discounts are limited to a multiple of the amount of your basis in

---

Key: Define your initial sweat equity as know-how or trade secrets to avoid the tax on services that are exchanged.

FIGURE 8.4   Section 351 Exemptions

Section 351 Exemptions from Tax for Contribution into a New Corporation

Warning! The contribution of property into your new corporation could be considered taxable unless you can meet the exceptions under Code Section 351. This checklist walks you through the major requirements of this section.

1. Was there an actual transfer of property?
   Yes / No

2. Was the property transferred by one or more persons?
   Yes / No

3. Were the transferors in control of the corporation immediately after the transfer?
   Yes / No

4. Was the exchange solely for stock in the corporation?
   Yes / No

5. Was the stock issued in proportion to the relative fair market value of the assets transferred?
   Yes / No

6. Did the basis of the assets transferred exceed the liabilities assumed?
   Yes / No

7. Did the corporation have a true business purpose for assuming the liabilities?
   Yes / No

If you answered all of the above questions as "yes," the transaction is tax-free. If your answer to any of the questions is "no," there still may be a way to make part of the transaction tax-free. Do not take this lightly! There could be hidden tax in the most innocent of actions.

the stock. In this case, you would want as much as possible shown as the value in the stock.

On the other hand, if you plan on continuing the business with ultimate leverage (business runs itself), then you would want to maximize the amount of loans to take advantage of the change in character of income available (changing the earned income into portfolio income). So, in this case, you would want as little as possible shown as the value in the stock.

S corporations and C corporations have capital stock. And only a C corporation has the distinction of being a separate taxing structure. If you form a partnership, then you have partner accounts and the issues of capital versus loans for initial funding are less significant. Of course, these entities do not have the ability to change the character of income or have the small business capital gains reduction.

Assets for a Note

You might want to contribute assets at fair market value in exchange for a note. This is especially true when you need to capitalize the new corporation with money. In this scenario, the corporation will promise to pay you back. That promise should be recorded both in the corporate minutes and in a properly executed note signed by a corporate officer. The note must have a reasonable interest rate. As the corporation pays the money back to the individual owner, there will also be interest paid on the note. This is one way in which a corporation can change the character of earned money (received by the corporation) into portfolio income (paper asset earning money) paid to you.

Here are three guidelines that help ensure that the notes are correctly set up:

1. Draw up a formal note and pay the interest when due. Be sure that the note has a maturity date.

2. Make sure that the note specifies at least the current minimum rate required by the IRS.

3. Loan only enough funds to pay for the immediate needs of the corporation, and make it an amount that obviously can be paid back soon.

You might also want to own intellectual property within a separate business structure, thus employing the philosophy of not wanting to put all your eggs in one basket. Intellectual property might include patented or copyrighted information, as well as systems that you could charge rights or royalties for. There can be two significant reasons for doing this: (1) You move a valuable commodity away from the business and set it up for future franchising (more income streams). (2) The payments for the use of the intellectual property will be an expense to the operating corporation and income to the other company.

In and Out of Partnerships

Most of this section has been devoted to the intricacies of corporate tax law. That is because the rules for partnerships are much easier in this area. Property can be distributed, for example, at basis to the owning partnerships without the need to deal with built-in appreciation that could occur. The same kind of distribution from a corporation to a shareholder must be done at fair market value. Partnerships are much easier to run.

Your Likely Exposure to Risk from Personal Acts

Americans today are the most litigious people who have ever existed on the planet. As a culture, we seem to always be on the lookout for someone to blame for every mistake or unfortunate circumstance. The result is increasingly larger settlements awarded by juries. In some cases, you may be concerned about danger that might result from actions of you or your family. The public perception of you and your wealth can be quite distorted if you own a business or are a professional person.

I have had clients sued when their horse kicked another horse, six months after a supposed fall at an apartment building, and when someone stumbled over a sidewalk crack in front of their house. If you have a concern about liability that might result from your personal life, there is something that you can do to protect your assets.

A limited partnership or limited liability company can protect you against these suits. It should be noted that LLCs are not uniformly accepted among states and you should consult an expert in your state regarding the specifics of LLCs in your area.

How a Limited Partnership Works

An owner of a limited partnership share really does not have any say in the running of the partnership. By definition, a limited partner is not involved in the management. That function falls to the general partner. The general partner determines when and if distributions are made to the limited partner. In real life, if your personal assets are held within a limited partnership of which you are merely a limited partner, you have no control over the distributions. If you were sued and a judgment was lodged against you, the most that the opposing side could receive would be a charging order. That means that the other side would stand in your place as a limited partner. Assuming the general partner is on your side, the other guy would know that distributions would not easily be forthcoming. Good attorneys know that. If they see a possible defendant who holds their assets in a limited partnership, they are much more likely to settle the lawsuit for cents on the dollar.

General Partner

At the beginning of the chapter when we discussed the asset protection available for your investments, note that we discussed how the limited partner was protected. The general partner has full liability. In this case, since the risk comes potentially from the business or investment, then the protection would come about by having a corporation (either S corporation or C corporation) serve as the general partner.

Other Ideas for Protection

Your mother might have told you not to put all your eggs in one basket. If you have businesses that could create liability, such as commercial buildings or apartments, you may want to separate these assets. In other words, if you own three apartment buildings, you might want to separate the three buildings into three separate limited partnerships to limit exposure. That way, if a lawsuit results from one of the buildings, they would not all be at risk.

Can Insurance Provide the Protection?

Some clients prefer to carry large amounts of umbrella policy insurance. These policies generally have limits of $1 million to $5 million. If you assess your risk as slight and have a high level of risk tolerance, and there are no other reasons (such as tax savings) to have other business structures, it may be that an insurance policy is the best answer for you. Again, don't do anything without an overall plan and without examining the proposed plan using a cost/benefit analysis.

Your Tolerance for Risk

The safest possible plan for your business and investment assets is to have every single asset completely in a separate business structure. It's an expensive and time-consuming process to have that level of asset protection.

Yet, I have clients that are so consumed by the fear of a lawsuit that they are willing to pay the extra price of holding each investment separately. For example, the husband has a dental practice where the practice is in an S corporation and all equipment is held in a separate LLC. He and his wife have five rental properties. Each of the properties is in a separate entity. That way, if a lawsuit comes about from any one aspect of the business or investment, the lawsuit risk is contained within that business structure.

I have other clients who will be perfectly happy with 10 properties in one LLC. The difference is their personal risk tolerance. The best plan in the world doesn't work if you aren't comfortable with it. Take the Risk Tolerance Quiz in Figure 8.5 to determine your own risk tolerance.

FIGURE 8.5   Risk Tolerance Quiz

Assess Your Risk Tolerance

The first part of this questionnaire, questions 1 through 5, contains questions that are modeled after more traditional investment risk assessment. Although this test is not specifically designed to determine your risk tolerance for your investments, the way you approach investments is likely to be the way you approach a number of things in your life. The latter part of the test examines the psychological factors that determine how we approach risk. Together, they can provide an indicator of how comfortable we feel with decisions we make regarding tax planning, strategy, and asset protection.

1. You would feel comfortable risking ____ percent of your investable money if the chance of doubling it was ____ percent.
    a. 0 and 0.
    b. 10 and 10.
    c. 25 and 25.
    d. 50 and 50.

2. What do you want your money to do for you?
    a. Grow as fast as possible; current income is not important.
    b. Grow faster than inflation; produce some income.
    c. Grow slowly and provide a nice income.
    d. Preserve principal, no matter what.

3. You have just heard that the stock market fell by 10 percent today. Your reaction is to:
    a. Consider reducing the proportion of your portfolio that is invested in equities.
    b. Be concerned and continue to monitor the market.
    c. Not to worry because the market is likely to go up again at some time in the future.

FIGURE 8.5 *(Continued)*

4. Which of the following best describes how you evaluate the performance of your investments?
   a. My greatest concern is this quarter's performance.
   b. The past 12 months are the most important to me.
   c. I look at the performance over several years to help form an opinion about an investment's attractiveness.

5. What is the worst one-year performance you would tolerate for your portfolio?
   a. −12 percent.
   b. −8 percent.
   c. −4 percent.
   d. Any loss is unacceptable to me.

Choose the response that most accurately reflects your feelings or behavior:

6. I generally prefer to stay in a familiar situation, rather than take a chance on a new situation:
   a. Exactly like me.
   b. Somewhat like me.
   c. Not very much like me.
   d. Not at all like me.

7. I am usually the one who gives in when my plans conflict with the plans of those around me:
   a. Exactly like me.
   b. Somewhat like me.
   c. Not very much like me.
   d. Not at all like me.

8. I often put off making financial decisions because I am afraid of making a mistake:
   a. Exactly like me.
   b. Somewhat like me.
   c. Not very much like me.
   d. Not at all like me.

9. I am optimistic about what the future holds for the economy:
   a. Exactly like me.
   b. Somewhat like me.
   c. Not very much like me.
   d. Not at all like me.

(Continued)

FIGURE 8.5 *(Continued)*

10. My lack of knowledge about investments keeps me from becoming more involved in financial planning activities:
    a. Exactly like me.
    b. Somewhat like me.
    c. Not very much like me.
    d. Not at all like me.

11. I often feel that I don't have enough control over the direction my life is taking:
    a. Exactly like me.
    b. Somewhat like me.
    c. Not very much like me.
    d. Not at all like me.

12. I would feel very embarrassed if anyone found out I made a major investment mistake:
    a. Exactly like me.
    b. Somewhat like me.
    c. Not very much like me.
    d. Not at all like me.

Scoring the Test:

For questions 1, 3, 4, 6, 7, 8, 10, 11, and 12, give yourself a "1" for every "a," "2" for every "b," "3" for every "c," and "4" for every "d."

For questions 2, 5, and 9, give yourself a "1" for every "d," "2" for every "c," "3" for every "b," and "4" for every "a."

12–23: You have a lower risk tolerance. Many times this is due to circumstances you might not even be aware of that are impacting you. Continue to get more information to correctly understand where real and imaginary risk occurs. Look for ways to reduce risk and contain the part that makes you uncomfortable.

24–36: You have a moderate risk tolerance. You can tolerate risk when you have a reasonable expectation that you will receive gain from taking the risk. Carefully assess possible gain and weigh it against the loss you might experience. There is range within the "moderate" title—you may be more comfortable with risk than the average person, but you will likely be the person to always want information before you move.

37–48: You have a high tolerance for risk. Not only do you not mind taking risk, you get bored if you don't have a certain risk factor in everything you do. You are happiest when there is a potential for "all or nothing." You will be able to handle risk in your financial life, but make sure you have done adequate homework to support the decisions and aren't foolhardily jumping just because something sounds exciting.

Exposure to Risk from Business

A business can be a risky venture. Protect your personal assets with the right business structure.

Corporate Veil

An S corporation, a C corporation, and a limited liability company, when properly administered, have a corporate veil between your personal assets and the risks that might come about as a result of daily business. For example, if your delivery van driver hits someone while running errands for your business, the repercussions from that accident will be contained within the business. To take advantage of the corporate veil, you can move the ownership of all tangible assets—such as personal property used in the business—into another business structure. This can also serve for tax planning as you create leasing income into another business structure and reduce earned income.

Determining the Best Business Structure for Your Business and Investments

- What is your current taxable income?
- What is the source of your current income? What are the future projections of that income?
- What are your hidden business deductions?
- Do you have dependents who may be employed?
- What are your short-term and long-term financial goals?
- What is your current and projected income from your business?
- What is the probability of your projected business income?
- What type of business is this?
- What plans do you have for proceeds from the business and from saved taxes?
- What exit strategies do you have for your business?
- How will you fund your business?
- What is your likely exposure to risk from personal acts?
- What is your risk tolerance?
- What is your exposure to risk from business?

Running Corporations . . . or Having Them Run You

I met Nick and Sue after they had already set up their business structures. In their case, they had gone to a seminar by a promoter who was neither a CPA nor an attorney, but he assured them he knew all of the secrets that no one else knew. And the best secret, he claimed, was a C corporation, which he would be glad to sell them in the back of the room.

After reviewing their First Step Financial Profile, I saw that they had total taxable income of $100,000 and yet, inexplicably, had five corporations and five partnerships. Many of these structures had no business purpose and so ran the risk of being considered sham businesses.

The other problem was that they had met a very good salesman and had mistaken him for an advisor. They had not assessed his credentials to determine if he had the necessary education and business and personal experience to provide truly good advice. Ever since they had bought all of the structures, they had been hopping from CPA to CPA trying to find one who could work with what they had. No one, including me, could do that. That was because they didn't have a viable plan. I've recently seen attorneys, or people who claim to be attorneys, selling similar products. Yet these same people either have never practiced law or haven't done so in a very long time. They have a business selling books, tapes, seminars, or corporations; they don't have the essentials to be good advisors. A big part of being a tax advisor is being able to put the theory into practice with the tax return preparation.

Nick and Sue also had based their plan on future goals not relevant to their current status. Their income was currently $100,000. Their plan was something that might have worked, if properly executed, if their income was much higher. They had broken the first rule of business, "Think big and act small."

They had also not taken full advantage of all of the tax-free benefits available to them. After they found how much their current business's taxable income really would be, we discovered that

(Continued)

> ### Running Corporations . . . or
> ### Having Them Run You *(Continued)*
>
> they needed only one C corporation. They had a start-up business that had current losses. We changed this business structure to an S corporation to take advantage of the losses.
>
> Nick and Sue were very concerned about risk from lawsuits. We completed one of the limited partnerships that had never been properly implemented to hold the equipment from their business. If we were starting over, we'd have probably chosen an LLC instead to hold the equipment.
>
> This simplified their tax plan, which had started with five C corporations and five limited partnerships. The new plan had a C corporation for the business, an LP to hold the equipment, and an S corporation for the start-up business.
>
> Unfortunately, dissolving the extra structures wasn't cheap. The first plan, which was improperly designed and implemented, cost them time and money. Once this was all behind them, though, Nick and Sue were able to move ahead with confidence in their new plan.

Final Note on Business Structures

The right business structure will save you taxes and protect your assets. The wrong business structure can be expensive to unwind and can actually cost you extra taxes. After your business structures are in place, it's necessary to keep them legal by following the proper corporate formalities.

Chapter 9

DISCOVER YOUR HIDDEN TAX LOOPHOLES

What's Deductible?

The IRS starts by defining a deductible expense in just 27 words:

> There shall be allowed as a deduction, all the ordinary and necessary expenses paid or incurred during the taxable year in carrying on any trade or business.

Now it gets tricky! What exactly is "ordinary and necessary"? It's all subject to interpretation, like much of the tax code. In this case, there have been numerous federal court decisions trying to interpret what those words mean. The consensus of that additional tax law gives us the following additional definitions:.

- *Ordinary expenses* are expenses that are normal, common, and accepted under the circumstances by the business community.
- *Necessary expenses* are expenses that are appropriate and helpful.

Those are the guidelines, and now it gets fun! Just about anything can be a deduction, if it helps your business. At my TaxLoopholes seminars, I often lead the group in a "discover your hidden deductions" interactive portion. Participants shout out the expenses they have in their personal lives and then, as a group, we come up with situations where these expenses could be deductible.

We've found ways to make your travel, kids, home, vacation, computer equipment, clothing and even pets deductible. It all depends on what you're doing with the business.

One time, though, a man in the front row was insistent in trying to find a way to write off his bed. I wasn't sure that we really wanted to discuss the business purpose for his bed in the seminar. So, I ended up just saying that not everything every time will be deductible. And that's true for your deductions. Not everything will always be deductible. There's an old saying that pigs get fat and hogs get slaughtered. Don't get slaughtered.

You might want to refer again to the First Step Financial Profile in Chapter 3 and then ask yourself, which of these items could be deductible? Review Appendix B for a list of common business deductions. Every time you consider a new purchase, ask yourself, "Is there a way that this could be a business deduction?"

Importance of Business Deductions

Most taxpayers understand the importance of deductions. This is an area that everyone, even employees, is constantly striving to derive more benefit from. Many ads use the "tax deductibility" of items as a reason to buy. Everyone is looking for ways to reduce their taxes by finding deductions.

In the case of a business owner, there are many more deductions available than for an employee. Highly compensated employees have *no* deductions available to them. But the business owner will always find something that is deductible, no matter how much the owner's income is.

Why look for deductions? It's simple; the more tax deductions your business can take, the lower your taxable income is and the lower the tax you must pay.

Commonly Overlooked Business Deductions

First, though, let's go over the most commonly overlooked business deductions. Chances are you already have these deductions available for your business.

Automobile

There are many ways to deduct the cost of an automobile. And that can be confusing. Using the values for the year 2004, here are the simple facts about autos:

- You can buy the car in your business. The business can deduct the cost of maintaining the car (gas, oil, repairs, tires, car washes, and so forth). Plus, the business can deduct the interest portion of any payments and then depreciate the car, using the limits established by the government. For vehicles purchased in 2003, the depreciation amounts are: year 1—$10,610; year 2—$4,800; year 3—$2,850; year 4 and later—$1,675.

- Your business can lease the car. However, most likely not all of the lease will be deductible. A portion will have to be added back for tax purposes. For example, a vehicle worth $30,000 will have to have a little more than $200 of the lease added back in the first year.

- You can buy or lease the car yourself and be reimbursed for mileage at the current rate. In 2004, the amount is $0.375 per mile. The payment is deducted from the business income, but is not considered income for you.

- If you buy a vehicle that is over 6,000 pounds gross vehicle weight, the luxury automobile limitation does not apply. In this case, your business can depreciate the vehicle just as though it was any other piece of equipment. That includes being able to make a Section 179 deduction of $102,000 (in 2004) right up front.

  TaxLoopholes Tip #1: Congress keeps talking about changing the "heavy vehicle" exemption. Check in at www.taxloopholes.com/loopholesoftherich for updates.

  TaxLoopholes Tip #2: A real estate investment is not eligible for a Section 179 deduction. However, if you set up your real estate investments so that you provide your own property management company, you will have created a business. The business can then take advantage of the Section 179 deduction.

Bad Debt

Bad debt is a commonly misunderstood deduction. It is most overlooked at the personal level, though, and not at a business level. An individual can write off as bad debt loans made to anyone that have no hope of collection. An individual can also take a deduction for expenses paid on behalf of others that will not be repaid. The burden of proof will be on whether the item is actually a gift. To prove a bad debt, you must attempt to collect just as you would with any other debt. I recommend that clients first have a note drawn up for each loan and then show proof of a collection attempt by sending a certified letter with a return receipt requested demanding payment.

Where most people will unintentionally overlook the bad debt expense deduction at an individual level, they will mistakenly try to take a bad debt expense deduction for a business when it is not allowed. The only way that a business can take a bad debt expense deduction is if the income was first reported and tax was paid on it. In other words, if your business is accrual-based, which means that accounts receivable are counted as income even if they have not been collected, then when that receivable is not collected, there is a bad debt expense. Most small businesses, however, are cash-based, which means that income is counted only when it is received. There cannot be a bad debt expense offsetting income, because the accounts receivable income was never recognized.

Business Start-Up

There are many expenses *before* you begin your business. And, unfortunately, since one of the steps is setting up your accounting system and the expenses occur first, you might forget them. Here is a checklist of common start-up expenses that you can deduct (or capitalize and amortize over 60 months). It is not complete. Use it as a memory jog for items you can deduct in your business.

- **Legal expenses.** These are costs that you pay to an attorney or document preparation service to prepare the initial paperwork for your business. They need to be amortized over 60 months. In other words, you can subtract $\frac{1}{60}$ of the cost each month. After the business is up and running, most legal fees are deductible immediately.
- **Business structure setup** (cost of corporation, etc.—amortized over 60 months). This includes the costs you pay to have special business structures set up, such as the cost of forming a corporation.

- **Filing fees.** These are the costs paid to the state and local agencies for the privilege of doing business and include business licenses, state filing fees, fees for lists of directors, and others. The exact fees will depend on the type and location of your business.
- **Accounting fees.** Hopefully, you will consult with an accountant and bookkeeper to get your books set up as soon as possible. Those costs are deductible.
- **Office equipment.** A great deal of office equipment is needed for a basic office in this electronic age. Computer, printer, fax machine, and phone are just a few of the items needed. Many people already have some of these items before starting a business. Your business can pay you the fair market value for these items from its proceeds, but you need to track the expenses first.
- **Office furniture.** Office furniture can include your desk, tables, chairs, and filing cabinets, as well as art you hang on the walls.
- **Cost of investigating business** (seminars, books, travel, advisors' fees). Prudent business owners take time to investigate and learn all they can about their business first. This can include going to seminars, buying books, subscribing to magazines, talking to advisors, dues to professional organizations, and travel to look at other businesses.
- **Office setup costs** (stationery, business cards, logo design). The costs of designing a logo, setting up a web site, preparing stationery, and so forth, are all part of the office setup costs.

Education Expenses

You can deduct education expenses when they are related to your current business. There are two ways to expense education: (1) as education that is required to maintain or improve skills and (2) under an education assistance plan. In the latter case, the Internal Revenue Code under Section 127 currently allows up to $5,250 in annual tax-free assistance to each eligible employee. The education need not be job-related. Children of owners can qualify if they are over the age of 21, are legitimate employees of the business, and are not dependents of the owners. You will need to have a separate written plan for this deduction, and you cannot discriminate among employees (samples are provided in Appendix D). Note that education that is required to maintain or improve skills does not require a written plan and is not subject to the limits of $5,250 per employee. However, we recommend that you include a note in your minutes authorizing such expenditures.

Entertainment Expenses

It's amazing to me how many clients fail to count their business entertaining expenses. Currently, 50 percent of *any* expense that is "directly related" to the business or "associated with" the business, and the entertainment takes place immediately before or after a business discussion, is deductible.

- The "directly related" test says that: (1) the main purpose of the combined business and entertainment was the active conduct of business; (2) you do conduct business with that person; and (3) you had more than a general expectation of getting income or other business benefit at some future time.
- Business that is held in a clear business setting and is for business purposes is considered directly related. Examples are: (1) entertainment in a hospitality room at a convention where business goodwill is created through the display or discussion of business products; (2) entertainment that is mainly a price rebate on the sale of your products (such as a restaurant owner providing an occasional free meal to a loyal customer); and (3) entertainment of a clear business nature occurring under circumstances where there is no meaningful personal or social relationship between you and the persons entertained (such as entertainment of business and civic leaders at the opening of a new hotel or play when the purpose is to get business publicity rather than to create or maintain the goodwill of the persons entertained).
- If you don't meet the "directly related" test, you may still meet the "associated with" test. You must show that the entertainment is associated with your trade or business and that it directly precedes or follows a substantial business discussion. In this case, you must show that you actively engaged in a discussion, meeting, negotiation, or other business transaction to get income or some other specific business benefit. The meeting does not have to be for any specified length of time, but you must show that

the business discussion was substantial in relation to the meal or entertainment. It is not necessary that you devote more time to business than to entertainment.

In some cases, though, 100 percent of the expense can be deductible. In this case, it needs to be provided for the "convenience of the employer."

- Occasional and sporadic meal reimbursements and supper money for overtime work are excludable from gross income.
- When a meal is provided so that employees are present for emergency work (emergency medical personnel who are on call, for instance), then the cost is 100 percent deductible.
- When a meal is provided because business operations require a short lunch period and employees don't have time to eat elsewhere (a short lunch period means less than one hour), then the cost is 100 percent deductible.
- If more than half the meals provided at the on-premises eating facility are provided for the employer's convenience, then the balance of the meals also are treated the same. In other words, if more than half of your employees eat tax-free, the rest do also.

Legal and Professional Fees

Fees that you pay to attorneys, tax strategists, accountants, bookkeepers, or other consultants can be deducted in the year you pay them. If the work clearly relates to future years, such as patent work, the fees must be deducted over the life of the benefit.

Travel Expenses

Deducting travel expenses has gotten more and more complex. Generally, when you travel for business, you can deduct many expenses such as the cost of the plane fare, costs of operating your car, taxi fare, lodging, meals, shipping, business meals, clothes cleaning, telephone calls, faxes, and tips. If you combine business and pleasure within the United States, the trip is still deductible if the primary purpose is business. You can determine primary purpose by counting the number of days for business compared to the number of nonbusiness days. If there are more business days than nonbusiness days, then you have a deduction. What is a business day? It is a day in which you do business—any amount. Document what you have done by making a note in your organizer or calendar. Keep copies of any literature or business cards you collect as part of your business.

Interest

If you use credit to finance business purchases (like many start-up businesses), especially in the beginning, you can deduct the interest. If you take out a personal loan such as a home equity loan to fund business needs, then that interest is also deductible. You will need to keep good records showing how the money or purchases were used in your business.

Moving Expenses

If you move your office, even if it is across the street, moving costs are deductible. Many new business owners make transitions from home to executive suite to their own suite of offices. That's a lot of moves and they are all deductible. Many new business owners also get confused on this deduction and assume that the moving expense rules are the same for a business as they are for an individual. They are not. An individual can take a moving expense deduction only if their new workplace is at least 50 miles farther from their old home than their old workplace was. A business is not subject to such restrictive rules.

Software

What would a modern business do without software? Don't forget this common expense, especially in your first year of business when you transfer all of the software you had previously purchased. The business should reimburse the cost to you, so it is a deduction.

Charitable Contribution/Promotion

If your business is formed under a flow-through entity (partnership or S corporation), your business can make a charitable contribution and pass the deduction through to you to claim on your individual tax return. There are some limitations as to how much you will be able to take in charitable deductions on your return. A C corporation can take deductions directly against its income, but is allowed in the current year only up to 10 percent of net profit. In many cases, there is actually a promotional aspect to what might be considered charitable contributions. For example, advertising in a program for an event sponsored for a local

---

Reduce Your Taxes Today!

- Create a legitimate business.
- Calculate the hidden business deductions you already have.
- Keep good documentation of your expenses.
- Change your current withholding through payroll.

---

charity could actually be called a promotional expense. Wherever possible, look for promotional expenses within charitable deductions, so that you do not have problems with the limitation on charitable donations.

Taxes

There are many taxes that are deductible for your business. For example, sales tax paid on supplies and equipment for your business, excise taxes, fuel taxes, payroll tax, real estate taxes, personal property tax, city taxes, and state income tax are deductible for your federal income tax. Your federal income tax is never deductible. The state income tax is not deductible for your state tax return.

Hidden Business Deductions

Now let's look at some common hidden business deductions. These are the things that you are already paying for with after-tax dollars. But with a business these can become legitimate business deductions.

I never recommend that clients invest in something just for the write-off. Your only return would be the tax savings. At the current highest tax rate, that means if you buy something for $1,000 the best you'll get is $350.

Boat

If your boat has a restroom and a kitchen, then it can qualify as a second home. It's not a business deduction, but the interest on payments would be deductible. A boat could also be a deduction if, again, it is needed as "ordinary and necessary." In other words, if you had a business that required that you have a boat—such as a photographer or fisherman or boat seller—it would be deduction. There is a famous story told by accountants of a man who went in to his accountant and said he wanted to write off a new yacht. His accountant told him that he could not deduct it unless he had a business that needed it. The client resolved to prove he could turn it into a business. So he started a business selling yachts . . . and made 10 times more money than he ever had in his other business.

Children

There are many expenses associated with your children. The best plan is to have your children employed in your business so that they can pay for their own expenses. In this way, you are able to deduct the cost of their salaries, and up to approximately $4,900 is not taxable to them (the amount changes each year). You may not want to stop there, though. If you are in a high tax bracket, it may make sense to have your child pay tax at their lower tax rate. You'll get the deduction at your high rate and they pay at their lower rate.

There are three things financial advisors want to see if you do employ your children (or other dependents) in your business:

1. A written job description.
2. A time card that shows the hours that have been worked.
3. Reasonable wages paid for the job performed.

TaxLoopholes Tip: Children under the age of 14 who receive unearned revenue are subject to the "kiddie tax." That means that they pay tax at your tax rate. However, children who make *earned* income (they work for it) are not subject to the kiddie tax, no matter how young they are.

Clothing

The cost of items that are considered uniforms is deductible, as is the cost of cleaning such items. In other words, if you put a logo on your polo shirt, it is likely a business deduction, both for the cost of the shirt as well as for the cleaning expense.

Gifts

Many gifts are really promotional gifts—the flowers you send as a thank-you or the gift certificate to a restaurant. These are more properly considered promotional items and are deductible as such.

Home Office

This deduction has gone through some wild swings in the past decade. Currently, a home office is allowed for anyone who has a business and meets the requirements of:

- A space with exclusive business use.
- Regular business use of the space.

The concern of a red flag over an audit because of this deduction is long past. In fact, using this home loophole, and others, is an integral part of the Jump Start! plan.

Medical Reimbursement

A medical reimbursement plan is one of the little-used strategies that are available to businesses that operate as C corporations. With a plan in place (you can find a copy in Appendix D), you can deduct reimbursements for medical co-payments, as well as dental, vision, orthodontia, therapeutic massage, and other costs. These benefits are fully deductible for the business and are not income for the recipient. The plan cannot discriminate against other employees and must cover 70 percent or more of all employees. If there are more than 100 employees, a Form 5500 is required to be filed.

Personal Care

Remember the rule of "ordinary and necessary." An actress can deduct the cost of hair and nail care. In Nevada, a showgirl was allowed to deduct her augmentation expense. The question to ask is whether the cost really does help the business—and even more importantly, does it pass the laugh test? In other words, can you write it down with a straight face?

Pets

The cost of pets can even be a business deduction. For example, the cost of keeping a watchdog is a deduction, as was proved in a tax court case in Hawaii, where a junkyard was allowed to deduct the cost of the dogs. Also, I have seen real estate brokers and land developers deduct the cost of keeping a horse when they use the animal to view property.

Travel/Vacation

See earlier in this chapter for write-off rules regarding travel within the United States. Of course, if you are in a business that has travel as an essential ingredient (for example, if you are a travel writer or photographer), you will have an easy time proving the business purpose of travel. If your spouse and children are also legitimate employees, then their travel is deductible also. Finally, if you have a corporation, you are required to have an annual shareholders meeting. The travel cost to these meetings is a legitimate expense of the corporation. There are different rules if your travel is outside of the United States. If you stay away more than seven days, then you will have to allocate your expenses between time spent on business and time spent on pleasure.

Tax Credits

Tax deductions reduce your taxable income. Since tax is calculated based on the amount of taxable income you have, having less taxable income is good for tax purposes.

Tax credits are even better. A tax credit directly reduces the amount of tax you pay. If you have $10,000 in tax credits, that means you will pay $10,000 less in tax. In contrast, if you have $10,000 in tax deductions and you're at the highest tax rate, you will pay only $3,500 less in taxes.

When you're putting together your tax loopholes strategy, don't forget the credits!

Work Opportunity Credit

The work opportunity credit provided a credit for wages paid to certain individuals in certain areas deemed "enterprise," "empowerment," or "community renewal." For a full review of the potential areas, see www.hud.gov/progdesc.

In most cases, you could get a tax credit equal to 40 percent of the first $6,000 paid to qualified individuals. Under current law, this provision expired December 31, 2003, but we may be seeing it come back soon. Check in at www.taxloopholes.com/loopholesoftherich to register for free updates on tax law changes.

Welfare to Work Credit

The welfare to work credit provided a tax credit equal to 35 percent of the first $10,000 of eligible wages to recipients of long-term family assistance paid in the first year and 50 percent of the first $10,000 of eligible wages paid in the second year. This provision expired December 31, 2003, but we may see it come back.

ADA Tax Credit

This credit is applicable to businesses with 30 or fewer full-time employees or not more than $1,000,000 of gross revenue. It is intended to help cover the Americans with Disabilities Act (ADA)–related business access costs. Anything that is done to create access or communication with vendors, customers, or employees with disabilities is applicable, including:

- Provision of readers for customers or employees with visual disabilities.
- Provision of sign language interpreters.
- Purchase of adaptive equipment.
- Production of accessible formats of printed materials.
- Removal of architectural barriers in facilities or vehicles.
- Fees for consulting services.
- Provision for access to the Internet for those with disabilities.

The credit is 50 percent of the amount spent for adapting existing facilities. The maximum credit per year is $5,000.

Hot Tax Loopholes for Businesses and Investors

Business owners get special treatment. Here are some other deductions that only business owners can take.

Group Life Insurance

Group life insurance coverage of $50,000 or less provided to you by your company is excludable from your income.

De Minimis Fringes

This means gifts literally of "little value." A Rolex watch is not a de minimus fringe. However, a turkey at Thanksgiving would qualify. It's a tax deduction for the company and is not income for the recipient.

Meals and Lodging for the Benefit of the Employer

The value of meals and lodging provided by your company to you, your spouse, and your dependents is not taxable income as long as the following three criteria are met:

1. The meals and lodging are provided at your employer's place of business.

2. The meals and lodging are provided for the convenience of your employer.

3. In the case of lodging (but not meals), you must accept the lodging at your employer's place of business as a condition of your employment. This means that you must accept the lodging to carry out the duties of your job properly, for example, if you must be available for duty at all times.

Lodging includes the cost of utilities such as electricity, gas, water, garbage collection, and the like.

Chapter 10

CONTROL WHEN AND HOW MUCH YOU PAY IN TAXES

Control

Do you feel like you don't have control over the amount of taxes you pay? Well, the Jump Start! plan can get you started on having that control. In fact, if you have a business and invest in real estate, and either you or your spouse can qualify as a real estate professional, you can have a plan where you pay *no* taxes. And, even better, you do it with the government's blessing because you are taking advantage of the legal tax loopholes within tax law.

By the way, if you currently have a business and invest in real estate and either you or your spouse qualifies as a real estate professional and you still pay too much in tax, it means one of two things (or both):

1. You don't own enough real estate.
2. You aren't taking full advantage of the tax loopholes.

Jump Start! Method to Pay No Taxes

The Jump Start! method uses business, real estate, and your home as part of the overall methodology for building wealth because these areas have the most tax loopholes. It is possible to get rich with stock investing. However, this is either done as a tax-deferral plan or as a stock trading business. The tax-deferral plan—IRA, SEP, defined benefit plan, 401(k) plan, and the like—gives you a tax deduction now in exchange for a higher tax rate later if your income increases. If you have a plan to be rich, a tax-deferral plan seldom makes sense. Of course, if your plan is to be poor and have a lower tax rate later, then the tax-deferred plan will work.

Under the Jump Start! plan, your business creates income after you've taken advantage of all tax-free benefits. That income is taxable. If you have held the business in a flow-through business structure, the taxable income is reported on your tax return. Now, here's the trick. If you or your spouse is a real estate professional, you can use paper real estate losses to fully offset the taxable business income. Otherwise, the losses from real estate are limited to just $25,000 if your income is under $100,000. If your income is over $150,000, you cannot use any of the real estate losses to offset your income.

Real Estate Professional Status

The real estate professional status is an integral part to this strategy. This means that you (or your spouse) are spending more time in real estate activities than any other occupation for which you are paid. There must also be a minimum of 750 hours per year spent in real estate activities.

Creating Real Estate Loopholes

The best real estate loophole is depreciation. Although we know that generally real estate goes up in value, the government says that it actually goes down in value. That's what depreciation is. In fact, they say that a residence is worthless in 27.5 years and a commercial building is worthless in 39 years. Land never depreciates, according to the government. That means that there is no depreciation allowed for land.

The secret, then, to tax-advantaged wealth building is to invest in

Wife Triples Family Income by Quitting Her Job

I first met my new clients, a full-time doctor and his wife who worked full-time as a nurse, about five years ago. Reuben and Clarice live in Florida, where he makes a very good living as a doctor. He has his own practice, so we were immediately able to maximize the tax-free benefits. However, as there was still considerable income left at the end of the year, they paid a lot in taxes. Additionally, because Clarice likes to keep active, she continued to work full-time as a nurse. Reuben and Clarice are raising three children, one of whom is developmentally challenged, so they have their hands full.

They both understand the issue of working hard for their money versus having their money work hard for them. By the time I met them as new clients, they had already begun investing in apartment buildings. They quickly discovered that in a hot real estate market it's hard to find easy cash-flowing deals. So they were instead buying properties that needed work, reasoning that the expenses to get the properties fixed up would help them on their taxes. The problem was that at their high income level, we couldn't take advantage of their real estate losses.

Clarice was almost as active in the real estate as Reuben was. We all discussed the feasibility of having Clarice become a real estate professional. Currently, she went to the job sites on a daily basis to check on the contractors, wrote all the checks for the work, met with interior designers, and continued to look for new properties to purchase. Added together, she clearly had the 750 hours she needed for the year. The problem was that she was not spending more hours in real estate than she was in nursing. So Clarice quit her job and kept good records of her real estate activities.

Their taxes dropped by $50,000 in the first year. That was more than Clarice had made as a nurse! With the extra time she had created, Clarice began taking more of a role in the real estate.

Now, five years later, the real estate pays Reuben and Clarice *more* than Reuben's income. Plus, through the use of real estate loopholes, they also pay half the tax they used to. More money and less tax—that's the beauty of the Jump Start! method.

real estate that has the maximum potential for depreciation Don't buy bare land or develop property and expect the same tax loopholes. Depreciation is available only for property that is in service; and that means it is in use as a rental.

The next two steps in the Jump Start! program discuss buying real estate and maximizing real estate loopholes to create cash that you put in your pocket without paying tax (see Chapters 11 and 12). There is also the benefit of creating so much depreciation in your project that it more than offsets the income you make from your property. That's how you create a paper loss. If you or your spouse is a real estate professional, you can take that loss against your other income.

Balancing Business and Real Estate

How much real estate is enough? A good rule of thumb is that you will be able to take a deduction for 4 percent of the full value of the real estate if you follow our plan for maximizing depreciation. So, say you have bought a building for $250,000; estimate $10,000 for depreciation. That depreciation first offsets against the income of the property. Just using a rough rule of thumb, let's assume that you put 10 percent down on the property ($25,000) and you are getting a cash-on-cash return of 20 percent. That would mean that you have $5,000 per year of positive cash flow. We're going to also assume, for purposes of our model, that you have an interest-only loan for maximum tax benefit. (Interest is fully deductible, while an amortizing loan payment, with principal and interest both, is only partially deductible.) That means you will likely also have taxable income of $5,000 per year. But wait! You can subtract the $10,000 depreciation from the $5,000 income and create a paper loss of $5,000. Of course, you've actually put $5,000 in your pocket. But the government will let you take that $5,000 loss against your other income. That's one of the benefits of Jump Start!

Based on this model, you now have $5,000 to offset business income. If you make $50,000 per year from your business, you'll need 10 such properties to offset your income. If you make $500,000 per year from your business, you'll need 100 such properties to offset your income. Generally larger properties will provide lower cash-on-cash returns. It's common to get a 10 percent cash-on-cash return for big properties. That means that a person with $500,000 worth of income will need approximately $1,650,000 in real estate to create enough offset to eliminate the tax altogether.

There is a warning, though! The accelerated depreciation method of Jump Start! means that you front-end-load your depreciation. After about five years, the amount of depreciation will be reduced. The best way to view this plan is as a long-term commitment to buy more real estate, at least every five years. That way you can keep replenishing your depreciation basis.

Seven Ways to Minimize Taxes

The preceding business/real estate/real estate professional scenario is the ideal world. Can everyone do that? No, and certainly not from the very beginning. Here are seven ways you can start to minimize the taxes you currently pay.

Business Structure Timing

The C corporation is the one entity that allows different year-ends. In other words, you can use a year-end for your corporation of any month-end. I strongly recommend that you use a year-end that is different than your personal return (December 31). That way you can make use of staggered year-ends for tax planning. Don't pay the government any sooner than you have to!

Timing Payroll Withholding

Wherever possible, pay your taxes through payroll withholding, not estimated tax withholding, and do it as late as possible. Estimated tax payments must pay your taxes ratably through the year. Let's say you have tax due of $100,000. The estimated tax payments must be paid quarterly and equally, or you run the risk of penalties. Payroll withholding, in contrast, can all be paid at the very end of the year, if you have a big enough bonus coming. This is another example of how not to pay the government too soon!

Wise Use of Tax Deferrals

Early on in *Loopholes of the Rich*, I told you the reasons I'm not a fan of tax-deferred pension plans. But they do come in handy in one instance—it's year-end and you didn't do your tax planning! In this case, tax deferrals might be your only hope. But I don't recommend it for a long-range strategy.

The same is true of the like-kind exchange for real estate. Using this tax deferral device, you can defer taxes when you sell your real estate investment property. You then roll over the basis of the property into another new investment property. The problem is that you continue to just roll over the same basis. Let's say you had owned a residential rental property for 10 years and then sold it using the like-kind exchange for a property of exactly the same sale price. You wouldn't pay tax on the transfer. You've just exchanged the position you had in one property for the same position in another. That means you're going to run out of depreciation in 17.5 more years. Do a few of these like-kind exchanges and you've lost the real estate loophole of depreciation.

Capital gains tax rates are lower than ordinary income tax rates. And currently, they are a lot lower. It might make more sense to sell the property and pay the capital gains tax now. You'll have to recapture depreciation as well, but you now have higher basis for more depreciation.

The one time that tax deferrals make sense is when we consider that they defer the taxes you pay. In general, that's a good thing. But we want to make sure you make wise use of that tactic.

Income Splitting with Business Structures

You can also control your taxes by making full use of income splitting loopholes. Income splitting is based on that fact that our tax system is graduated. The first dollar you make is taxed at a lower rate than the last dollar you make, unless you don't make a lot of taxable dollars. Our first tax bracket, as an individual taxpayer, is zero. The next bracket is 10 percent, then 15 percent, and so on until we hit the maximum rate in 2004 of 35 percent.

Income splitting loopholes take advantage of the graduated tax rates of others. In other words, we want to move some of our 35 percent taxed money into another tax bucket that starts off at 0 percent or 15 percent.

One of the most misunderstood loopholes for income splitting is by the use of a C corporation. C corporations are so different that they get their own chapters later in the book in Part III. But one of the benefits of a standard C corporation is that the first $50,000 of income in this structure is taxed at 15 percent. That means if you can set up your business income to go through a C corporation, or divert one of the parts of your business into a separate C corporation, you can then take advantage of the rate difference between your tax bucket and your corporation's. That loophole alone can save you $10,000 or more annually!

The C corporation has a graduated system, so you want to be careful not to leave too much income in the C corporation. Otherwise, the higher rate of the corporation will negate any advantage of moving the money from your personal tax rate.

Also, be careful of this strategy if you have a business with a high income. For example, if your business nets $350,000 and you run the entire business through a C corporation, you'll need to pull out $300,000 in salary. That means that you have payroll taxes on $300,000 to pay. On the other hand, if you had been able to use an S corporation and a C corporation for the business, you could have had just the $50,000 go to the C corporation and the rest go to the S corporation. The S corporation could then have distributed the $300,000 to you partly in the form of salary (subject to payroll taxes) and partly in the form of distribution (*not* subject to payroll taxes). The Medicare portion of your payroll taxes has no cap and it costs 2.9 percent. It might not be huge but 2.9 percent of $150,000 would more than pay the annual latte bill for both my husband and me!

Income Splitting with Dependents

If you currently are supporting dependents, pay them with before-tax money! This includes your children as well as anyone else you help support—nieces, nephews, parents, and the like.

If you can legitimately employ them in your business, you can then take their salaries as a deduction against your income and effectively move the income to their lower tax buckets.

See Figure 10.1 for a demonstration of how you can combine the income splitting loopholes for both dependents and C corporations to immediately reduce your taxes.

Depreciation

We talked earlier about depreciation and how it could be used to create passive real estate losses that will offset your business income.

What if you can't make use of the passive real estate losses? If that is

FIGURE 10.1   Income Splitting Loopholes

the case (and this is important), do not maximize the depreciation. If you do, and create the losses, they will be suspended until you sell the property.

I see the problem again and again with people who have studied some of our TaxLoopholes products and are excited about the prospect of accelerating depreciation. However, if they don't have advisors working with them who fully understand the strategy, they may create a loss that not only is useless but actually costs more in taxes.

It is better to *not* accelerate the depreciation; instead, wait until a future date when circumstances might change. If you have a year in which you can take the loss (either you or your spouse qualified as a real estate professional or your income has fallen below $100,000), then you can catch up past depreciation in that year.

Carryforward Losses

Sometimes I see tax returns for new clients that have a lot of carryforward losses. Unfortunately, there aren't a lot of strategies to do after the fact for most tax situations.

Carryforward losses generally come about in one of five ways:

1. Net operating loss (NOL). This is a loss that your business has experienced. You have a choice of carrying this loss back and then forward, or merely carrying it forward. This is a good kind of loss, because it can be used immediately to offset business income. In some cases, you can even sell your NOL to another taxpayer for their use. This transaction will cost some money and require sophisticated legal and tax advice, so it's generally used only for high-end losses.

2. Passive loss. This loss may come about because real estate losses exceed real estate income and the taxpayer cannot use the loss to offset other income. This is a bad loss—you're not going to be able to use it until you sell the property.

3. Investment expense. Generally these expenses come about from margin interest on stock trading accounts or fees related to investment accounts. Unfortunately, the only way you can use this expense is against other investment income. Another bad carryforward loss, it's hard to use it up.

4. Capital loss. This one is perhaps the most devastating. You've lost money on a stock or investment sale and now you can only offset against capital gains or take the loss at $3,000 per year. A new client came to me a year ago who had over $1,000,000 in carryforward capital loss. Unless he hurries up and makes some money, it will take him more than 330 years to use the loss up!

5. Loss in excess of basis. If you have invested money in a project and the project loses money, you can take a deduction only up to the extent of your investment. In some cases, debt that you are responsible for can also be used to create basis, so you get more deduction. As an example, let's say you invest $10,000 in a limited partnership that loses money. In fact, you receive a K-1 form that says your portion of the investment lost $20,000. You can take only $10,000 as a current loss. The rest is a loss in excess of basis that should be tracked on a schedule. It's not a great type of loss, but it's not a bad type of loss, either. It didn't cost you any money and you can carry it forward.

Beware the Ticking Tax Bomb— Alternative Minimum Tax

There is one warning for your tax plan. Currently, there is an alternative tax, called the Alternative Minimum Tax (AMT), that is beginning to affect more and more taxpayers making more than $50,000 per year. The tax loopholes for AMT are different. It's also a very sneaky tax. You often don't know you'll be subject to it until after the year has ended and your accountant prepares your tax return.

AMT—Problem Now, Disaster Later

The Alternative Minimum Tax (AMT) was designed as an alternative tax for the rich who were able to take advantage of tax loopholes. Until it was put in law, the rich had been able to use tax loopholes to completely offset all income and pay no tax. That's why this tax was designed. It was a way to make sure that the rich paid *something*!

Fast forward to today: The tax loopholes have kept coming. In fact, the best tax loopholes come when you have a business and/or invest in real estate. Even better tax loopholes information is now available for everyone who wants it! (That's the resources that TaxLoopholes.com provides.) You no longer need to be rich to take advantage of these loopholes. That means more people are also becoming susceptible to AMT.

Inflation continues to push income upward. This increase in taxable income is called "bracket creep." The income tax brackets have been adjusted to take inflation into account. The AMT brackets have not. More middle-income people (as many as 17 million people!) will soon become subject to AMT.

It's a ticking tax bomb for unsuspecting American taxpayers. Will it affect you? Complete the TaxLoopholes AMT Test in Figure 10.2 to find your answer.

What Is AMT?

AMT is an alternative type of tax. If, after taking the TaxLoopholes AMT test, it looks like you might be subject to this tax, you will need to calculate the alternative tax using a different base of income. There are two AMT tax rate brackets—26 percent and 28 percent. The rate(s) will be multiplied by the new AMT income base. The two amounts—AMT tax and income tax—are then compared. You will pay whichever is higher.

So, the best income tax planning for regular taxes in the world won't help you if AMT kicks in. At a minimum, you'll have to pay the AMT tax.

The best tax loopholes strategy, then, first determines if AMT is a possibility. If it is, then AMT tax planning should be done.

Filing Requirements

Form 6251—Alternative Minimum Tax for Individuals—is a complicated form that is used to report your AMT calculation. The IRS estimates that this form will take more than six hours to complete. And you might need to complete this form even if you don't have to pay the tax!

The test to determine if you need to complete Form 6251 is the same test that is used to determine if you might be subject to AMT.

How Do You Calculate AMT?

AMT is computed by starting with the regular taxable income from your individual tax return, Form 1040. You then increase or decrease the taxable income with AMT adjustments and tax preference items.

Some examples of adjustments are:

- Taxes claimed as itemized deductions.
- Accelerated depreciation.
- Capital gains tax rates.

FIGURE 10.2 TaxLoopholes Alternative Minimum Tax Test

TaxLoopholes Alternative Minimum Tax Test
Instructions
Line numbers are based on the 2003 Form 1040.
Go through each line through #37 on page 1 and page 2 of your Form 1040 and your Schedule A. Are these numbers realistic for your current year? If not, change to the current estimated amount.
Complete the following calculations:

1. Enter amount from Form 1040, line 35 (Adjusted gross income) _____

2. Enter amount from Form 1040, line 37 (Itemized deductions) _____

3. Enter amount from Schedule A, line 4
    (Total medical and dental expenses)
        LESS
        2.5% of Form 1040, line 34 _____
        (Adjusted gross income)
        Total _____

4. Enter Schedule A, line 9 (Total taxes) +
    line 26 (Net miscellaneous expenses) _____

5. Subtotal _____

6. Enter applicable amount:
        Single or head of household—$40,250
        Married filing jointly—$58,000
        Married filing separately—$29,000 _____

7. Subtract line 6 above from line 5

8. Enter applicable amount:
        Single or head of household—$112,500
        Married filing jointly—$150,000
        Married filing separately—$75,000 _____

9. Subtract line 8 from line 7 _____

10. Multiply line 9 by 25% _____

11. Add lines 7 and 10 _____

12. Is the amount on line 11 more than:
        Single, married filing jointly, head of household—$175,000
        Married, filing separately—$87,500
    If yes, you need to complete Form 6251 with your tax return.
    If no, there is one more test.

13. Enter amount from Form 1040, line 40 (Taxable income)
    minus tax from Form 4972 and minus Form 1040, line 43
    (sum of tax and alternative minimum tax) _____

14. Multiply line 11 by 26% _____

15. Is line 14 more than line 13?
    If yes, you need to complete Form 6251.

AMT Loopholes Warning: If you are in the lower (10 percent or 15 percent) tax bracket and have substantial capital gains income (being taxed at the lower 5 percent rate), you will likely be subject to AMT. That's because the AMT capital gains rate is higher than the regular capital gains rate at the lower income levels. AMT is not merely a problem for the rich anymore!

AMT can be assessed at both the individual level as well as the corporate level. The tax planning will differ for these two types of AMT tax.

When Loopholes Aren't Loopholes Anymore—Tax Preference Items

The government views certain loopholes as "tax preference items." These loopholes are the items that are added back to the regular taxable income to determine the income subject to AMT. In other words, you may be able to take a deduction against income on your tax return, but then will need to add it back into your income calculation for AMT purposes.

Loopholes Strategies for Individual AMT Planning

What are some strategies to reduce the impact of AMT? First, determine how real the possibility of AMT is for you. This is an important first step because the loophole strategies for reducing AMT are often *exactly opposite* to the loophole strategies for regular income tax. If you think you might be subject to AMT and apply AMT loophole strategies, you'll wind up paying more tax than you would have to if it turns out that you won't be subject to AMT. And the opposite is true as well. If you think you won't be subject to AMT, and then it turns out that you will be subject to this tax, you'll find that you wasted a lot of loopholes and will pay more tax.

> *AMT Loopholes Strategy:* Determine if you will be subject to AMT. Tax planning for AMT is different from tax planning for regular income tax.

After you've determined whether you might be subject to AMT, look up what AMT tax preference items will be applicable. Remember that the tax preference items are the items that will be added back to your taxable income to calculate your AMT income.

Following are some common tax preference items for individual taxpayers.

State and Local Taxes

State, local, and other taxes paid and claimed as itemized deductions are added back to the taxable income when calculating AMT income. In other words, you don't get an AMT deduction for these taxes.

If possible, a taxpayer should avoid paying deductible state and local taxes in a year in which AMT is likely to be assessed. Instead, pay the taxes in a year in which the ordinary income tax rate is applicable.

There are two general situations for AMT and state and local taxes.

First, if a taxpayer is subject to AMT for the current year, but expects to be subject to regular tax the following year, the taxpayer should defer tax payments until the following year. One potential pitfall is that deferral of payments may lead to underpayment penalties at the state or local level.

Another possible scenario would be if the taxpayer is subject to regular tax during the current year, but is expected to be subject to AMT during the following year. In this case, it would be best to accelerate state and local tax payments into the current year. The IRS and state government are only too happy to get paid early, so there is no penalty for this practice. However, you should use caution when using this approach since the IRS will not allow a deduction for state and local income taxes unless the taxpayer can prove that he or she reasonably anticipated that the taxes would be owed.

Charitable Contributions of Appreciated Property

Finally, good news regarding AMT! One great tax loophole regarding charitable giving is that you can take a deduction for the fair market value of appreciated property. In other words, let's say you buy a piece of art for $10,000. Now, years later, the art is worth $50,000. You decide to donate this to a charitable organization. Prove that it's worth $50,000 and you have a deduction for $50,000!

Here's more good news: You no longer need to make an adjustment for AMT for the donation of appreciated property. This is one loophole that's applicable for both regular tax and AMT.

Incentive Stock Options

One of the biggest surprises for employees of dot-com companies prior to the dot-com crash is the way incentive stock options (ISOs) were taxed for AMT purposes.

The grant or exercise of an ISO does not generate regular tax. The tax is instead deferred until the stock acquired by exercising the option is sold. You then pay tax on all of it at once.

It's different, however, for AMT purposes. The income is recognized when the ISO is exercised. The amount by which the fair market value of the share at the time the option is exercised exceeds the option price is treated as an AMT adjustment.

For example, let's say you have a stock where the option price is $20. The stock is currently trading at $50. You will have an AMT adjustment for $30 per share of stock.

During the dot-com bust, some taxpayers got caught in the AMT/regular tax problem as they exercised their ISOs, paid AMT, and then found the stock dropping in value. In fact, I met one employee of a large dot-com company who ended up paying $120,000 in tax when he made only $100,000 in income! His stock plummeted in value the next year.

Prior to the stock market drop, the standard advice had been to exercise options because stock always went up in value. It was worth the price, some advisors reasoned, to pay AMT in order to have capital gains treatment later. (The capital gains tax treatment comes from having a holding period of longer than one year.) That standard advice is not standard anymore after many people were caught in the same trap as the employee just mentioned.

I'll go one better on that standard advice: Always avoid standard advice. People are different and circumstances are different. Don't get caught when someone just assumes you are average.

Medical Expenses

Medical expenses may be deducted for AMT purposes, but they must exceed 10 percent of adjusted gross income. For regular tax purposes, medical expenses in excess of 7.5 percent of gross income can be deducted.

Just as with any of the AMT timing strategies, it might be best to defer or accelerate discretionary medical expenses so that you are taking the expenses in the year that gives you the most favorable tax treatment.

Of course, if you have a business operating as a C corporation, you can take 100 percent of the medical expenses using a medical reimbursement plan.

Mortgage Interest

In order to have the regular mortgage interest deduction for income tax count against AMT income as well, you must also prove that the debt (for the interest) was used for acquisition indebtedness. In this case, acquisition indebtedness means that the debt was incurred to purchase, construct, or improve the taxpayer's first or second residence and is secured by that residence.

If you refinance your residence, the interest on the debt will still be deductible as long as the amount of the loan is not increased.

AMT Loopholes Tip: AMT planning for mortgage interest is difficult. You may be subject to AMT one year and not the next. Yet mortgages are generally long-term decisions. This might be one case where you can't plan for every eventuality; instead try to avoid AMT whenever possible.

Miscellaneous Itemized Deductions

Miscellaneous itemized deductions for the individual tax form include reimbursed employee expenses, expenses for the production of income, tax return preparations, and safe-deposit box fees. These items are added back for AMT purposes.

If possible, avoid paying these types of expenses in an AMT year. Instead pay them in a regular year and accelerate them to pay early in a regular year if you expect AMT in the next year.

Net Operating Losses

If a taxpayer has a loss from a business in a given year, this is called a net operating loss (NOL). That loss can be carried back two years to apply against income and forward for 20 years from the year in which the loss was incurred. The loss is claimed as a deduction in the year to which it is carried.

It is also possible to have an NOL for AMT purposes. This is a separate calculation and is based on AMT. The AMT NOL is generally known as the ATNOL.

Because the ATNOL is carried forward along with the NOL, both the regular tax and the AMT effects must be considered when developing a strategy to best utilize the NOL.

Passive Losses

The losses from passive activities such as real estate can be used to offset only passive income when it comes to AMT. The loophole strategy of materially participating in the real estate and then using the real estate professional status to take a full offset of real estate passive losses against other income will not work for AMT.

There are even tougher rules for passive farming activity losses. A taxpayer who is not a material participant (and therefore is passive) may not take the losses against other income for AMT purposes.

The definition of passive farming activities states that it is a "farming tax shelter." The farming tax shelter is further defined as a farm syndicate or passive farm activity in which the taxpayer is not a material participant. This includes a partnership engaged in farming that:

- Has offered for sale, in a registered offering, interests in the enterprise.
- Has allocated more than 35 percent of the enterprise's losses to limited partners or entrepreneurs.

That means that the common estate planning technique of family limited partnerships may actually trigger an AMT issue for farm properties!

There are some potential AMT tax loopholes available. The taxpayer will be considered to be active even if a partnership has been formed if the taxpayer (or family members):

- Had previously participated in the management of a farming business for at least five years.

- Has a principal residence at the farm.
- Is participating in the management of another farming activity.

Loopholes Strategies for Business AMT Planning

Businesses also face AMT challenges. Here are some potential traps along with AMT loophole strategies.

Alcohol Fuels Credit

There is a tax credit available for vehicles that use alternative fuels such as alcohol. This tax credit is not available for AMT.

AMT Loopholes Tip: If AMT is a possibility, make sure that deductions and tax credits work both for regular tax *as well as* for AMT calculation. If they are just for regular tax considerations, then realize that the timing of those deductions and credits needs to be in years when you will be subject to regular tax—not AMT.

Depreciation

The AMT depreciation adjustment affects most taxpayers. It not only causes some to become subject to AMT, it also makes the depreciation calculation more complex. The AMT depreciation adjustment is an issue not only during the time when the property is held (to calculate whether regular tax or AMT will apply) but also when the property is sold. The property's adjusted basis must be computed under AMT rules to determine the gain or loss from the sale and the difference between the regular tax gain or loss and the recomputed AMT gain or loss.

For personal property placed in service after 1998, depreciation is computed over the same periods for both regular tax and AMT. The method of depreciation is different, though. In the case of AMT, the method is something called the 150 percent declining balance method. It then switches to the straight-line method as soon as the straight-line method becomes higher. This means that in the beginning the AMT depreciation calculation will be smaller. As the property ages, the regular tax depreciation will become the smaller of the two. In the beginning there will be an amount added for AMT purposes due to depreciation. Later, the amount added will be reduced until there is no adjustment needed.

AMT Loopholes Tip: If you use the straight-line method for your regular tax calculation, you will not need to make the AMT adjustment.

AMT Loopholes Tip: Another strategy is to use the netting rules when computing the AMT adjustment. Depreciation for all property is combined when you calculate the AMT income. This allows the netting of excess regular tax deductions for property that is recently placed in service with excess AMT deductions on property placed in service in earlier years. For example, assume you own five buildings. Only one of those properties was recently put into service. The older four buildings will have more AMT depreciation under the straight-line depreciation method in the current year. Your new property will have higher regular tax depreciation. By netting the total depreciation, you are able to offset the depreciation differences so that there is no AMT adjustment later.

Gain from Sale of Qualified Small Business Stock

If you sell qualified small business stock (stock of a small business C corporation), you can exclude up to 50 percent of the gain. However, the tax for AMT purposes often kicks in. Depending on when you sell the stock and when you first acquired it, you might have to include 42 percent of the excluded gain as a tax preference item (sold before May 6, 2003, or after 2008) or 28% of the excluded gain (small business stock in which the holding period began after December 31, 2000).

Sound confusing? In this case, the regular tax calculation is confusing because of changing laws based on the holding period and the sales period. If you add in the additional complications of AMT, it gets even more confusing.

In this particular case, the benefit of the exclusion isn't as good as it used to be because of the lowered capital gains rate. It might make more sense to forgo this particular exemption if it throws you into an AMT situation.

Mining Exploration and Development Costs

For regular tax purposes, a taxpayer may expense mining exploration costs. This is one of the loopholes that savvy investors use.

However, a taxpayer may *not* take a current deduction for mining exploration costs for AMT purposes. These costs are instead capitalized and then amortized over a 10-year period.

To avoid a tax preference item for AMT purposes, it is possible for a taxpayer to elect to capitalize the expenses and then amortize them over a 10-year period for both regular tax and AMT purposes.

The benefit of this strategy is that it may let the taxpayer continue calculating taxes using the regular tax method, thus avoiding having to use the AMT.

Research and Experimentation

Generally when you incur costs in developing a product, you must capitalize the expenses. There is a loophole that allows taxpayers to deduct research and experimentation (R&E) expenses in the year in which they are paid or incurred (rather than having to capitalize them). The R&E loophole allows you to:

- Immediately deduct the R&E cost to match up with the current cash outlay.
- Take the deduction in an easy way. There is no election required.
- Take the deduction and *not* recapture the deduction if the technology or asset is later sold.

However, if the taxpayer does not materially participate in the R&E activity, then the expense must be capitalized and amortized over 10 years for AMT calculation.

That's the problem with the R&E deduction, but there are two strategies for this expense.

AMT Loopholes Strategy #1: First, make sure that the AMT issue is real in your case. If it is, you can instead capitalize the asset and amortize it over 60 months, beginning when the taxpayer first has a benefit from it. In this case, the R&E expensed amount would not be added back for AMT purposes. The downside of this election is that once it's made, it takes the IRS's okay to change it.

AMT Loopholes Strategy #2: Again, first make sure that the AMT issue is real in your case. If it is, another option is to capitalize the R&E expenses and then amortize them over a 10-year period beginning with when the expenses were first incurred. In essence, this is the same treatment that the AMT adjustment would have created, so there is no change needed. However, by taking a proactive stand in taking the deduction the way AMT would require, you might be able to avoid the AMT issue completely for other expenses and avoid filling out the arduous AMT form.

Tax-Exempt Interest on Private Activity Bonds

Interest on certain private activity bonds issued after August 7, 1986, is exempt from regular tax but treated as a preference item for AMT purposes. An example of this type of bond would be a bond used to finance a water treatment or a sewage treatment plant.

There aren't a lot of loopholes strategies for this one. The best way to handle it might be to give the bond to a child. Just make sure the child is 14 years of age or older so that you don't have to deal with the kiddie tax issue. (Kiddie tax applies to children under the age of 14 who have unearned revenue.)

Chapter 11

SMART REAL ESTATE INVESTING

Investing with a Business

I f you've been faithfully following the Jump Start! steps, you have a business that has the right type of business structure, is maximizing tax-free benefits, and is beginning to control when and how much it pays in taxes. Now is the time to look at other ways to maximize the cash from the business by investing it in real estate.

Building for the Business

The best strategy of all with your business and real estate is to buy the building your business is in. Then, charge your business rent for use of the building. There are three benefits to this strategy:

1. Changes earned income into passive income.

2. Creates real estate passive income to offset other real estate losses that might have been disallowed previously.

3. Builds equity in a building.

I love this strategy!

Home Office for the Business

Your business can also take an expense for the business use of your home. This is just one of the many home loopholes that are discussed later (see Chapter 14). Meanwhile, though, consider taking full advantage of the home office. It's another way to take money from your company, tax free, as you build value in real estate.

Investing without a Business

Some of my clients want to start with Jump Start! Step 4 right away. They don't have a business and have no desire to have one, at least right now. How can they get involved in real estate right from the start?

In this case, we look for ways to maximize real estate income and take advantage of the real estate loopholes as we go. The strategy will be different based on a couple of factors: (1) whether they qualify as real estate professionals and (2) amount and type of other income they receive.

Real Estate Professional Status

The real estate professional status is a critical test in determining your strategy with real estate investing. If you're a real estate professional, then we want to maximize your depreciation and look for ways to create passive losses. If you're not, we want to see good cash flow properties where the depreciation will completely offset the income from the properties, but not a cent more.

What Type of Investor Are You?

One of the common misconceptions with real estate investing is that all real estate means passive income. But, actually, the IRS has tests that determine the type of real estate investor you actually are. We've been discussing the real estate professional status throughout *Loopholes of the Rich*. But the other two definitions you need to be aware of might be new to you: (1) real estate dealer status and (2) real estate developer status.

Real Estate Dealer Status

The IRS determines real estate dealer status based on the *intent* of the taxpayer holding or buying the property. The characterization of gain or loss on the sale or exchange of real property turns on whether the property was held primarily for sale or investment. The courts have come up with their top 15 items that they look for in determining the status:

1. Taxpayer's purpose for acquiring, holding, and selling the property.
2. Number, frequency, and continuity of sales.
3. Duration of ownership.
4. Time and effort expended by the taxpayer in promoting sales.
5. Taxpayer's use of brokers.
6. Extent of improvements and subdivision made to facilitate sales.
7. Ordinary business of the taxpayer.
8. Extent and value of the taxpayer's real estate holdings.
9. Extent and nature of the transactions involved.
10. Amount of income from sales as compared with the taxpayer's other sources of income.
11. Taxpayer's desire to liquidate landholdings unexpectedly obtained.
12. Taxpayer's overall reluctance to sell the property.
13. Amount of advertising.
14. Use of a business office for sales.
15. Taxpayer's control over any sales representatives.

Of these, the most important issue appears to be the number, frequency, and continuity of sales. In other words, if you sell a great deal of property, you might be considered a dealer and thus subject to taxation as a self-employed individual.

It is possible to be treated as dealer on one property and an investor for another. In this case, the IRS will look at the taxpayer's intent with that particular property. For example, they will look for sales activities that show that property was held primarily for sale if they are attempting to prove dealer status. These activities would include advertising, For Sale signs, a sales office, and employment of sales personnel.

Best Defense for Real Estate Dealers

If you are considered a real estate dealer, then the income you make will be subject to a self-employment tax. You might consider holding the real estate within a limited partnership (only the general partner would be subject to self-employment tax) or a corporate structure.

The biggest problem with real estate dealers occurs when you sell the property and carry back a note. If you are a dealer, you cannot defer your gain from the sale until you receive money. That type of tax treatment, where the gain is recognized as you receive payments, is called the installment sale tax method. However, if you are a dealer, you can't take the installment sale tax method to defer the tax. You must recognize and pay tax on the gain as soon as the sale occurs, no matter when you get the money.

Real Estate Developer Status

The real estate developer status is another issue for many novice real estate investors. Say, for example, you find a great piece of land and decide to subdivide and develop it, or, as clients of mine did, determine that it would make a fantastic mobile home park in an area that desperately needed affordable housing and had the proper zoning. In my clients'

Real Estate Developer by Mistake

Bob and Ruth had found 20 acres with zoning that could easily be changed into that of a mobile home park. The 20 acres would translate into 60 spaces that would rent quickly for an average rent of $200 per month. That meant a gross income of $12,000 per month. There would be some maintenance, landscaping, and management costs. At the very high end, these costs would be $3,000 per month. One of the spaces would be provided to an on-site manager, reducing the gross income by $200. They were looking at potential income of:

Gross rent	$11,800
Vacancy costs	−1,800
Maintenance costs	−3,000
Monthly gross	$ 7,000

Reprinted with permission from *Easy Accounting for Real Estate Investors* by Diane Kennedy, 2004.

(Continued)

Real Estate Developer by Mistake (*Continued*)

The cost of the property was $200,000 and the owner would carry a note at 8 percent with 20 percent down. Bob and Ruth estimated the improvements would cost $10,000 per space and they had gotten tentative approval for a construction loan with 30 percent down. Bob and Ruth had the necessary $40,000 for the down payment for the purchase and felt they could liquidate some other resources (i.e., sell some stocks) to obtain the $180,000 they needed for their 30 percent portion of the construction loan.

They had always heard that real estate provided paper losses that could offset their other income and so weren't worried about the tax consequences of selling their stock. After all, they reasoned, they were spending the money on another business venture.

At tax time, though, they discovered the tax truth of what they had done. The land was not depreciable. That meant that the $200,000 ($40,000 of it in cash) was all booked as an asset with no expense to offset it. The construction was considered land improvements and would be expensed or depreciated once it was completed. So, at the end of the first tax year, they were three-fourths of the way completed with the project. They had liquidated stock, which incurred capital gains tax, and had drained all of their resources to develop the property. They had spent $220,000 and none of it could be written off. That was because Bob and Ruth were developers, much like someone building an apartment house, and none of their investment would be depreciated until it was put in service.

Additionally, Bob and Ruth discovered that the interest from the land note and the construction project was capitalized with the asset. It was not currently deductible and would instead be amortized and expensed over time. The money was flowing out, they were investing in a business, and none of it was deductible . . . yet. They had a horrible tax surprise the first year.

Reprinted with permission from *Easy Accounting for Real Estate Investors* by Diane Kennedy, 2004.

Developer? Who, Me?

Tom and Cecilia had a successful real estate investment and property management enterprise. They had a staff of four people who helped them with the ongoing maintenance and bookkeeping for their investments. They wanted to keep growing their business, but had reached a point where they simply couldn't find the deals on more real estate investments. So they decided to build new properties.

Tom had a contractor's license and they already had the beginnings of a staff to work with the subcontractors he needed.

They bought their first parcel and began construction on a multiunit apartment building. At tax time, though, they discovered that they couldn't take a deduction for any of the payments on the land, the down payment, or the out-of-pocket expenses for construction. And they also discovered even worse news. A large portion of the administrative expenses and salaries for their employees was now no longer deductible.

The construction of the apartment building made Tom and Cecilia now subject to uniform capitalization on all of their administrative expenses, even those that used to be deductible through the rest of their real estate investment business.

Reprinted with permission from *Easy Accounting for Real Estate Investors* by Diane Kennedy, 2004.

---

case, they did stumble on an eventual gold mine, but the business almost didn't survive because of the tax issues.

You are a developer if you buy a property and then do work before you put it into service. This could be true if you buy vacant land and then develop it. It would also be true if you bought a home and fixed it up before you rented it out. You would be treated as a developer during the time that you held the property before it was put in service. During this time you would not be able to take the depreciation deduction.

One more issue for some real estate developers is something called Uniform Capitalization rules. This area is a very complicated and little understood part of tax law. Basically, if you qualify as a real estate developer, you will be forced to capitalize certain percentages (up to 100 percent!) of almost all general and administrative expenses. That means you might not only have to wait to depreciate the property but also have to capitalize all carrying expenses *plus* the general and administrative costs such as office rent, car leases, and all of the other expenses that go into making your business work. Beware of the real estate developer status! If this status is applicable to you, verify that your tax advisor has experience with Uniform Capitalization and work closely with him or her to determine the tax consequences prior to tax time.

Impact of Other Income

There are two choices here—you either have other sources of income beyond the real estate income you hope to create or you don't. If there is no other income, your tax planning will be very easy indeed—as long as you are using real estate as a holding strategy. If you are a real estate dealer or a real estate developer, then you have a business, whether you like it or not.

If you have other income, be careful to balance your other income with possible passive losses from the property. The only way you'll get the full benefit is if you or your spouse is a real estate professional.

Using Leverage

One of the fundamental strategies with Jump Start! is leverage. Real estate provides easy leverage of money. Look for all of the ways you can maximize the money you have in your property. Leverage of money is really good debt when it comes to your real estate investments. This is the kind of debt that can make you rich.

At heart I'm still a conservative accountant, so to offset the extensive leverage that my husband and I use for our own plan we keep a minimum of three to six months of expenses and debt payments for all properties in a very liquid account. Currently, we have gone to a stronger cash position because we are expecting—in fact, hoping for—a real estate correction. We'll always use as much leverage as possible with our properties. And, for us, that means refinancing properties frequently where there has been significant appreciation. We want to keep our money working hard for us.

Holding Title

One of the questions you'll have to deal with when you buy your real estate investment property is how you want to hold title. Holding title is different from using a business structure. If you use a structure (which is what we recommend), the issue of holding title has changed, as it becomes a case of how you want to hold ownership in the entity. But that's an entirely different conversation.

Joint Tenancies

If you and another person own a property, you are probably joint tenants. That means that you have an undivided interest in the property. So does your joint tenant.

The undivided interest means that each joint tenant owns the entire property and has equal rights to use all of the property. A joint tenant cannot sell their interest in the tenancy without destroying the joint tenancy.

Property held as a joint tenancy cannot be seized easily. That's because there is ownership held by another tenant. However, it is possible for the courts to change the way title is held to another form of tenancy—a tenant-in-common. Tenant-in-common interests are held separately so a creditor can then just take over a tenant-in-common's individual ownership.

Joint Tenancy with Rights of Survivorship

Another benefit of joint tenancy is the right of survivorship. Survivorship provides joint tenants rights that differ from those enjoyed by tenants-in-common. A tenant-in-common has a separate ownership in the property, so they can leave their interest to an heir upon their death. Joint tenants have a complete ownership, so they don't have an interest that they can bequeath an heir. Upon the death of a joint tenant, the surviving tenant automatically owns the entire property. This automatic transfer feature is called a "right of survivorship."

The right of survivorship is the reason why married couples often use joint tenancies. There is an automatic right for a surviving spouse to inherit the property. Married couples know that they inherit, even if there is no will. The spouse will not pay estate tax on the inheritance.

Community Property

In community property states, there is an additional way that married couples can hold title to their property—as community property assets. This is often a more favorable way for married couples to own property because it allows the spouse to not only inherit the property without estate tax, but also be able to take a step-up in basis. That means that the surviving spouse inherits at current fair market value for the property and thus would have no tax due upon an immediate sale.

Tenants-in-Common

A joint tenant's interest in the property is undivided, whereas a tenant-in-common's interest is divided. In other words, if Tom and Gabe are 50–50 partners and hold a property as tenants-in-common, they each own 50 percent of the property.

Suddenly the Tenant-in-Common designation has gained popularity, thanks to a new IRS ruling regarding like-kind exchanges where there have been multiple owners. If you and a few of your friends buy a property together, you need to hold the property as tenants-in-common or you will not be able to do a like-kind exchange individually upon sale. If you want to use an LLC to hold your interest, you would have to first set up the tenants-in-common and then would have one of the tenants be your LLC. Your partners could then own their individual tenancy in either their own name (no asset protection) or their own individual LLC.

Land Trust

Land trusts seem to be the darling of the seminar circuit these days. They are great devices for privacy and for transferring ownership, but they do not offer asset protection. The privacy comes about because title is recorded in the name of the trustee of the land trust, not in the names of the beneficiaries—or true owners—of the trust.

If you are the beneficiary of a land trust, no one will be able to find you through a search of public records. The fact that the search does not turn up any ready assets to proceed against may well deter litigation.

However, a land trust does not protect you from liability. If a tenant is injured on property in which you are the personal beneficiary of a land trust, you will be personally responsible. If you are sued due to something unrelated to the property, your beneficial ownership in a land trust may be reached. And if you are asked in court if you have any interests in real estate, you must disclose that you own a beneficial interest in a land trust.

Business Structures for Real Estate

Now that we've covered ways to hold title to your property, let's cover the ways that you can protect that ownership. First, though, a warning: Make sure you know what type of investor you really are. If you are a dealer or developer, you have a business and need to consider business structures for business, not business structures for real estate.

The best business structures for real estate are LLCs (limited liability companies) or LPs (limited partnerships).

The LLC can have one member (in states that allow a single-member LLC) or many members. The members can be individuals, living trusts, or even corporations. An LP has one general partner and one or more limited partners. The general partner needs to have another type of entity to hold the general partner position to get full asset protection. An LLC is easier than an LP in most cases. Use an LP if you are in a state that doesn't have as strong LLC law or that has a large fee for the LLC.

You will want to set up the LLC or LP in the state in which the real estate is located.

Transfer Property into an LLC or LP

You might have property already in your name or you might be currently buying a new piece of real estate investment property and have discovered that the lender wants you to have the property in your name.

Now how do you get the property into the LLC or LP?

First, ask your lender to let you transfer the property into an LLC or LP. If he or she says no, you might ask to speak to a supervisor. If the answer is still no, go to Plan B. It is necessary to ask the lender first because most, if not all, mortgages have a "due on sale" clause. That means if the ownership transfers, the entire mortgage is immediately due and payable. An innocent transfer could mean you suddenly have to come up with hundreds of thousands of dollars.

I do not recommend that you "record the transfer anyway" and hope the lender doesn't catch on. First of all, it's dishonest and I don't recommend dishonesty at any time. Secondly, it does leave you open in case the lender catches on. Interest rates have experienced record lows recently, and when they rise, expect lenders to look for ways to get out of the low rates. That might mean searching records to look for transfers such as these so they can claim the due on sale clause and demand payment or refinance.

My preferred method of transfer is to use the land trust. Set up a land trust with yourself holding the position of trustee, trustor, and beneficiary. The land trust, which is just another form of living or revocable trust, does not trigger the due on sale clause. Then you can later transfer your beneficial interest to an LLC. This transfer is not recorded in the public records.

Chapter 12

REAL ESTATE LOOPHOLES TO TAKE MONEY OUT OF YOUR PROPERTY

Four Ways to Make Money from Real Estate

You will generally make money four different ways from the real estate you own. These four ways are:

1. Cash flow from the property.
2. Tax benefits of ownership.
3. Debt pay-down.
4. Appreciation.

Cash Flow from the Property

The first, and I think the most important, benefit of real estate ownership is the cash flow. Cash flow is the money you get from the property from rent after subtracting all regular expenses. Typically, we look at the cash-on-cash return from a property. The cash-on-cash return is calculated by first calculating the annual cash flow, then dividing it by the cash that you have invested in the property.

So, as an example, let's say that you have a property that has annual rents of $10,000. Your annual expenses (mortgage, property tax, insurance, repair allowance, and the like) total $8,000, so you have an annual cash flow of $2,000.

The cash invested (comprised of the down payment, settlement costs, repair costs, and the like) totals $20,000.

The cash-on-cash return in this case is 10 percent. That is calculated by dividing $2,000 by $20,000.

The cash-on-cash return is generally calculated when you first purchase a property. But if you want to have velocity on your real estate investing, regularly assess a new cash-on-cash return.

If you refinance to pull more cash out of the property, what would be your new cash-on-cash return? Or, assuming you do not refinance, divide your current return by the amount of money you now have invested in the property after it has appreciated.

Using the previous example, this time assume that the property has gone up in value by $100,000. That means that the cash you really have invested in the property is $120,000. (I'm assuming that there hasn't been any debt pay-down.) Now, if your cash flow from the property is $2,000 you have an effective cash-on-cash return of only 1.7 percent ($2,000 divided by $120,000).

If you refinanced the house, the cost would go up, but you would also be able to pull cash out for another investment.

My husband and I calculate the cash-on-cash return on an annual basis for all of our properties so that we can clearly identify where we need to improve our investment strategies.

By the way, I've seen people try to play games with cash flow by putting large down payments on a property or by paying off a property completely. In my book, if a property can't be justified using traditional financing, it's not a cash-flowing property. If your strategy with it is something else (planning for appreciation or development), then be sure you're comfortable with it and you're clear with yourself and your advisors that this is your strategy.

Tax Benefits of Ownership

Owning real estate provides tax benefits as well. Tax benefits are perhaps the best cash of all because you don't need to pay tax on tax benefits. They truly are after-tax benefits.

Depreciation

The biggest tax benefit of all is depreciation. The theory of depreciation is that your real or personal property gradually degrades in time. In the case of personal property, such as vehicles, this theory is very true. Anyone who has ever purchased a car and immediately seen the value decrease can attest to the validity of depreciation for personal property. But real property is another story. Does it really go down in value? In some areas yes, but generally over time real property appreciates. It goes up in value.

This is an example of a loophole that Congress has provided for real estate investors. Even though we know property, if bought right and maintained to its fullest potential, will go up dramatically in value, Congress lets you take a deduction for a reduction in value. The IRS provides tables to calculate how much the depreciation will be for your property. With the right structure and strategy, this phantom loss can be used to dramatically decrease your taxes.

Classes of Property

First, you will need to determine the class of the property involved with your investment. (*Class* is a term used by the IRS to determine the depreciable life of certain assets.) This is a very critical procedure that unfortunately most investors and their accountants don't do correctly. Here are the steps:

1. Break out the value of the land, separate from the structure. *Tip:* Many times the value of a bare lot in the area plus the cost of the construction do not equal the total purchase price. One technique the professionals use is to compare the assessor's statement of value for the land and building with the purchase price. Use the ratio that the assessor used for land versus building times the total purchase price for your property to determine the ratio between land and building value. Land is not depreciable.

2. Break out the value of personal property items within your building. The best way to do this is to have an appraiser help you with the value of these items. If you can't find an appraiser in your area, use the fair market value of the personal property items and then compare that value with the total cost of the building. Generally, it's hard to substantiate more than 30 percent to 40 percent of total building value in personal property items. Personal property items are depreciated over a shorter life, typically ranging from 7 to 15 years.

3. The value of the structure is the total price less land less personal property. This value is then depreciated as real property. Currently, real property used in residential rental properties is depreciated over 27.5 years and real property used in commercial properties is depreciated over 39 years. If property was placed in service prior to May 13, 1993, there will be different depreciation lives.

4. The depreciation for the real and personal property is then subtracted from your operating income for the property. (Operating income means that you have deducted the costs of the property, such as mortgage interest, property tax, insurance, homeowner's dues, utilities, and repairs, as well as your business expenses in running the property.)

5. In some states, such as California, you are also required to keep depreciation schedules using the state's assignment of life. This is where you really need to have a good tax software program. Otherwise, you are going to compile a lot of spreadsheets!

How to Catch Up Past Accelerated Depreciation

Many taxpayers miss Step 2. They forget to take out the value of the personal property! It is estimated, based on the review of past records of new clients of my CPA firm, that more than 90 percent of those returns make this very common mistake. This omission costs the taxpayers thousands of dollars each year. If you have made this common mistake in the past, don't despair! You can recover the past depreciation on your next tax return by filing Form 3115 and attaching a statement to your tax return.

What Happens When You Sell

When you sell your property, you will be required to recapture the depreciation at ordinary income tax rates. You then pay the capital gains rate on the difference between the basis and the sale price (less costs). Or you can delay the tax through the use of a Section 1031 like-kind exchange.

Common Mistake

Another mistake is much more potentially damaging. Some taxpayers have made the mistake of *not* deducting depreciation on their investment property. If you've made this mistake, correct it immediately by filing to take the past depreciation with your next tax return. If you don't take the depreciation when you should, the IRS will assume that you took it anyway. You'll have to pay tax on the "recaptured depreciation" when you sell even if there's nothing to recapture!

How Does Depreciation Help You?

Depreciation is a phantom expense. It means that you can offset the income from your property with an expense that doesn't cost you cash. You have a choice in how you calculate how much depreciation you take against your cash flow. You can take the standard 27.5 years for residential (exclusive of land) and 39 years for commercial (exclusive of land) if your strategy is to take a minimum amount of depreciation because otherwise your venture is thrown into a loss. Or you could allocate value to personal property so that you can maximize your depreciation.

The choice depends on your tax strategy.

Tax Credits

Tax credits are reductions against the tax you pay. Depreciation, which we love, is a reduction against taxable income. Tax credits are the most bang for the buck that you can get.

There are three types of tax credits that we see on a regular basis: historic property rehabilitation, pre-1936 construction rehab, and ADA improvements.

Historic Property Rehabilitation

If you rehabilitate a property in a federal, state, or city historically designated area or the property itself has been historically designated, you might be eligible for a historic property tax credit.

There are some requirements: The property must still have 75 percent of the walls left standing and you must spend more money on the rehab than you did purchasing the property.

Additionally, if you sell the property within five years of doing the work, you will need to recapture the tax credits.

But for the property that qualifies that you plan to keep for at least five years, this is a great deal! For every dollar you spend, you will receive a 10 percent tax credit. So, if you spend $10,000, your tax credit is $1,000. Of course, you still get to depreciate or expense (as appropriate) the rest of the expense.

Currently, in Phoenix, Arizona, there are old homes downtown that the city must move. If you have a lot in a historic neighborhood, the city will sell you the house for $1. Of course, you need to pay the cost to move the house to your lot and then you'll have rehab work to do. All of that rehab work would qualify for the tax credit! Not a bad deal.

Pre-1936 Construction Rehabilitation

Hand in hand with the historic property rehabilitation, there is another tax credit available for rehab work done on properties that were constructed prior to 1936. You can use this extra 10 percent tax credit in conjunction with the historic property rehabilitation or it can be used separately in the case of a pre-1936 property that hasn't gotten the historical designation.

The total rehab tax credit is 20 percent of improvement costs. And, again, if you keep the property for five or more years you do not have to recapture the tax credit when you sell.

Americans with Disabilities Act Tax Credits

Just as you can get ADA tax credits for equipment used for your business that assists handicapped customers, vendors, or employees, you can also receive ADA tax credits for improvements you make to your property that provide access.

The ADA tax credits are limited to 50 percent of the total expense. The first $250 of expense is not allowed and the amount of ADA tax credit is limited to $5,000 per year.

If you're remodeling your investment property, consider separating the ADA compliance changes.

Debt Pay-Down

Until recently, mortgages that included principal and interest were the only types of loans readily available. In the beginning of the loan, the principal pay-down is a small amount of the payment. As the loan ages, the principal portion increases significantly.

I think that the small amount going to pay down the debt at the beginning makes people forget to calculate the debt pay-down portion as building equity.

This is a benefit, but only if you take advantage of it. If you are interested in fully leveraging your money with more velocity, you will want to either convert to an interest-only loan or access that equity through refinancing or second mortgage loans on a regular basis.

Appreciation

There are some parts of the country where appreciation is running so high that rents simply can't keep up. It's tough to find a property that will provide cash flow in those areas. In general, when an area has appreciation rates higher than the cost of living adjustments, eventually it will be hard to find a property that provides positive cash flow.

In general, my husband and I use one of two strategies in those areas: (1) In the rent to own program we have a rental for two to three years. The tenant/buyer exercises at the end of that period and we all share in the appreciation. Meanwhile, we've gotten a small positive cash flow on the property. (2) We buy and resell properties. We make hay while the sun shines!

The best indicator of future appreciation is to look at the past appreciation. If an area has seen great appreciation and the same upward statistics are continuing (people are moving into the area and the economy appears strong), then chances are you'll experience above-average appreciation.

Your property has gone up in value—now what? You can sell the property, refinance it, or simply keep it with the higher equity value.

If you're interested in velocity, you'll want to keep the money moving. So my least favorite idea is to just keep the equity building.

You can refinance (or put a second mortgage on the property) to access the equity. Take the money and invest in more real estate or just take it to live on. If you invest the money, the interest on the loan will be deductible. If you take it to live on, you won't be able to deduct the interest, but either way you won't have to pay tax on the money you received.

Finally, you can sell it. If you do a straight sale and you have held it for one year and one day, you will receive capital gains treatment on the sale. That means a lower tax rate. If you held it for less than one year, then you will pay tax at the ordinary income tax rate. And, if it is determined that you are a real estate dealer, you will also have to pay self-employment tax.

You could also sell the property and do a like-kind exchange into another piece of real estate.

You have numerous options for taking money out of your property. The key, though, with real estate is to get started! There is an old Chinese proverb that asks, "When is the best time to plant a tree?" The answer is, "Ten years ago. But the second best time is today." Just like planting a tree, the second best time to start your real estate investing is today. Get started.

Chapter 13

BUYING A HOME THE RIGHT WAY

Buying a Home

The final module in the Jump Start! program is your personal residence. For many people, buying a home is the biggest financial decision they will ever make. There is also a great number of people whose only investment strategy is to buy a home. The Jump Start! method purposely puts the personal residence as the third module after building a business and investing in real estate.

It is possible to make your home part of your tax-advantaged wealth-building plan, but it is necessary to view your home differently than other people view theirs. It starts with how you buy your home.

View your home as a real estate investment, because that's what it really is if you take advantage of the home loopholes. Buy a house in an area that is having good appreciation and buy it with good negotiation so you get the best deal possible. Select your home with resale in mind.

I have had clients who moved from their hometowns to other cities (and states) where real estate investing was more lucrative. That alone, I know, is a radical thought: to move away from friends, family, schools, and familiar surroundings just because an investment might be better in another area.

It could also mean that you stay in the city you're in now, but that you make the commitment to move every few years to maximize the benefit of your home loopholes.

Protecting Your Home

Since your home has some of your investment money tied up in it, make sure you are protecting that equity.

There are three primary ways that you can protect the equity in your home, in addition to insurance:

1. Homestead exemption.
2. Single-member limited liability company.
3. Debt.

Is insurance enough? In today's world of outrageous lawsuits and high jury awards, I'm not sure you can be comfortable that the insurance you have is enough. This is especially true if you are a high-lawsuit-risk professional such as a doctor or business owner. The problem is that if you have a high profile and people think you're rich, then you're at risk for frivolous lawsuits.

Homestead Exemption

The homestead exemption protects the equity in your home. The amount of the exemption (or protection) varies by state. If you're in a state that has an unlimited homestead exemption such as Florida or Texas, you're in good shape. Check the amount of your homestead exemption with the local county recorder's office or assessor's office. If you have more equity in your home than your homestead exemption covers, read on for more ideas on how to protect your equity.

Single-Member Limited Liability Company

The LLC is becoming a familiar business structure for holding real estate investments. The LLC is not an entity with a specific taxing structure. It can actually elect how it wants to be taxed. That's the benefit for real estate. The LLC elects to be taxed as a typical flow-through entity for real estate with no self-employment tax issues and provides good asset protection for the owner.

The IRS issued a new Treasury Regulation in 2002 that stated that a personal residence could now be held within a certain type of LLC and not jeopardize the home loopholes. Prior to that, the home loopholes were in jeopardy if the home was put in an LLC for asset protection purposes.

The IRS states that the LLC must be a single-member LLC and "disregarded for income tax purposes."

It is possible for a married couple to own a single-member LLC by holding the single-member unit together. In other words, "John and Sally" own one of the membership units instead of John owning one and Sally owning one.

The second requirement for the LLC, that it is "disregarded for income tax purposes," means that you would not apply for an employer identification number (EIN) with the IRS and you would not file a tax return for the entity. What could be easier?

There are two potential issues with the single-member LLC plan, though. First, in states where there is a high cost to maintaining an LLC, the benefit of the asset protection must be weighed against the cost. Secondly, the issue still remains of how to get the property into the LLC without triggering a due on sale clause on your mortgage.

The land trust strategy would work in this case. The title for your home is transferred into a land trust. This can be done without triggering a due on sale clause. You then change the beneficial interest from your own name to that of the single-member LLC.

Debt

Debt is asset protection. Many people are under the mistaken belief that their assets are protected by having more equity. That's why they pay extra every month to pay off their mortgage. Equity actually protects the bank. Consider what happens if you pay extra money each month toward paying down your mortgage. In this example, let's assume that at the end of 10 years, you've paid your loan down by another $50,000.

Now you lose your job and you can't pay the mortgage. Worse still, the real estate market has gone soft, meaning that it's hard to sell the property. The bank soon forecloses on your property. The extra money you put down on the property just gave them more equity when they foreclosed on you. What if instead you had taken that extra money and put it into another investment or even just in a savings account? You would have had the money available now to make the payments while you searched for another job, got your business going, or sold your house. The extra equity in your property was illiquid and so did you no good. Equity protected the bank.

On the other hand, let's assume that you instead keep debt as high as you can on your property by refinancing whenever equity builds up due to debt pay-down and/or appreciation. You take the extra cash you are able to pull out with the refinance and use it to build your business or invest in real estate. Or, under the Jump Start! plan, use the money for living expenses so that the business income can be invested in real estate with the best tax advantages.

Besides putting into play the concepts of leverage and velocity, using debt will protect your house. If you can keep enough debt on your home to reduce the equity to the homestead exemption limitation in your area, you have created great asset protection. Anyone looking to sue you would be dissuaded because of the debt and the homestead exemption.

Mortgage Interest Deductions

Generally, your mortgage interest is deductible as an itemized deduction on your personal tax return. The qualified residence interest is interest paid or accrued based on acquisition indebtedness or home equity indebtedness that is secured by your personal residence. If you have seller-provided financing for your property, you will need to report the name, address, and taxpayer identification number of the person you pay.

The mortgage interest deduction is available for (1) your principal residence and (2) an additional residence selected by the taxpayer. Typically this second residence is a vacation home, recreational vehicle, or boat. As long as the second residence has a bathroom, a place to sleep, and a kitchen, the debt on it will qualify for the second residence mortgage interest deduction.

The mortgage interest deduction must be related to acquisition indebtedness. Acquisition indebtedness is any debt that is (1) incurred in acquiring, constructing, or substantially improving any qualified residence, and (2) secured by such qualified residence. The total amount that can be treated as acquisition indebtedness for a principal residence and a second residence is $1,000,000 ($500,000 in the case of a married individual filing a separate return). Any interest on otherwise qualifying debt that exceeds $1,000,000 is not qualified residence interest.

How do you prove that the debt was used in acquiring, constructing, or substantially improving your residence? A debt's qualification as acquisition indebtedness is determined under either the general tracing rules or a special 90-day rule. Thus, if the use of borrowed funds can be traced to acquisition, construction, or substantial improvements, the interest is qualified residence interest up to the debt limit of $1,000,000. Debt incurred prior to commencing construction or improvement of a qualified residence must be traced to such use.

A mortgage may also be considered as acquisition indebtedness if the debt is incurred within 90 days before or after the debt is incurred. Debt incurred after construction or substantial improvement begins may qualify to the extent of construction or improvement expenditures made not more than 24 months before the debt is incurred. Debt incurred within 90 days of completion of the residence or improvement also may qualify to the extent of construction or improvement expenditures made within the period beginning 24 months before the residence or improvement is completed and ending when the debt is incurred.

Home Equity Debt

Home equity indebtedness is any debt secured by a qualified residence that is not acquisition indebtedness. The amount of deductible interest must be on home equity indebtedness that does not exceed $100,000 ($50,000 for a married person filing a separate return). It also may not exceed the difference between the fair market value of the residence and the amount of acquisition indebtedness.

Mortgage Interest Loophole

Prove that the additional debt you have taken out secured against your property is used for your business or investments and you have converted the debt to a business or investment debt. It is necessary to be able to prove that the debt was used for another project and so, again, we need to be able to meet the tracing rules to be able to deduct the associated interest.

Good recordkeeping should provide the trail between the debt and the use of funds for another project.

Mortgage Points

Often a new loan will include mortgage points, a fee that you pay for use of the money. Points can be qualified residence interest if paid in conjunction with a debt that is secured by a residence of the taxpayer. Points paid in connection with the acquisition, construction, or improvement of the taxpayer's principal residence are generally deductible in the year paid. Points that do not qualify for current deductibility are deducted ratably over the indebtedness period. In other words, if the points don't qualify to be immediately expensed, you must amortize the points over the length of the loan. If the loan is for 30 years, you will amortize the points over 360 months. If you then later refinance that loan, the remaining balance of the points is immediately deductible.

In order to take an interest deduction, you must show you actually paid the interest. In order to take the current points deduction, you must pay points at the loan closing out of your own separate funds. You can't just pay the points by borrowing the money from the lender. However, if you pay an amount at closing at least equal to the amount of points required, the amount will be treated as paid directly by the taxpayer, even if the amount paid includes down payments, escrow deposits, earnest money, or other funds to be paid at closing. Thus, for example, if at the closing for the purchase of a new principal residence you make a payment of $2,000 for closing costs, the entire payment can, in effect, be allocated to any points charged by the mortgage lender for purposes of determining if you paid the points from your own funds.

Cash-basis taxpayers paying points are ordinarily limited to deducting the points ratably over the period of the indebtedness. However, one type of prepaid interest that remains currently deductible is points paid on any indebtedness incurred in connection with the purchase or improvement of a taxpayer's principal residence. To qualify for this exception, the payment of points must also be an established business practice in the area in which the taxpayer incurs the debt, and the amount paid for points cannot exceed the amount generally charged in that area for points.

The IRS has come up with six guidelines that must be met in order to take the current deduction for points paid. Under these guidelines, the IRS will allow you to currently deduct your points if:

1. The Form HUD-1 clearly designates the amounts as points payable in connection with the loan.

2. The amount is computed as a percentage of the indebtedness incurred by the taxpayer.

3. There is an established business practice in the local area to charge points on residential mortgage indebtedness and the amount charged does not exceed the amount generally charged.

4. The amounts are paid in connection with the taxpayer's acquisition of his or her principal residence.

5. The loan is secured by the principal residence.

6. The points are paid directly by the taxpayer.

Vacation Home

Have you ever dreamed of having a second home by the beach or in the forest? If so, join the crowd of people buying second homes. The fact, though, is that a vacation home generally isn't a great investment. It's a little like buying the really fancy sports car. Treat it as a reward for a job well done and pay for it with passive income.

There are some things you can do to make the vacation home less of an expense, though. First of all, consider the mortgage interest expense. Mortgage interest paid on a second home (i.e., any residence other than the taxpayer's principal residence) is fully deductible only if the home meets the requirements of a qualified residence and the owner elects to treat it as such.

Many times vacation homes are also partially rented out. If the personal use exceeds the greater of 14 days or 10 percent of the number of rental days, then you have a building with personal use. A pro rata portion of vacation home expenses can offset the rental income, but you can't create a loss in the building. In this case, the vacation home becomes a little bit of a hybrid. You can't take a paper real estate loss on a personal-use vacation property, even if as a real estate professional you would normally be able to take the deduction. And you can't get the principal residence capital gains exclusion or do a like-kind exchange upon sale.

If you have more than two eligible dwellings, you can alternate the selection of the second residence among homes in order to maximize the interest deduction.

You may find that your personal use of a dwelling is close to the threshold at which it would cause the dwelling to be considered used as a residence. For example, a ski condominium may have been rented at fair rental 180 days and used for personal purposes 12 days as of December 15 of the tax year. The taxpayer plans to use the condominium for personal purposes for about a week during the holiday season. If you stay for 6 days, for a total of 18 personal use days, the dwelling will not have been used as a residence in that year. Staying an extra day will cause the dwelling to have been used as a residence because the 19 days of personal use exceed 18 days, 10 percent of the number of fair rental days. In this type of situation, you might want to not stay the extra time so the property will qualify for rental status that year.

One more consideration on the vacation home has to do with the $1 million cap on qualified residence indebtedness. If your primary home has a large mortgage, you might not be able to take much, or any, of the mortgage deduction for your vacation home. In this case, it definitely makes sense to convert the vacation home to a rental property by passing the "days of use" test.

Recordkeeping Requirements for Your Principal Residence

Most people know that they will at some point need to have accounting records for their business and real estate investments. But it's not common knowledge that you'll also need records for your personal residence. Current law says that a married couple filing jointly can exempt $500,000 of gain from the sale of a residence that they have lived in for two of the previous five years. If you're single, the exemption amount is $250,000. But you have to be able to prove that is all the gain you had!

Let's say you're married and sell your house for $550,000. If you bought the house for $100,000 and have lived in it for the requisite time, then you won't have any tax impact. But you will have to prove that you actually did buy the house for $100,000. Plus, if the gain on your house is close to the maximum amount, congratulations and be ready to prove your basis, which includes the cost of all improvements to the property.

Just as with your other real estate investment records, you will need to box up the temporary files and keep them for a minimum of five years after filing the appropriate tax return. You might consider keeping the records for a full 10 years in case there are any legal questions related to the ownership of the property. We recommend that you shred all documentation when you get rid of it. There is a lot of personal information included with those records and you don't want that falling into the wrong hands!

Keep the permanent records until the property is sold. At that time, combine the permanent files with your temporary files for the year. After the recommended holding period, shred them along with the other temporary records.

If this is the only real estate property you own, or intend to own, it's probably not necessary to invest in accounting software. However, if you are investing in real estate or own a business, you likely will want to use accounting software, anyway. If you've got the software, I recommend that you set up a personal financial statement for yourself, just as if you were a business. In this way, you can track the money that comes in and budget the money that goes out. If you run your financial life like a business, holding yourself accountable for the same standards of operation, you will find that you become more financially successful!

High Income Warning

As your income increases over the IRS's "high income" limit ($139,500 for a married couple filing jointly in 2003), you lose the ability to take certain itemized deductions. One of those expenses is mortgage interest. As your income goes up, you lose the normal deductions. That's why the Jump Start! plan, which includes business and real estate, is so important to wealth building.

Chapter 14

HOME LOOPHOLES SO YOUR HOME PAYS YOU

Does Your Home Work for You?

T he second biggest expense for the average American is their home. Many people slave away at a job they don't really like and work harder than they want in order to afford their home. How would you like to have your home work for you? If you do it right, your home can provide a tremendous source of home loopholes that add to your tax-advantaged wealth-building plan.

Yes, you will have to do things differently to take advantage of these loopholes. But, isn't that the point? Most people work for their houses. Follow a different strategy and you can live in a beautiful home and have your home work for you! That's what home loopholes can do for you.

HomeLoophole #1—Live in Your Home for Two Years

Congress has given us a terrific tax gift! For the past seven years, you have been able to take tax-free gain on the sale of your home of up to $250,000 for a single filer and $500,000 for married, filing jointly. In order to take advantage of this tax-free exclusion, the rule is that the property must have been used as the principal residence for two of the previous five years. The five-year period runs backward from the date of the sale of the property.

The calculation for the two-year period is actually a total of days— 730 days. But it's not that straightforward. Short temporary absences for vacations or seasonal absences are counted as periods of use, even if the individual rents the property out during those periods of absence. Note that any absence over one year is not considered a temporary absence. That means that you could live in your home for one month, move out for 11 months (during which time you rent the property), move back for one month and then rent it out for another 11 months and qualify as having it as your principal residence for two years.

For a married couple, the ownership test is met if either spouse meets the ownership test. However, if one of the spouses has taken advantage of this loophole on another property within the previous two years, the couple must wait two years from the date of the sale to take advantage of this exemption on the current property. Otherwise, the gain exclusion is limited to $250,000 (the amount of exclusion for a single taxpayer). So, if you get married and your new spouse has not taken advantage of this exclusion within the past two years and you have lived there for two years, you have the full $500,000 gain exclusion.

I have clients in my CPA firm who don't even work anymore. All they do is buy a property, fix it up, and wait two years until they can sell it and take the gain tax-free. Of course, that type of plan needs good financing, credit lines, or a cash reserve to pull off!

HomeLoophole #2—Live in Your Property for Less Than Two Years

In December 2002, the IRS issued a Treasury Regulation that added some great loopholes for the principal residence if you haven't lived in the property for the full two years. Prior to this Treasury Regulation, the only guidance we had was in the Internal Revenue Code itself:

> If the sale or exchange of the residence is due to a change in the taxpayer's place of employment, health, or, to the extent provided in regulations, unforeseen circumstances, a taxpayer who does not otherwise qualify for the exclusion is entitled to a reduced exclusion amount.

But the initial IRC regulation, at Prop. Reg. Section 1.121-3(a), didn't explain what "unforeseen circumstances" meant!

Most tax practitioners used the "unforeseen circumstances" loophole very cautiously. We were then all astonished to see how liberal the IRS's view was when the new regulations came out. In this new regulation, the IRS defines "unforeseen circumstances" as: involuntary conversion of the home (for example, the government takes your property for a freeway on-ramp), natural or man-made disasters or acts of war, death, cessation of employment, change in employment or self-employment, divorce or legal separation, or multiple births resulting from the same pregnancy.

Notice the "change in employment or self-employment." This could mean you are laid off or demoted at your job. It could also mean that you start, change, or end a small part-time business. In fact, if you want to move from an appreciated property in which you have lived for less than two years, perhaps the best strategy is to start a small home-based business. All you need is a "change in self-employment."

The "reduced exclusion amount" from the Internal Revenue Code means that you can then exempt an amount equal to the pro rata portion of time lived in the house times the total possible gain exclusion, but no more than the total gain. In other words, let's say that John and Corrine had lived in their home for only one year and had reason under this clause to qualify for the special circumstances. The fraction allowable would be 50 percent (1 year/2 years). They could then take an exemption for half of the possible gain (50% × $500,000 = $250,000). If they had gain of $100,000, they could exclude all of it. If they had gain of $300,000, they could exclude only $250,000.

HomeLoophole #3—Live in Your Property for *More* Than Two Years

Do you need to move to take advantage of the value of your home? The answer is "no." You can simply refinance the property to take the value out of the property. If the current market interest rates are higher than your existing loan, consider getting a home equity loan instead. (Read Strategy #7 to make sure it's fully deductible.)

Once your gain (sale price minus basis minus cost of sale) approaches

$250,000 if you're single or $500,000 if you're married, it's time to sell and buy the next property.

If you're in a midrange-priced home in an average appreciating area, it's likely that you won't hit that maximum gain amount for five or more years. As with most financial decisions—do the math!

HomeLoophole #4—Renting Rooms

I have clients who have bought large, fixer-upper homes at huge discounts through preforeclosure processes. Often they have a much bigger house than they want or need, and some relish the idea of a congenial roommate.

If you rent out part of your home, you've created a business opportunity for yourself just the same as if you had a business operating out of it. The difference is that this is not a home office. In this particular case, you would have a rental property that is reported on Schedule E. That means that you can now deduct the pro rata portion of home-related expenses against the rental income as well as the depreciation for the space.

And when you sell your principal residence, you can exclude the gain on the pro rata portion of the home.

Of course, that begs the question: What if you rent out the main portion of the home, maintaining just a small room as your personal residence in which you reside one month out of 12? As long as you own the home for two years, you've got a full tax-free gain exclusion by combining HomeLoophole #4 and HomeLoophole #1!

HomeLoophole #5—Defense for High Income Loss of Deductions

One of the worst surprises that can happen at tax time is when a taxpayer discovers that his bonus or raise meant he couldn't take the tax deductions he used to get! As your income increases over $139,500 (in 2003), you will begin to lose your itemized deductions. The lost itemized deductions are calculated as 3 percent of the amount of your adjusted gross income that is over $139,500, but no more than 80 percent of the total amount of itemized deductions.

Certain itemized deductions are not subject to this limitation: the deduction for medical expenses, the deduction for investment interest, the deduction for casualty or theft losses, and the deduction for gambling losses.

A strategy to avoid this loss of deductions is to look for ways to move the mortgage interest deduction *off* the Schedule A. One of the best ways to do that is through the use of the home office deduction. The home office deduction allows you to deduct a pro rata portion of the mortgage interest and property tax on a separate schedule (depending on what type of business entity you are using for your business).

HomeLoophole #6—Home Equity Loan Full Deductibility

Many people are using home equity loans to cash out excess equity from their homes. This money is then used for investments or for personal expenses. They've been told that the mortgage interest will be deductible so it's a way to convert nondeductible consumer debt interest (credit cards, car loans, and the like) into deductible mortgage interest.

Then, at tax time, they discover that a home equity loan isn't always tax-deductible. The same problem exists for the primary mortgage as well. The issue is that you cannot deduct interest on a loan (or loans) associated with the acquisition indebtedness that exceeds $1 million. Additionally, you cannot deduct interest related to home equity debt in excess of $100,000.

Here's the home loophole that solves that problem: Prove that the additional debt was used for investment or business purposes and the interest has just moved from your Schedule A (itemized deductions) to the appropriate business form.

For example, let's assume that you have a property that was originally purchased for $500,000, with a loan for $400,000. The value goes up to $700,000 and you take out a home equity loan for $200,000. Under normal circumstances, you would be able to deduct only half of the interest attributable to the home equity loan. However, you know this home loophole and so take the deduction for the other half of the interest by proving that $100,000 of the equity drawdown went to buying a multi-unit apartment building. The interest related to the $100,000 is then deductible as a regular interest expense for your real estate investment.

HomeLoophole #7—Controlled Entity Sale to Step Up Depreciation

The next three home loopholes all relate to the concept of having a controlled entity that is something separate from you. Let's start with the discussion of what a controlled entity is. In this case, the controlled entity could be an S corporation, C corporation, or multiowner LLC. You would not want to put the asset into a C corporation because the real estate would be an appreciating asset. (Never put appreciating assets inside a C corporation.)

This strategy has not been proven to work, but the barriers to using it have been removed. Prior to the Tax Reform Act of 1997, a taxpayer was able to defer gain realized from the sale or exchange of a principal residence if a replacement residence was acquired during the period beginning two years before the sale and ending two years after the sale. The cost of the replacement residence had to be equal to or more than the sale price of the previous residence. The IRS addressed the sale to a controlled entity in two Private Letter Rulings and concluded that the sale of a principal residence was allowed into a closely held corporation as a legitimate part of the transaction for the tax deferral. However, the IRS did note that if a subsequent sale would create a taxable event at ordinary income tax rates, then the corporation would face the same circumstances at a later date.

All of that changed when the new law came into effect as shown in HomeLoophole #1. There is no longer any tax-deferred gain hanging over the taxpayer's head. It is simply a tax-free gain provided all other residence requirements are met. There is one more part to this strategy: There must be a bona fide sale. This means that the sale price can be supported and that there is proper documentation. The best of all worlds would be if there were also new financing in place by the purchasing entity. But, through the use of creative seller-financing documentation, loans can often be assigned or "wrapped."

All of this leads up to the huge benefit of this home loophole. You can now sell your personal residence into a multiowner (say you and your spouse) LLC at the appreciated value. As long as the gain is less than $250,000 (if single) or $500,000 (if married filing jointly), you don't have any tax. But the LLC has the property at the increased value for more depreciation.

This has just become a great way to grow your real estate fortune! Don't sell your house—move out and turn it into a rental with increased depreciation, and no tax consequences on the increased basis.

HomeLoophole #8—
Controlled Entity Sale to
Sell Apportioned Property

One of the great benefits of the new Treasury Regulation is the ability to subdivide your property and still get the tax-free benefit. Here's how it could work. Let's say that you have a home sitting on a 40-acre parcel. At some point, the zoning changes so that you can sell 39 of the acres to a developer for a $300,000 profit! At this point, you will still have the home and the remaining acre. A year later, you sell the home and the remaining acre for a $150,000 profit. What part of this sale was taxable?

Under the new Treasury Regulation, you can take the $500,000 (married, filing jointly) tax-free gain on the combined gain, provided you have sold the remaining part of the split sale within two years. In other words, under this Treasury Regulation, the total gain ($300,000 + $150,000) was tax-free, provided the home was sold within two years of the sale of the land. But what if you sold the home two and a half years later? You've now got taxable gain!

Here's a way around that: You can sell the home to a controlled entity in order to lock in the gain. The controlled entity (an S corporation or a dual-ownership LLC) buys at the higher fair market value (no taxable event for you) and the entity just holds the property until the sale date. The only possible problem would be if the entity sells in less than a year for a much greater value. In that case, the sale would be at ordinary income tax rates because it was held for less than one year. Of course, if you had sold the house and lost the tax-free gain you would have then had a capital gains rate on *everything*. It's one of those issues where you need to just do the math based on your best assumptions to guide your decisions.

HomeLoophole #9—Controlled Entity Sale to Save Two-Year Residency

HomeLoophole #1 tells us that you can take out tax-free gain if you have lived in your home for two of the previous five years. But what do you do if you've turned your home into a rental and the three-year window to sell is rapidly closing? That means that you're about to lose the provision unless you move back into the house or follow HomeLoophole #9.

Now we have another solution: You can sell the house before your two years out of five years residency runs out and still control the property if you sell the property into a controlled entity. This gives you tax-free gain, stops the clock from ticking on the three-year window, and provides a higher basis for increasing the depreciation deduction.

Jump Start! Your Wealth

We've now completed the entire Jump Start! Your Wealth program. There are three main categories of loopholes—business, real estate, and home; three wealth-building strategies—leverage, velocity, and cash flow; and seven steps that will jump-start your money, no matter where you are today.

The reason the plan works is because you have multiple streams of income flowing through to you in the most tax-advantaged way possible. And you have three asset categories (business, real estate, and your home) appreciating. It's also the safest plan because you have taken into account the proper business structures at each step of the way and you have diversified yourself in the market. If real estate cools down, you have a business that can pick up the slack. I have found in my own plan that the business and real estate climates frequently stair step each other. Recently the real estate market has been running really hot and it's been harder for us to find big cash-flowing properties. So we've switched to appreciation strategies for our real estate as we maximize our home loopholes and business growth. When the real estate market cools, we'll be well positioned to take advantage of lower prices and the resulting even higher cash flow opportunities.

Keep your plan flexible and be willing to make quick changes when markets and new investments create new opportunities.

PART III

New Tax Strategies for C Corporations

Chapter 15

AVOID C CORPORATION PITFALLS

C corporations provide some unique benefits for their owners and some unique problems as well. In this chapter, we'll look at common problems and the loopholes strategies that avoid them.

How Do You Form a C Corporation?

In the United States, the right to incorporate comes only from state governments. You cannot incorporate under the federal government, only under state law. That means that there are at least 50 different nuances to corporations.

Every S corporation and C corporation starts its corporate life as a C corporation. Each C corporation can then make a special election to be taxed as a flow-through entity, the S corporation. If you don't make that election, then your corporation remains a C corporation.

Corporate State

You can incorporate in any state, but you may have to later be "accepted" into another state as a "foreign" corporation. For example, say you incorporate your Colorado-based business under Nevada state law. Then, to do business in Colorado, it will have to be accepted to do business in Colorado. Colorado would consider it a foreign corporation, because it was incorporated in another state.

There are two primary differences in how states view corporations. First, they differ in how they impose tax. Some states (such as Nevada) currently (2004) have no state tax for corporations. Other states (such as California) not only have a state tax for corporations, they also use different tax law for determining how the tax is assessed. In essence, a corporation that operates in a state with different tax laws must prepare two different tax returns, which are calculated using different amounts of income and expense.

Second, the states have different corporate laws and applicable court cases that have determined how asset protection, shareholder disclosure, and other items are handled. In other words, corporations formed in Colorado and Nevada might have completely different statutes and liability protection for their shareholders.

Delaware has more corporations than any other state. The state of Nevada is a close second attracting companies looking for no state income tax and nondisclosure of shareholders. Nevada is not the darling that it once was, however, as the state has recently been looking for ways to tax the corporations formed in the state.

Corporate Elections That Must Be Made within the First Year

Timing is everything. When it comes to certain elections, there are limited windows of time when you can make the choice. This is often where having a strong advisory team will really come into play.

Critical Timing

There are a number of items that you must elect within the first few months of your new C corporation. If you don't meet the deadlines, the IRS, state government, or federal government will choose for you. Sometimes it is possible to change the elections or choices made for you, but it is often very costly and time-consuming.

Selection of Accounting Period

In the case of a C corporation, you can choose a year-end that is different from the standard December 31, or calendar year-end.

You can elect the year-end by selecting it on Form SS-4, which you fill out when you apply for your employer ID number.

Selection of Accounting Method

You select the accounting method to be used for your corporation when you file your first corporate tax return. Your choices will be cash method, accrual method, or a hybrid method.

If your business has average annual sales of less than $5 million, you are free to choose which accounting method to adopt as long as you don't have inventory. If you stock an inventory or have sales over $5 million, you will be required to use specific forms of accounting.

Most small businesses choose the cash method, as long as it is allowed. The cash method counts revenue when you receive the cash and expenses when you pay them. It's a simpler form of accounting.

Election to Amortize Start-Up
Expenses and Organizational Expenses

The election to amortize your starting expenses can be made only with the initial corporate tax return. Organizational expenses are the costs of organizing any entity and include the cash outlays for legal fees, entity setup fees, and so on. Start-up expenses are amounts incurred in connection with preopening expenses, initial legal services, organizational meetings, initial fees paid to state and local agencies, and other similar expenses.

An election is made with the first return to amortize the expenses ratably over 60 months, starting the first day that the corporation is actively engaged in business.

S Corporation Election

If it is determined by your tax strategist that an S corporation is the best structure for you, you have a limited time in which to make your S corporation election. This is done by filing a statement with the IRS within the first two and a half months of operation (in some cases, extensions can be granted) that is signed by all shareholders (and their spouses if they reside in a community property state).

How Will You Get Money Out of Your C Corporation?

There are two kinds of money problems—not enough money and too much money! In the case of your C corporation, you can have too much money. One of the strategies to use with a C corporation is to take advantage of the separate taxing structure and leave income within the corporation. Now, how do you access it? My favorite ways to access the money are:

- Tax-free benefits.
- Salaries.
- Loans.
- Money partner.

Tax-Free Benefits

First, look for tax-free benefits available from the corporation. These are the benefits that the corporation can pay for you for which it takes a deduction and you don't pay tax. This is the best of all worlds!

Salaries

A salary paid to you is a deduction for the corporation and income for you. It's generally income tax neutral because of the offsetting deduction for the corporation. Use this way to balance out the income tax brackets so that you are paying the lowest tax rates both for yourself and for the company.

Loans

Your company can lend money to you. Be careful with this, though. If you are taking out your cash in the form of loans and not sufficient salary, the IRS can come back in and recategorize the payments as dividends.

Even better, have your company lend money to your investment LLC or LP. This way the company is just making an investment like any other form of investment, and it provides the cash for the investment.

Money Partner

Your C corporation can become a money partner by providing the cash for an investment. Form an LLC in which both you and your company are members. The corporation provides the money and you provide the management.

There are other potential tax traps for your C corporation. Make sure you review the following items carefully or you might just get caught in a trap that costs you more tax.

Double Taxation

Double taxation occurs when income is first taxed at the corporate level and then at the personal level, with no offsetting deduction for the corporation. In other words, the income is taxed twice.

Double taxation occurs only when dividends are paid. Most expenses that a corporation pays are deducted against the income of the corporation, so there is no double taxation.

It is also possible to have liquidating dividends when a corporation is liquidated. For example, if your corporation sells off all of its assets and then you immediately dissolve the corporation, you will receive something that the IRS calls a "liquidating dividend." There is no deduction for the corporation because it doesn't exist anymore; you have to pay tax on the gain from the sale of assets, and then you have to pay tax personally for the dividend income received.

Double taxation through dividends can also occur when a corporation doesn't have proper documentation. If benefits are paid on behalf of the shareholder without the proper plans in place and without the proper documentation (such as resolutions, filing systems, and so on), the IRS will determine that the benefits are really dividends and tax them as such.

Controlled Group

A controlled group issue comes about when the same person or group controls multiple corporations. When a controlled group issue occurs, the corporations are collapsed into just one corporation for tax purposes. There is only one tax rate table. The benefits of multiple corporations go away. It's possible to also have a controlled group issue for multiple companies even if they aren't all C corporations. In this case, if the same person or group controls multiple business structures and you put a non-discriminatory benefit plan in place, then you must include all other employees of all other controlled group companies in the plan.

The IRS caught on pretty quickly to the trick of using multiple corporations to take advantage of the graduated tax rates for each corporation. The trick would have been (if it worked) to keep $50,000 of income in each C corporation so that you never pay more than 15 percent in tax. The IRS said no, and that's why it came up with the concept of controlled groups. In essence, if one or more of the same people maintain control of a group of corporations, they are considered to be just one corporation. This has become a significant problem for many people when they simply buy a corporation setup plan without the overview of their entire plan.

The key to avoiding controlled group status is to avoid having control with any small group of people. One way to do that is to have unrelated persons (unrelated by blood or marriage) own a portion of the corporation. For example, if we had decided that Ted and Ellen needed C corporations, we could have set Ellen up with a corporation and Ted with a corporation in which 51 percent or more of the stock was owned by someone unrelated to Ted. If you follow this strategy, make sure you have a buy-sell agreement so you can buy back the stock in case something goes awry.

Personal Service Corporation

A qualified personal service corporation (QPSC) is subject to a flat tax of 35 percent and has a lower threshold ($150,000) for accumulated earnings tax. A personal service corporation is defined as a specific type of company where the shareholder/employer provides his or her own services for the corporation. Not all personal service activities are considered qualified personal service corporation activities.

In many states, professionals who want to incorporate their practices must create what is called a professional corporation.

The list of professionals required to incorporate as professional corporations is different in each state. Usually, though, mandatory QPSC incorporation requirements apply to these professionals:

- Accountants.
- Engineers.

- Health care professionals such as audiologists, dentists, nurses, opticians, optometrists, pharmacists, physical therapists, physicians, and speech pathologists.
- Lawyers.
- Psychologists.
- Social workers.
- Veterinarians.

The designation of professional corporation is important because the IRS considers professional corporations to generally also be personal service corporations. Additionally, the IRS has recently expanded the description of "personal service" to include consulting or any other type of work that requires the personal service of the owner-shareholder.

Take the qualified personal service corporation test in Figure 15.1 to determine whether you will escape being stuck with this designation.

FIGURE 15.1   Qualified Personal Service Corporation Status Test

Qualified Personal Service Corporation Status

Instructions: If your business qualifies as a personal service corporation (PSC) due to the type of work performed, use this checklist to determine if you are subject to the qualified PSC rules. If you answer yes to questions 1–3, you have a qualified PSC and are subject to the 35 percent flat tax rate as well as subject to the lower accumulated earnings threshold.

1. Is the corporation a C corporation?

   Yes / No

2. Is 95 percent or more of all employee time spent in the performance of services in one or more of the personal service fields listed in the text? (Divide hours worked in the personal service activity by total hours worked for all employees in the year.)

   Yes / No

3. Is 95 percent or more of the value of the stock of the corporation owned by employees involved in qualifying personal service activity? (Divide value of shares owned by personal service employees by value of shares owned by employees and nonemployees.)

   Yes / No

If you take the test and fail, then the C corporation is probably not for you. Generally, the S corporation designation is the best one for qualified personal service activities.

Personal Holding Company

A personal holding company is a corporation that has been established for the main purpose of collecting dividends, interest, and other solely passive investment income. The income for a personal holding company is currently taxed at 15 percent, but will rise to the highest individual income tax rate after 2008.

The IRS defines a personal holding company as a corporation in which 60 percent or more of the corporate income is personal holding company income and which has five or fewer individuals who own 50 percent more of outstanding stock.

Personal holding company income includes dividends, interest, royalties, annuities, rents (unless they constitute 50 percent or more of the adjusted income of the corporation), and personal service contracts where the person performing the work is specified.

The personal holding company issue has become much less of a concern since the tax rate has dropped. If the laws change back, or at the very least by 2008, we will need to start watching this issue for C corporations.

Accumulated Earnings

When a corporation has exceeded a certain amount in earnings that are retained in the corporation, an additional tax is assessed on the corporation.

Every C corporation runs the risk of being subject to an additional accumulated earnings tax equal to the highest individual tax rate. This amount is assessed on the accumulated earnings in excess of $250,000 ($150,000 for personal service corporations). This tax is in addition to the regular income tax paid by the corporation.

The accumulated earnings tax is a much-litigated portion of tax law and, increasingly, the case law does not mirror the Internal Revenue Code and IRS regulations. The simple definition, from the tax code and regulations, states that accumulated earnings are the previously taxed income in the corporation reduced by any net capital gains. In other words, they are the retained earnings held by the corporation without any capital gains reflected.

There has been significant case law supporting the Bardahl formula, which basically says that accumulated earnings are the working capital of the company. The working capital, or Bardahl formula, approach defines working capital as the amount necessary to run your company.

The necessary working capital for your business can be used to reduce the accumulated earnings. For example, if you discover you have a total of $350,000 in accumulated earnings in your company for a potential 35 percent tax on $100,000 (the excess over $250,000), you may also find that your company has working capital needs of $100,000. You're fine this year. But next year, as your company makes more money and accumulates more earnings, your risk of this excess tax will also increase.

Besides the working capital, your company can also withhold a certain amount for projected growth and investment in the business and can take an accumulated earnings deduction for life insurance paid on the lives of key officers of the company.

You do not actually report the calculation of working capital needs. If the retained earnings on your corporate return show an amount over $250,000, your corporation may get a letter from the IRS that asks about the accumulated earnings. You will be a long way ahead of the game if you can immediately offer copies of your working capital calculation, additional forecasted needs for the company, and corporate minutes that substantiate all of it.

Chapter 16

NEW C CORPORATION TAX LOOPHOLES STRATEGIES

Hot New Tax Strategies for C Corporations

Tax law is always changing and that means new tax strategies are always coming up. If you're interested in learning about the latest tax strategies for free, go to our web site at www.taxloopholes.com. You'll learn how you can become part of the *Loopholes of the Rich* Reader Club to receive updates on strategies outlined in this book. Plus, you'll have the opportunity to present feedback and ask questions.

C corporations have undergone some very dramatic changes just as a result of a few simple tax rate changes. Here are some of the hot new tax loopholes strategies for C corporations.

Double Taxation Is Still Less Tax

One of the biggest problems for C corporations in past years has been the double taxation issue. As we discussed previously, the double taxation issue means that the dividends your C corporation pays you are not tax-deductible for the corporation and yet they are taxable income to you. That's what is meant by double taxation.

But let's see what happens to that tax in light of recent tax law changes. Currently, the dividend tax rate is no more than 15 percent. Let's take the worst-case double taxation scenario and compare business structures for a business that has $50,000 of taxable income after your salary.

You could put the business in an S corporation and then have the income flow through to you at your highest tax rate. We'll assume that is the 35 percent highest federal tax rate. Your tax would be 35 percent of $50,000 or $17,500.

Or you could put the business in a C corporation, pay the tax, and then take the money out in the form of a dividend. Your C corporation would pay tax of 15 percent on the $50,000 for a total of $7,500. The income then is paid to you as a dividend. The dividend income is taxed at a maximum of 15 percent, for a total of $7,500 in taxes. That means you've paid a total tax of $15,000. The worst-case scenario saves you $2,500! Double taxation is actually better in this case.

Take Back Lost Passive Losses with Your C Corporation

If you don't have the ability to offset your real estate losses against your other income, maybe you can use a C corporation to help you do so.

Congress enacted Code Section 469 in the 1986 tax act primarily to eliminate tax shelters, in which individuals used large depreciation deductions and similar tax allowances generated from highly leveraged investments to deduct against their taxable salary and professional income. These rules apply only to closely held C corporations and certain personal service corporations.

The limited rules on the 1986 tax act indicate that it is possible to pair active taxable income with passive activities generating tax losses within a C corporation. That means you can now offset the passive losses from the real estate with your earned income. This approach, however, would seem to be attractive only in very special circumstances. It would require a constant stream of tax losses from the passive activities. I would also be concerned about the asset that is generating the passive losses. If it's appreciating, we don't want to hold it within a C corporation.

Change the Character of Income

One of my favorite all-time strategies with a C corporation is to use it to "upstream" income. The basic plan is that either an income stream or a function is diverted to a C corporation and the original business then pays a fee to the corporation for this service.

Here are two examples of how that could work:

1. A doctor has a regular medical practice but also subleases out space to a drug-testing company. He is compensated for use of space, plus access to the doctor's clients for clinical trials. This is a function that is separate from his regular practice of medicine, which he holds in an S corporation. This separate function can operate in a C corporation. He now receives both flow-through income and salary from his medical practice while the C corporation receives approximately $50,000 per year in income that is taxed at 15 percent.

2. A family has begun an eBay business that has just exploded with opportunity. They are making a lot of money through their company and now are looking at other ways of holding their business other than an S corporation. Because the husband is involved more in just the shipping of the products while working his full-time job and the wife dedicates her time to running the business, they decide to have the husband set up a separate corporation. He then begins subcontracting the shipping function and selling shipping products to others. Her S corporation pays a fee for the service. His C corporation makes income from her company as well as a few other eBay clients that he has picked up.

The Seven Secrets of C Corporations

A C corporation is a unique type of structure with special tax laws and the ability to pay tax at its own rate, instead of at your individual rate. That means there are unique benefits to using the C corporation as your structure. Here are my favorite reasons to use a C corporation.

Own Tax Rate

No matter how you look at it, the C corporation tax rate is graduated and if you can move $50,000 from your personal tax bracket of 35 percent to that of a C corporation's tax bracket of 15 percent, you will save $10,000 in taxes. And that's not just $10,000 today. It's $10,000 year after year, as long as the tax rates and your income remain constant.

Medical Reimbursement Plan

Your C corporation can form a medical reimbursement plan that pays for all medical co-payments, dental and vision care, orthodontia, therapy, even therapeutic massage—all with before-tax money. The trick is that you can't discriminate with the plan. If you (or another company in which you have controlling interest) have full-time employees, you will need to provide the same benefits to them that you receive.

Disability Insurance

Your C corporation can pay for disability insurance for you. It's tax free to you and a deduction for them.

Accumulate Dividend Income

As we saw, this is one of the hot new tax strategies based on the change in tax laws. Don't let the fear of how you will take money out of your corporation stop you from having a C corporation. Of course, it is better to have other plans for taking money out of your corporation.

Receive Dividend Income

Your C corporation can receive dividend income and pay a whole lot less in tax. If there is no ownership in the corporation paying the dividends, only 30 percent of the dividend income is taxable. If your corporation owns 20 percent or more of the company paying the dividends, only 20 percent of the dividend income is taxable.

Ability to Borrow from Pension Plans

If you have a pension plan just sitting there losing money, no doubt you've wondered how you can access that money to do other things.

One of the best little-known secrets of C corporations is that you can set up a corporate pension plan and roll your other pension plans into it. Then, because it's a plan that has been set up in a corporation, you can borrow from your pension.

Generally I don't recommend borrowing against your pension if you work for someone else because if you leave your job you will have to pay the money back immediately. But, if it's your own company you're much safer with this plan.

Ability to Go Public

The C corporation is the only entity that has the ability to go public. If you're planning to grow big, sooner or later you'll need a C corporation.

When *Not* to Use a C Corporation

Does that mean that the C corporation is the best structure for every scenario? Absolutely not! Here are five scenarios where I would generally *not* recommend a C corporation:

1. Your business has losses. A C corporation doesn't work if you have losses because you lose the ability to offset the loss against other income.

2. Your business has high income. The C corporation will need to distribute most of the income out to you in the form of salary. That means you'll pay high payroll taxes. If you instead use an S corporation for the business you will be able to flow some of the income through to you in the form of a distribution. *Note:* A C corporation would work well in this case for part of the income that comes from the business.

3. Your business is a qualified personal service corporation. In this case, you're pretty much stuck with a professional LLC, a professional LLP, or an S corporation.

4. Your business is a personal holding company. I don't recommend holding appreciating assets inside a C corporation. The individual capital gains rate is much less than the rate paid at the corporate level. There is also the issue of having to liquidate the company if its only purpose is to hold an asset. Appreciating assets are better held within an LP or an LLC.

5. You want a very simple structure. A C corporation will require better and more diligent bookkeeping. If that's not your strong suit and you don't plan on hiring someone to do it for you, I don't recommend a C corporation. Some of the biggest accounting nightmares I've ever seen have been when someone tried to use a strategy of the rich without the support and diligence that are necessary.

C Corporation Choices

A C corporation provides unique choices and opportunities. It's not the best structure for every use and it's not the worst structure ever invented. It's just one more possible tool in your tax loopholes tool kit.

PART IV

Take Your Loopholes and Still Sleep at Night

Chapter 17

ELIMINATE IRS RED FLAGS

Reduce the Likelihood of an Audit

T he IRS uses patterns and statistics in deciding which taxpayers to audit. By decreasing the red flags on your tax return, you can significantly reduce your chances of being audited. Here are some of the ways to avoid red flags:

1. Make sure there are no math errors on your return.

2. If at all possible, don't put down round numbers such as $10,000 or $4,000 on your tax return.

3. Make sure you put down on the tax forms the exact amount reported to you from the following forms—*even if they are wrong* (write the correct amount in a separate entry on the form):

- W-2 (wages and salaries).
- W-2G (gambling winnings).
- 1098 (mortgage interest paid).
- 1099-INT (interest earned).
- 1099-DIV (dividends earned).
- 1099-B (proceeds of sale)—allocating basis.
- 1099-MISC (rents, royalties, prizes and awards, and nonemployee compensation).
- 1099-R (pensions and IRA withdrawals).
- Form 5498 (IRA contribution information).

4. Attach all required schedules. For example, if you give noncash gifts having a value in excess of $500 to charity, you are required to attach a schedule.

5. Make sure you have the correct principal business or professional activity code on your business return. The wrong code will result in your return being compared to dissimilar businesses. See Appendix C for a list of the business codes.

Special Circumstances

Another thing the IRS will look for will be that there is inventory and uniform capitalization of costs where there are sales of products. Many retailers don't properly record their inventory and many businesses that also happen to sell products don't even show inventory. The IRS is onto them!

Uniform capitalization has been around for a number of years, but I am amazed at how many tax preparers either don't understand how to apply this principle or ignore it. You don't need to know how to do the calculation, but make sure your tax preparer does!

Uniform capitalization (also discussed in Chapter 11) requires certain taxpayers to capitalize direct costs and an allocable portion of indirect costs. It covers any reseller who does not alter the form of the property, self-constructors who produce property for use in their own trade or business, and producers who acquire inventory and then change the form of the inventory before selling it. Resellers who have less than $10 million in gross sales per year are exempt. If you manufacture products, your gross sales exemption is much lower. Check out the current law with your tax preparer.

Business Form

Although you don't want to make economic decisions simply based on audit statistics, the fact is that a Schedule C business (sole proprietor) has the highest likelihood of audit.

Following are the percentages of returns audited by the IRS, by year:

	1997	1998	1999	2000
Individuals	0.61%	0.46%	0.31%	0.49%
Schedule C (sole proprietors)				
$25,000 to $100,000 in income	2.04%	1.44%	1.01%	0.93%
$100,000 and above in income	3.44%	2.85%	2.08%	1.48%
Corporations				
Less than $250,000 in assets	1.16%	0.75%	0.44%	0.28%
$250,000 to $1 million in assets	3.49%	2.49%	1.65%	1.07%

The other fact you see from studying this chart is that the number of company audits is going down. The IRS is concentrating on certain pockets of known problems and is reducing the number of face-to-face audits.

How Does the IRS Select You for Audit?

The IRS makes a series of computer checks on your tax return when it is first received. Each time your return has a problem with one of the checks, you're running the risk of having an audit. The best way to avoid an audit is to stay under the IRS radar screen during these checks. And, of course, comply by taking only the legal tax loopholes available.

The first computer check is looking for math errors. Don't assume that there are no math errors on your return simply because a computer program was used to prepare it. Take the time to add up the columns and verify that the totals are properly carried to the appropriate schedules.

The second computer check is looking for unallowable items and verifying third-party-reported information. This is the check that makes sure you've calculated your exemptions properly and aren't exceeding allowable deductions per the form. This is also the time when the IRS will try to match up the wage, interest, dividend, and sales information received from other sources. Look for the IRS to start matching K-1s from partnerships and S corporations as well. They want to make sure that you're reporting everything that other people have said you should report. And if there's a discrepancy—guess who gets the audit!

TABLE 17.1   Average Deductions Claimed for 2001 Based on Adjusted Gross Income

	$15K–$30K	$30K–$50K	$50K–$100K	$100K–$200K	Over $200K
AGI total	$21,960	$39,087	$69,466	$131,630	$539,328
Itemized deductions	$11,817	$12,847	$16,346	$ 25,230	$ 69,548
Medical	$ 5,616	$ 5,489	$ 5,532	$ 10,780	$ 35,927
Taxes paid	$ 2,311	$ 3,052	$ 5,108	$ 9,713	$ 38,931
Interest paid	$ 6,406	$ 6,783	$ 8,330	$ 11,817	$ 23,260
Charities	$ 1,875	$ 1,906	$ 2,429	$ 3,761	$ 17,842
Itemizers' %	16%	38%	70%	91%	94%

The next check is the one that most people fear. It's a check performed by the Questionable Items Program and this is the one that can cause a full-blown audit. Some of the audits are selected completely at random and some are called because the return simply doesn't fit the normal criteria.

An average 2001 return claimed the amounts shown in Table 17.1. The farther your numbers are away from the average, the more likely the audit.

If you have a business, the IRS will check your reported deductions against other businesses of your type. It will use the principal business code that you've reported for determining what types of businesses are like yours.

Avoid IRS Red Flags

- File on time (or with timely extension).
- Be thorough.
- Be neat.
- Be sure math is correct.
- Be consistent.
- Fill in all blanks that should be filled in.
- Balance out deductions to reasonable amount compared to income.
- Sign your return.
- Mail return receipt requested.

Chapter 18

HOW TO HAVE A PAINLESS IRS AUDIT

What to Do If You Get a Letter from the IRS

irst of all, you are not going to jail! But don't ignore the letter, either. Action is needed. It just needs to be reasoned and logical action. I always instruct my clients to immediately fax to me any correspondence they receive from the IRS. That serves two purposes: (1) gets it out of their hands, so they can stop worrying, and (2) serves notice to someone who knows how to deal with it.

You Get a Letter

There are three general types of IRS audits:

1. Mail audit.
2. Office audit.
3. Field audit.

The mail audit typically occurs when there is a discrepancy within the return (such as a calculation error) or with third-party information (such as 1099s). Usually, these audits merely require submitting backup information, documents, and an explanation.

An office audit normally is for W-2 wage earners and some small business owners. The taxpayer is required to bring substantiating documentation for the return to the local IRS office for analysis. The office audit typically lasts one day or less. Immediately upon receipt of an office audit notice, the taxpayer should consult their tax preparer.

Field audits, where one or more IRS revenue agents come to a taxpayer's office, are usually reserved for corporations, partnerships, and limited liability companies, although complex sole proprietorships are also subject to field audits. The auditor has to go to the office of the taxpayer because the documentation and legal issues are voluminous and complex. The taxpayer should expect to obtain proper representation, as well as further accounting assistance to prepare for the audit.

Maybe They Made a Mistake

Don't assume that the IRS is right if you get a notice. There are some common areas where the IRS's technologies have not kept up and they consistently make errors. Some common errors by the IRS:

- An IRS worker may mismatch information on W-2 forms with information on Form 1040.
- Employers can currently file W-2 returns on their employees either using a standardized W-2 form or via magnetic media (tapes). In some cases, with large employers, they must file using the magnetic media. When they do, they can use a nonstandardized W-2 form, which will not always be readily apparent to the temporary IRS worker who is working on the crunch of mail that arrives during tax time. There are simply too many forms to look at, and they might miss one, which kicks the return out for a letter. Nothing was done incorrectly; it is simply a case of human error and a system that doesn't support the IRS worker.
- The total that the IRS enters from Form 1099 may be more than the gross income actually reported.
- Calculation of interest and penalty due may be incorrect. If you receive a statement showing interest or penalty, as well as tax due, first verify that the total tax due is accurate. Then, recalculate the interest and penalty due.

What If You Get an Incorrect 1099?

You may occasionally get an incorrect Form 1099. What you do about it will depend on what the error is.

- Social Security number is incorrect: Contact the issuer to have them send a corrected Form 1099 with correct Social Security number.
- Income is stated incorrectly: Contact the issuer to have them send a corrected Form 1099. If they refuse, include the amount shown (if more) on your return and then subtract the difference with a note that the Form 1099 was issued incorrectly.

What If the IRS Is Wrong?

The IRS is incorrect more often than they probably want to admit. If they are, always follow these three steps: (1) promptly answer their correspondence; (2) send copies of documentation proving your point; and (3) mail return receipt requested.

Before the Letter Arrives

Reduce the risk from an IRS audit before you even get a letter by always having proper documentation, corporate minutes, properly executed agreements, and copies of invoices and canceled checks neatly filed.

The IRS will expect you to produce the following documents:

- Bank statements, canceled checks, and receipts.
- Books and records. A good accounting software program such as QuickBooks Pro will provide the necessary information, as long as the information has all been accurately and competently entered.
- Appointment books, logs, and diaries. Businesses generally track appointments using calendars, business diaries, or appointment books that are shown either manually or on computer programs. These can provide excellent additional proof for business expenses.
- Automobile records. A log is the best way to track business use of an automobile, but it is not strictly required by the tax code. Another plan would be to keep all gas and repair receipts in an orderly fashion

with notations of trips showing how the car was used for business. A less accurate way is to simply add up the gas receipts and divide by the number of miles per gallon that your car averages.

- Travel and entertainment records. You must have a written record of the specific business purpose for the travel or entertainment expense, as well as a receipt for it. For entertainment, the amount of each separate expenditure must be substantiated.

How Long Do You Need to Keep Records?

Following is a snapshot look at various records and the recommended time to retain them. (See also "Suggested Record Retention List" in Appendix D.) The major categories are:

- Supporting records. You must keep records until the statute of limitations for the return expires. Ordinarily, the statute of limitations for an income tax return expires three years after the return is due to be filed or is filed, or two years from the date that tax is paid, whichever is later. In some cases, you must keep records indefinitely. For example, if you change your method of accounting, records supporting the necessary adjustments may remain applicable for an indefinite time.
- Employment tax records. You must keep all employment tax records for at least four years after the date on which a tax return becomes due or the tax is paid, whichever is later.
- Tax returns. You should keep all copies of your filed tax returns for all years. They will help you in preparing your future tax returns, and in making computations if you later file a claim for a refund. They may also be helpful to the executor or administrator of your estate, or to an IRS examiner if your original return is not available.

Good Records

The law requires that you keep good records so that you can prepare complete and accurate tax returns. You must be able to substantiate items of income, deductions, and credits. (See also "Suggested Record Retention List" in Appendix D.)

Review the following:

- Identify sources of income. You may receive money or property from a variety of sources. Your records should identify the sources of your income. You need this information to separate taxable income from nontaxable deposits.
- Keep track of expenses. You may forget an expense unless you record it when it occurs. You can use your records to identify expenses for which you can claim a deduction.
- Prepare tax returns. You need records to prepare your tax return. Good records will help you file quickly and accurately.
- Support items reported on tax returns. You must keep records in case the IRS has a question about an item on your return. If the IRS examines your tax return, you may be asked to explain the items reported. Good records will help you explain any item and arrive at

---

Targeted Businesses

There are some types of businesses that the IRS has specifically targeted as being poor record keepers. If you have one of these businesses, make sure you have good records to stop a problem before it begins. The following targeted businesses and business-related issues are directly out of the IRS agents' manual:

Air charters.
Attorneys.
Bed-and-breakfasts.
Gas retailers.
Mortuaries.
Entertainment.
Independent used car dealers.
Taxicabs.
Trucking.
Employment tax—Classification of workers as independent versus employee.

(Continued)

Targeted Businesses (*Continued*)

Alaska commercial fishing.
Architects.
Bars and restaurants.
Foreign athletes and entertainers.
Entertainers.
Ministers.
Mobile food vendors.
Rehabilitation tax credit.
Resolution Trust Corporation (RTC)—cancellation of indebtedness.
Wine industry.
Beauty and barber shops.
Auto body and repair.
Reforestation.
Pizza restaurants.
The Port Project.
Grain farmers.
Passive activity losses.
Oil and gas.
Tobacco.
Cattle.
Entertainment—music.
Garment contractors.
Artists and art galleries.
Bail bond industry.
Coal excise tax.
Commercial banking.
Commercial printing.
Computers, electronics, and high-tech.
Farming—specific income issues and farm cooperatives.
Furniture manufacturing.
Garment manufacturing.
Hardwood timber.
Retail liquor.
Tour buses.
Tip reporting—hairstyling.
Tip reporting—gaming.
Tip reporting—food service.

the correct tax with minimum effort. If you do not have records, you may have to spend time getting statements and receipts from various sources. If you cannot produce the correct documents, you may have to pay additional tax and be subject to penalties.

Prepare

The single answer for how to reduce risk from IRS audit is to properly prepare for the audit. With good, neat, and easily accessible records, the concern will be reduced. If keeping good records is not your strongest suit, then turn that function over to a competent bookkeeper. Bookkeepers are trained in how to keep track of documentation. Follow their lead!

Common Errors for Businesses

If you are audited by the IRS, the agents' handbook will direct them to look at specific items. These follow:

- **Internal Revenue Code Section 7872—Imputed interest rules.** The IRS agent is looking for loans to and from stockholders and their corporations that have been made at below-market interest rates. They also will look to see that the property interest income or expense has been recorded. The answer to this is to make sure you have proper documentation for loans and that interest has been recorded. The IRS publishes a list each year of minimum interest for loans. For 2004, interest at 6 percent or more would be safe.
- **IRC Section 3121—Disguised compensation.** The agent is looking for payments that have been made in lieu of wages, such as management fees or contract fees. Be careful that you do not mix nonemployee compensation with personal compensation.
- **IRC Section 162—Trade or business expenses.** The IRS is looking for inappropriate or clearly personal expenses that have been expensed in the corporation. Above all, look for reasonableness in the expenses you show on your return. Don't put huge amounts as "miscellaneous" or lump amounts together that would look more normal when separated out.

- **IRC Section 3509—Employer's liability for employment taxes.** The IRS is looking for the failure of employers to classify workers correctly thereby avoiding employment taxes.
- **IRC Section 1101—Adjusted basis for determining gain or loss.** The IRS is checking here to make sure that the totals shown on your depreciation schedule match the numbers shown on your balance sheet.
- **IRC Section 301—Distributions of property.** The IRS makes sure that assets that have been distributed to shareholders have been reported at the assets' fair market values. They will specifically examine below-market sales to related parties. Of course, the answer to this problem is to never put potentially appreciating property into a C corporation. These should instead be held within a structure that can be taxed as a partnership.
- **IRC Section 1231—Sales of trade or business property.** The IRS Form 4797 is used to report these sales and it is extremely complex. The IRS has also discovered that many tax preparers make math errors on this report.
- **IRC Section 531—Accumulated earnings tax.** The best way to handle this potential problem is to prepare for it as discussed in Chapter 15.
- **IRC Section 61—Gross income.** The IRS will look for the gross profit margins (gross profit equals sales less cost of goods) that are out of alignment with other similar businesses.
- **IRC Section 471—Inventories.** The IRS is looking for inventory that has been understated (increasing cost of goods sold). To protect against this challenge, take an actual physical inventory each year and keep records of how this is done and calculated.
- **IRC Section 3121—S corporation shareholders.** In this case, the IRS is looking for 2 percent or more shareholders within an S corporation who receive distributions or excessive rent payments in lieu of reasonable salaries.
- **IRC Section 1366—Pass through to shareholders.** The IRS requires that certain benefits paid to shareholders be reported separately to shareholders and that these shareholders adequately track basis and correctly calculate debt basis.

Targeted Business Forms

The IRS has categorized certain types of business structures as more likely to be subject to fraud and are specifically targeting them for audit. These are:

- Business trusts.
- Equipment or service trusts.
- Family residence trusts.
- Charitable trusts.
- Foreign trusts.

For more information regarding the IRS's view of these types of businesses, see www.irs.gov for Publication 2193, *Too Good to Be True Trusts*.

A Final Word

Tax planning, above all, must make sound economic sense. Don't make the ends (less tax) justify the means (all that it takes to get there). For one thing, the means may be much more expensive than the benefit. Weigh carefully the decisions you make for your own tax strategies. Assess your goals and the skill of your assembled team, and look at the cost-benefit of any changes. The costs can be seen in many areas—lost sleep, more team needed, unease, and, of course, the actual hard cost of operations.

Are You Planning to Be Rich?

You *can* make the decision today to make significant changes in your financial life. Follow the five STEPS as you use the tax-advantaged wealth-building strategies of the Jump Start! method and carefully consider your tax planning. Loopholes do exist. They are there for you, too. Make the most of what is available to create the financial life you've always dreamed of. Live rich!

TAX LOOPHOLES STRATEGY SUCCESS STORIES

Y ou've learned about loopholes and the Jump Start! method for using leverage, velocity, and cash flow to create tax-advantaged wealth building. In this special report, we'll look at some real-life examples of how people have put loophole ideas into use.

How Can You Learn from These Success Stories?

These loopholes strategies are examples. That's it. No one case in this book will be exactly like yours, so you shouldn't use these examples as an exact blueprint for your own tax-savings plan. Instead use these examples to spark ideas for conversations with your advisors.

Hints for Getting the Best Results

Take notes as you read through these examples. Identify:

- Specific deductions that were taken.
- Strategies to change the type of income.
- Business structures used.
- Current situations for the clients.
- Your personal situation and how it is similar and how it differs.

What one idea can you take from everything you have read in *Loopholes of the Rich* that could transform the way you pay taxes? Now, how can you put it into action today?

In the following four examples, we'll cover some real-life tax savings success stories.

Story #1: Creating Phantom Income through Bad Planning in an S Corporation

Sometimes a plan is put into place that *increases* the amount of tax paid. In other words, conventional tax planning would have created less tax than the bad plan did. Why does bad tax planning occur? Typically, bad tax planning occurs when there is a breakdown in communication between the taxpayers and their advisor. There are a number of reasons for this. Some of the problems might be:

- There was a lack of current and accurate financial statements.
- The taxpayers got good advice, but tried to implement the plan by themselves.
- There was inconsistent communication with the advisor.
- The tax strategy firm did not prepare the tax return.
- The advisor was too busy to create a proactive plan.
- No regular follow-up system was in place.
- The taxpayers were trying to do their own tax planning without current information.

An S corporation is a pass-through entity. In other words, the income passes through to the shareholders and is reported on their individual tax returns. If there is a loss, the loss can be used to offset other income the shareholder has. However, the loss can offset the shareholder's income *only* "to the extent of basis." Basis is created when the shareholder buys shares in the corporation, contributes, or otherwise puts their own money or other assets at risk. What you put into the corporation determines the amount of loss you can write off each year. That is because basis should be calculated each year, when your S corpora-tion's tax return is prepared.

If your loss is more than the basis in the property, you will not be able to deduct the entire loss. The excess loss is "suspended" and rolls forward until the time that there is a change in circumstances.

A couple came to see me who had a successful business. Their S cor-poration made about $200,000 in profit, but they seemed to be paying tax on much more than that. A quick look at their S corporation return and their personal return told why. Their current accountant had ad-vised them to take salaries totaling $250,000 per year. That amount was reported as income on their personal return. It created a loss for their S corporation of $50,000, which is the difference between the profit of $200,000 and the salaries deduction of $250,000.

The problem was that the loss was more than the couple's basis in the corporation. They were not able to take the deduction for the $50,000 loss. They did, however, have to pay tax on the $250,000 in salary.

The bad tax planning had created a "phantom" income of $50,000. They didn't have the money, but they had to pay tax on it!

The Solution

We lowered their combined salary to a more reasonable amount to re-flect their actual work in the business. The rest of the income then flowed through as income to their personal return. This could be used to offset previously suspended losses. For the next few years, they will actu-ally receive more income (and cash) than they pay tax on.

It was a simple solution that put quite a lot of money in our new clients' pockets.

Figure A.1 demonstrates the before and after plan. We reduced their combined salary to below the company's total amount of net income. The company now has taxable income, which flows through to the indi-vidual owners' tax return through the Schedule K-1. This flow-through income offsets some of the previous year's suspended loss—so, no tax. We were able to reduce the clients' taxes by more than $40,000 by using this strategy.

FIGURE A.1   S Corporation Before and After Diagrams

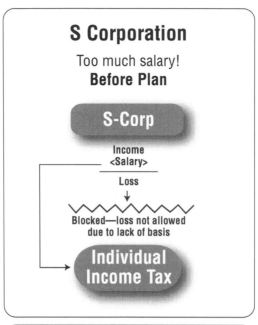

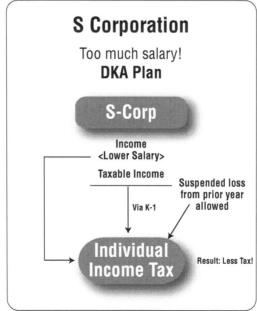

Story #2: Part-Time Business

The real loopholes come from having your own business. But how can you take advantage of business loopholes if you're a full-time employee? For many people, the answer is to start a part-time business. The key is to make sure you are in business to make money, not merely for the tax breaks. In tax law, the rule is never to have the "tax tail wagging the economic dog." This means that there must be a business purpose with the full intent to someday make money.

Once you have made the choice to begin a business, you need to learn the basics of your business as well. A part-time business still means a full-time commitment to the IRS requirements.

Brian and Amy were married. Both had full-time jobs working for someone else. But they were concerned about the economy and how long they'd have those jobs. As a result, Brian and Amy started a part-time business to create more income for themselves.

Business Structure

They anticipated a small loss in the first few years. The S corporation was the best structure for them because it allowed the losses to flow through to their personal return and offset some of the employment income.

Hidden Business Deductions

They also discovered tax benefits along the way. When Brian and Amy first came to us, we reviewed their itemized list of expenses and discovered the following new business expenses:

- **Home office.** Brian and Amy had a room in their home that had exclusive business purpose. This wasn't a corner of the dining room or the family room; it was a room that was used exclusively for their part-time business. Because they had an S corporation, Brian and Amy deducted the home office expenses as a percentage of home-related costs. Their home office was 10 feet by 15 feet, or 150 square feet. The total home was 1,500 square feet, so their home office was 10 percent of their total home area. That means that 10 percent of the mortgage interest, property tax, insurance, utilities, janitorial expenses, and the like would be deductible. The home office expenses would be deductible only to the extent of income from the business. In other words, the home office expense cannot force the business into a loss.

- **Home office equipment and furniture.** Brian and Amy also had a number of items they had contributed to their home office for the business. These items included a computer, software, printer, fax machine, cell phone, desk, artwork, and a file cabinet. Brian and Amy listed these items and came up with a fair market value for each item. The new business paid the couple for these contributed items. It was a tax deduction for the business and tax-free income for Brian and Amy. The total value was $5,000.

- **Cell phone.** Brian and Amy's part-time business required that they have contact with customers and vendors, so they needed to have cell phones for the business. They had a flat-rate service of $39 per month for each phone.

- **Medical insurance.** Brian's employer covered part of the couple's medical insurance cost. Amy didn't have any medical insurance through her job. The business reimbursed Brian for the employee portion of the insurance premium, which amounted to $100 per month.

- **Education.** Brian and Amy were very serious about succeeding with their business. Plus, they wanted to learn more about how to successfully protect their business from excess tax and lawsuits. As a result, they bought books and tapes and attended seminars. The cost of these seminars was deductible.

Benefit

Brian and Amy's total hidden business deductions were $7,868 and, at their marginal federal tax rate of 28 percent, this meant that the savings from their new business totaled $2,203 in the first year. Brian and Amy couldn't deduct their entire home office during the first year, though, as these deductions would have created a loss for their part-time business. They were able to carry the loss and the home office expense forward to the next year.

You can see the change in their plan in Figure A.2.

FIGURE A.2   Part-Time Business Diagram

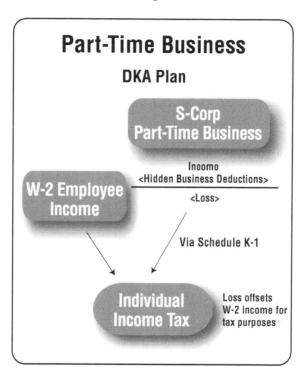

Story #3: Business Creates Passive Income with Intellectual Property

What is your business really? I asked this question of a new client, a very successful chiropractor. John made more than $500,000 per year in his practice. Through our conversation, John explained that he had a very systemized approach with his patients. He also was known as a practitioner who worked with people who wanted to be well and not sick. As a result, he prescribed exercise programs and pain management systems. As we talked, I realized a key word for John was *systems*. John has a written system of his practice's approach to treating patients. John's written system was unique enough that he had plans to expand his practice.

Action

We worked with John to finalize the legal requirements to separate his written system from his practice. In conjunction with his intellectual property attorney, we established John's written system as a separate asset, which he held in a C corporation. John's medical practice operated through an S corporation, and paid a fee to the C corporation to use John's written system. John soon opened new offices that also paid a fee to his C corporation for the use of his written system.

Benefit

John had a good tax plan in place and was taking advantage of all of the deductions currently available to him. But, by transferring income from his S corporation to the C corporation, we were able to move $100,000 of taxable income from his individual tax rate to the C corporation rate. He was able to save $13,000 in federal taxes by using this plan.

Figure A.3 demonstrates how John's plan changed after using this strategy. In the "before" plan, all of the income flows through to the individual tax return either as a salary or via the K-1.

In the "after" diagram, the licensing fees for use of the system are a deduction to the S corporation and income for the C corporation. That means John has been able to move income from his personal return to the C corporation, taking advantage of the lower corporate tax rate.

Story #4: Corporation Buys Real Estate

When I met with James and Cheryl, their first question was how they could use a corporation to buy real estate with pretax dollars.

Can it be done? Yes. But, there are a few steps involved in the process.

The Problem

The first challenge was in getting James and Cheryl pointed in the right direction for their business structure. They had heard the rich used

FIGURE A.3 Intellectual Property Before and After Diagrams

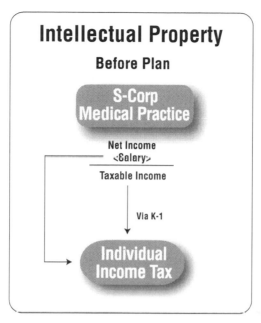

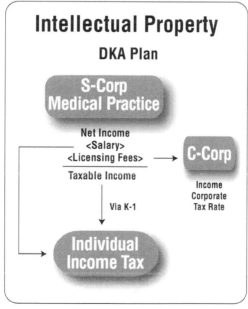

C corporations and since they planned to be rich, they figured they needed a C corporation as well. However, simply buying what the rich have won't make you rich.

The Process

We first went through the details of James and Cheryl's three-year-old business. They had just begun to make good money with their marketing consulting business. James and Cheryl provided services from the office space that they rented. The income was still a little uncertain. But we did discover a number of hidden business deductions that reduced their taxable income by $20,000. At their 28 percent tax rate, this provided a tax savings of $5,600. James and Cheryl had operated as a sole proprietorship and so paid self-employment tax on their $150,000 taxable income. As joint owners, both had self-employment tax. This added an additional $22,950 in taxes.

Our first plan was to form an LLC, which elected to be taxed as an S corporation. The LLC gave James and Cheryl protection of the assets of the business by providing "charging order" protection. This meant that any judgment that came as a result of their personal assets or actions could not go against their business.

The Benefit

James and Cheryl paid $17,000 less in tax with this new system. They were happy, even though they still wanted to know how they could eventually have a C corporation.

Future Plans

The next step for James and Cheryl was to buy a building for their business. Their plan was to take a distribution to make the down payment. James and Cheryl would hold the building in a separate LLC that would elect partnership taxation. The S corporation would pay rent (which was deductible for the S corporation) to their LLC. Their LLC would then have income (in the form of rent) that could be offset by depreciation. If we created a passive loss from the LLC for James and Cheryl, they would likely not be able to deduct it against other income. So our plan would be to make the rent as high as is reasonable for the S corporation. The higher rent meant a bigger deduction for the S corporation.

FIGURE A.4 Business Buys Real Estate Diagram

The higher income in the new LLC, even if it resulted in a flow-through taxable income after depreciation, was part of our plan. In this way, James and Cheryl began to see how real estate could be bought with money that was effectively before tax. The rent was a deduction.

If we added a C corporation to their tax strategy later, we could either use the same strategy of paying rent or actually make the C corporation a member in an LLC that holds real estate. The C corporation would receive the flow-through benefit of depreciation because it was a member.

Figure A.4 demonstrates how the rental expense reduces the taxable income that distributes through the S corporation. This means lower tax. The rent is income through the LLC, but that income is offset by the depreciation on the building.

300+ BUSINESS DEDUCTIONS

Business Tax Deductions

Instructions: Check each tax deduction that applies to your business.

A

	Abandonment of property used for business purposes
	Accounting and auditing expenses, such as:
	Auditing of your books and accounts
	Costs of bookkeeping
	Costs of tax strategy preparation
	Costs of preparing and filing any tax returns
	Costs of investigation of any tax returns
	Costs of defense against any IRS or state agency audits or challenges
	Accounts receivable, worthless
	Achievement awards—requires plan:
	Longevity award
	Safety award
	Sales award
	Advances made to employees or salespeople where repayment is not expected
	Advances to employees canceled as bonus
	Advertising expenses, such as:
	Premiums given away

	Advertising in:
	Newspaper
	Magazine
	Radio
	Other media
	Prizes and other expenses in holding contests or exhibitions
	Contributions to various organizations for advertising purposes
	Cost of displays, posters, and so on to attract customers
	Publicity—generally speaking, all costs including entertainment, music, and so on
	Christmas presents to customers or prospects—de minimis rule
	Alterations to business property, if minor
	Amortization
	Attorney's fees and other legal expenses involving:
	Tax strategy
	Drafting of agreements, resolutions, minutes, and so on
	Defense of claims against you
	Collection actions taken against others
	Any other business-related legal activity
	Auto expenses for business purposes, such as:
	Damage to auto not covered by insurance
	Gasoline
	Oil
	Repairs and maintenance
	Washing and waxing
	Garage rent
	Interest portion of payments
	Insurance premiums such as fire, theft, collision, liability, and so on
	Lease payment
	License plate
	Driver's license fee
	Depreciation

	Wages of chauffeur
	Section 179 deduction, for qualified vehicle

B

	Bad debts—if previously taken into income
	Baseball/softball/soccer team equipment for business publicity
	Board and room to employee:
	All meals and lodging if for employer's benefit
	Temporary housing assignment
	Board meetings
	Bonuses as additional compensation to employees
	Bookkeeping services
	Building expenses, used for business, such as:
	Repairs to building
	Janitorial service
	Painting
	Interest on mortgage
	Taxes on property
	Water
	Rubbish removal
	Depreciation of building
	Heating
	Lighting
	Landscaping
	Burglary losses not covered by insurance
	Business, cost of operating office
	Business taxes—except federal income taxes

C

	Cafeteria plan—requires written plan
	Capital asset sale—losses

	Car and taxi fares
	Casualty damages, such as:
	Bombardment
	Fire
	Storm
	Hurricane
	Wind
	Rain
	Ice
	Heat
	Drought
	Forest fire
	Freezing of property
	Impairment or collapse of property
	Charitable contributions
	Checking account bank charges
	Child care—requires written plan
	Children's salaries
	Christmas presents to employees, customers, and prospects for advertising or publicity purposes, or goodwill, or if customary in the trade
	Collection expenses, including attorney's charges
	Commissions on sales of securities by dealers in securities
	Commissions paid to agents
	Commissions paid to employees for business purposes
	Commissions paid to salespeople
	Condemnation expenses
	Contributions (deductible if made to organization founded for the following purposes, subject to some limitations):
	Religious
	Charitable
	Scientific

	Literary
	Educational
	Prevention of cruelty to children and animals
	Convention expenses, cost of attending conventions
	Cost of goods
	Credit report costs

D

	Day care facility
	Depletion
	Depreciation
	Discounts allowed to customers
	Dues paid to:
	Better Business Bureau
	Chamber of Commerce
	Trade associations
	Professional societies
	Technical societies
	Protective services association

E

	Education assistance—requires written plan
	Embezzlement loss not covered by insurance
	Employee welfare expenses, such as:
	Dances
	Entertainment
	Outings
	Christmas parties
	Shows or plays
	Endorser's loss
	Entertainment expenses

	Equipment, minor replacements
	Equipment purchases—may require capitalization and depreciation
	Equipment repairs
	Exhibits and displays to publicize products
	Expenses of any kind directly chargeable to business income, such as:
	Renting of storage space
	Safe-deposit boxes
	Upkeep of property
	Books to record income and expenses or investment income
	Experimental and research expenses

F

	Factoring
	Fan mail expenses
	Fees for passports necessary while traveling on business
	Fees paid to:
	Accountants
	Agents
	Brokers
	Investment counsel
	Professionals for services rendered
	Technicians
	Fire loss
	Forfeited stock
	Freight charges

G

	Gifts to customers—limit $75
	Gifts to organized institutions, such as:
	Charitable
	Literary

	Educational
	Religious
	Scientific
	Group term insurance on employees' lives
	Guarantor's loss

H

	Health insurance
	Heating expense
	Hospitals, contributions to

I

	Improvements, provided they are minor
	Insurance premiums paid
	Interest on loans for business purposes, such as:
	Notes (bank discount on note is deductible as interest)
	Mortgages
	Bonds
	Tax deficiencies
	Installment payments on auto, furniture, and so on
	Margin account with broker
	Inventory loss due to damages
	Investment counsel fees

L

	Lawsuit expenses
	Legal costs
	In defense of your business
	In settlement of cases
	Payment of damages

	License fees
	Lighting
	Living quarters furnished to employees for business's benefit
	Lobbying costs
	Losses, deductible if connected with your business or profession, such as:
	Abandoned property
	Accounts receivable
	Auto damage caused by fire, theft, heat, storm, and so on
	Bad debts
	Bank closed
	Bonds
	Buildings damaged
	Burglary
	Business ventures
	Capital assets
	Casualties: fire, theft, heat, storm, and so on
	Damages to property or assets
	Deposit forfeiture, on purchase of property
	Drought
	Embezzlements
	Equipment abandoned
	Forced sale or exchange
	Foreclosures
	Forfeitures
	Freezing
	Goodwill
	Loans not collectible
	Theft
	Transactions entered into for profits

M

	Maintenance of business property
	Maintenance of office, store, warehouse, showroom, and so on
	Maintenance of rented premises
	Management costs
	Materials
	Meals, subject to limitation
	Membership dues
	Merchandise
	Messenger service
	Moving cost
	Musician expenses

N

	Net operating loss—may be carried back to previous years' income for refund and/or forward against future years' income
	Newspapers

O

	Office expenses, including:
	Wages
	Supplies
	Towel service
	Heating and lighting
	Telephone and telegraph
	Repairs
	Refurnishing, minor items
	Decorating
	Painting

	Office rent
	Office rent—portion of home used for business
	Office stationery and supplies

P

	Passport fees
	Pension plans—must be properly drawn
	Periodicals
	Physical fitness center
	Plotting of land for sale
	Postage
	Professional society dues
	Property depreciation
	Property maintenance
	Property repairs
	Publicity expenses

R

	Real estate expenses of rental or investment property, including:
	Taxes on property
	Insurance
	Janitorial services
	Repairing
	Redecorating
	Painting
	Depreciation
	Supplies
	Tools
	Legal expenses involving leases, tenants, or property
	Bookkeeping

	Property management
	Utilities
	Commissions to secure tenants
	Maintenance—heating, lighting, and so on
	Advertising for tenants
	Cost of manager's unit, if on-site and at owner's convenience
	Rebates on sales
	Refunds on sales
	Rental property expense, such as:
	Advertising of vacant premises
	Commissions to secure tenants
	Billboards and signs
	Rent collection expense
	Rent settlement—cancel lease
	Rents paid, such as:
	Business property
	Parking facilities
	Safe-deposit boxes
	Taxes paid by tenant for landlord
	Warehouse and storage charges
	Repairing of business property, such as:
	Alterations, provided they are not capital additions
	Casualty damages, replaced, provided they are not capital additions
	Cleaning
	Minor improvements
	Painting
	Redecorating
	Repairing of furniture, fixtures, equipment, machinery, and buildings
	Roof repairs
	Royalties

S

	Safe-deposit box rental
	Safe or storage rental
	Salaries (including bonuses, commissions, pensions, management fees)
	Sample room
	Selling expenses, such as:
	Commissions and bonuses as prizes
	Discounts
	Entertainment
	Prizes offered in contests
	Publicity and promotion costs
	Rebates
	Services, professional or other necessary for conduct of business
	Social Security taxes paid by employers
	Stationery and all other office supplies used
	Subscriptions to all trade, business, or professional periodicals
	Supplies, office or laboratory

T

	Taxes, all taxes paid except federal income taxes, such as:
	City gross receipts tax
	City sales tax
	State gross receipts tax
	State sales tax
	State unemployment insurance tax
	Federal Social Security tax
	State income tax
	State unincorporated business tax
	Real estate tax
	Tangible property tax

	Intangible property tax
	Custom, import, or tariff tax
	License tax
	Stamp taxes
	Any business tax, as a rule
	Auto registration tax
	Safe-deposit box tax
	Membership dues tax
	Gasoline tax
	Admission tax
	Telephone and telegraph expenses
	Traveling expenses (includes: meals, taxi fare, rail fare, airfare, tips, telephone, telegrams, laundry and cleaning, entertainment for business purposes)

U

	Unemployment compensation taxes paid by employer
	Uniforms furnished to employees

W

	Wages
	Workers' compensation fund contributions

IRS PRINCIPAL BUSINESS AND PROFESSIONAL ACTIVITY CODES

The IRS compares businesses, their income, and their expenses based on the type of business activity they have. Following is the list of business codes that the IRS recognizes. You or your tax preparer will have to select from the following list when you file your corporate or partnership return. Take the time to check the list to find the best fit for your type of business. Careful selection can be the single most powerful way to avoid unnecessary IRS audits.

Agriculture, Forestry, Fishing, and Hunting

Crop Production

111100	Oilseed & Grain Farming
111210	Vegetable & Melon Farming (including potatoes & yams)
111300	Fruit & Tree Nut Farming
111400	Greenhouse, Nursery, & Floriculture Production
111900	Other Crop Farming (including tobacco, cotton, sugarcane, hay, peanut, sugar beet, & all other crop farming)

Animal Production

112111	Beef Cattle Ranching & Farming
112112	Cattle Feedlots
112120	Dairy Cattle & Milk Production

112210   Hog & Pig Farming
112300   Poultry & Egg Production
112400   Sheep & Goat Farming
112510   Animal Aquaculture (including shellfish & finfish farms & hatcheries)
112900   Other Animal Production

Forestry and Logging
113100   Timber Tract Operation
113210   Forest Nurseries & Gathering of Forest Products
113310   Logging

Fishing, Hunting and Trapping
114110   Fishing
114210   Hunting & Trapping

Support Activities for Agriculture and Forestry
115110   Support Activities for Crop Production (including cotton ginning, soil preparation, planting, & cultivating)
115210   Support Activities for Animal Production
115310   Support Activities for Forestry

Mining

212100   Oil & Gas Extraction
212110   Coal Mining
212200   Metal Ore Mining
212310   Stone Mining & Quarrying
212320   Sand, Gravel, Clay & Ceramic, & Refractory Minerals Mining & Quarrying
212390   Other Nonmetallic Mineral Mining & Quarrying
213110   Support Activities for Mining

Utilities

221100   Electric Power Generation, Transmission, & Distribution
221200   Natural Gas Distribution
221300   Water, Sewage, & Other Systems

Construction

Building, Developing, and General Contracting
233110   Land Subdivision & Land Development
233200   Residential Building Construction
233300   Nonresidential Building Construction

Heavy Construction
234100   Highway, Street, Bridge, & Tunnel Construction
234900   Other Heavy Construction

Special Trade Contractors
235110   Plumbing, Heating, & Air-Conditioning Contractors
235210   Painting & Wall Covering Contractors
235310   Electrical Contractors
235400   Masonry, Drywall, Insulation, & Tile Contractors
235500   Carpentry & Floor Contractors
235610   Roofing, Siding, & Sheet Metal Contractors
235710   Concrete Contractors
235810   Water Well Drilling Contractors
235900   Other Special Trade Contractors

Manufacturing

Food Manufacturing
311110   Animal Food Manufacturing
311200   Grain & Oilseed Milling
311300   Sugar & Confectionery Product Manufacturing
311400   Fruit & Vegetable Preserving & Specialty Food
         Manufacturing
311500   Dairy Product Manufacturing
311610   Animal Slaughtering & Processing
311710   Seafood Product Preparation & Packaging
311800   Bakeries & Tortilla Manufacturing
311900   Other Food Manufacturing (including coffee, tea, flavorings,
         & seasonings)

Beverage and Tobacco Product Manufacturing

312110   Soft Drink & Ice Manufacturing
312120   Breweries
312130   Wineries
312140   Distilleries
312200   Tobacco Manufacturing

Textile Mills and Textile Product Mills

313000   Textile Mills
314000   Textile Product Mills

Apparel Manufacturing

315100   Apparel Knitting Mills
315210   Cut & Sew Apparel Contractors
315220   Men's & Boys' Cut & Sew Apparel Manufacturing
315230   Women's & Girls' Cut & Sew Apparel Manufacturing
315290   Other Cut & Sew Apparel Manufacturing
315990   Apparel Accessories & Other Apparel Manufacturing

Leather and Allied Product Manufacturing

316110   Leather & Hide Tanning & Finishing
316210   Footwear Manufacturing (including rubber & plastics)
316990   Other Leather & Allied Product Manufacturing

Wood Product Manufacturing

321110   Sawmills & Wood Preservation
321210   Veneer, Plywood, & Engineered Wood Product Manufacturing
321900   Other Wood Product Manufacturing

Paper Manufacturing

322100   Pulp, Paper, & Paperboard Mills
322200   Converted Paper Product Manufacturing

Printing and Related Support Activities

323100   Printing & Related Support Activities

Petroleum and Coal Products Manufacturing
324110 Petroleum Refineries (including integrated)
324120 Asphalt Paving, Roofing, & Saturated Materials Manufacturing
324190 Other Petroleum & Coal Products Manufacturing

Chemical Manufacturing
325100 Basic Chemical Manufacturing
325200 Resin, Synthetic Rubber, & Artificial & Synthetic Fibers & Filaments Manufacturing
325300 Pesticide, Fertilizer, & Other Agricultural Chemical Manufacturing
325410 Pharmaceutical & Medicine Manufacturing
325500 Paint, Coating, & Adhesive Manufacturing
325600 Soap, Cleaning Compound, & Toilet Preparation Manufacturing
325900 Other Chemical Product & Preparation Manufacturing

Plastics and Rubber Products Manufacturing
326100 Plastics Product Manufacturing
326200 Rubber Products Manufacturing

Nonmetallic Mineral Product Manufacturing
327100 Clay Product & Refractory Manufacturing
327210 Glass & Glass Product Manufacturing
327300 Cement & Concrete Product Manufacturing
327400 Lime & Gypsum Product Manufacturing
327900 Other Nonmetallic Mineral Product Manufacturing

Primary Metal Manufacturing
331110 Iron & Steel Mills & Ferroalloy Manufacturing
331200 Steel Product Manufacturing from Purchased Steel
331310 Alumina & Aluminum Production & Processing
331400 Nonferrous Metal (except aluminum) Production & Processing
331500 Foundries

Fabricated Metal Product Manufacturing

332110   Forging & Stamping

332210   Cutlery & Handtool Manufacturing

332300   Architectural & Structural Metals Manufacturing

332400   Boiler, Tank, & Shipping Container Manufacturing

332510   Hardware Manufacturing

332610   Spring & Wire Product Manufacturing

332700   Machine Shops; Turned Product; & Screw, Nut, & Bolt Manufacturing

332810   Coating, Engraving, Heat Treating, & Allied Activities

332900   Other Fabricated Metal Product Manufacturing

Machinery Manufacturing

333100   Agriculture, Construction, & Mining Machinery Manufacturing

333200   Industrial Machinery Manufacturing

333310   Commercial & Service Industry Machinery Manufacturing

333410   Ventilation, Heating, Air-Conditioning, & Commercial Refrigeration Equipment Manufacturing

333510   Metalworking Machinery Manufacturing

333610   Engine, Turbine, & Power Transmission Equipment Manufacturing

333900   Other General Purpose Machinery Manufacturing

Computer and Electronic Product Manufacturing

334110   Computer & Peripheral Equipment Manufacturing

334200   Communications Equipment Manufacturing

334310   Audio & Video Equipment Manufacturing

334410   Seminconductor & Other Electronic Component Manufacturing

334500   Navigational Measuring, Electromedical, & Control Instruments Manufacturing

334610   Manufacturing & Reproducing Magnetic & Optical Media

Electrical Equipment, Appliance, and Component Manufacturing

335100   Electrical Lighting Equipment Manufacturing

335200   Household Appliance Manufacturing

335310 Electrical Equipment Manufacturing
335900 Other Electrical Equipment & Component Manufacturing

Transportation Equipment Manufacturing
336100 Motor Vehicle Manufacturing
336210 Motor Vehicle Body & Trailer Manufacturing
336300 Motor Vehicle Parts Manufacturing
336410 Aerospace Product & Parts Manufacturing
336510 Railroad Rolling Stock Manufacturing
336610 Ship & Boat Building
336990 Other Transportation Equipment Manufacturing

Furniture and Related Product Manufacturing
337000 Furniture & Related Product Manufacturing

Miscellaneous Manufacturing
339110 Medical Equipment & Supplies Manufacturing
339900 Other Miscellaneous Manufacturing

Wholesale Trade

Wholesale Trade, Durable Goods
421100 Motor Vehicles & Motor Vehicle Parts & Supplies Wholesalers
421200 Furniture & Home Furnishings Wholesalers
421300 Lumber & Other Construction Materials Wholesalers
421400 Professional & Commercial Equipment & Supplies Wholesalers
421500 Metal & Mineral (except petroleum) Wholesalers
421600 Electrical Goods Wholesalers
421700 Hardware & Plumbing & Heating Equipment Supplies Wholesalers
421800 Machinery, Equipment, & Supplies Wholesalers
421910 Sporting & Recreational Goods & Supplies Wholesalers
421920 Toy & Hobby Goods & Supplies Wholesalers
421930 Recyclable Material Wholesalers

421940   Jewelry, Watch, Precious Stone, & Precious Metal Wholesalers

421990   Other Miscellaneous Durable Goods Wholesalers

Wholesale Trade, Nondurable Goods

422100   Paper & Paper Product Wholesalers

422210   Drugs & Druggists' Sundries Wholesalers

422300   Apparel, Piece Goods, & Notions Wholesalers

422400   Grocery & Related Products Wholesalers

422500   Farm Product Raw Material Wholesalers

422600   Chemical & Allied Products Wholesalers

422700   Petroleum & Petroleum Products Wholesalers

422800   Beer, Wine, & Distilled Alcoholic Beverage Wholesalers

422910   Farm Supplies Wholesalers

422920   Book, Periodical, & Newspaper Wholesalers

422930   Flower, Nursery Stock, & Florists' Supplies Wholesalers

422940   Tobacco & Tobacco Product Wholesalers

422950   Paint, Varnish, & Supplies Wholesalers

422990   Other Miscellaneous Nondurable Goods Wholesalers

Retail Trade

Motor Vehicle and Parts Dealers

441110   New Car Dealers

441120   Used Car Dealers

441210   Recreational Vehicle Dealers

441221   Motorcycle Dealers

441222   Boat Dealers

441229   All Other Motor Vehicle Dealers

441300   Automotive Parts, Accessories, & Tire Stores

Furniture and Home Furnishings Stores

442110   Furniture Stores

442210   Floor Covering Stores

442291   Window Treatment Stores

442299   All Other Home Furnishings Stores

Electronics and Appliance Stores
443111   Household Appliance Stores
443112   Radio, Television, & Other Electronics Stores
443120   Computer & Software Stores
443130   Camera & Photographic Supplies Stores

Building Material and Garden Equipment and Supplies Dealers
444110   Home Centers
444120   Paint & Wallpaper Stores
444130   Hardware Stores
444190   Other Building Material Dealers
444200   Lawn & Garden Equipment & Supplies Stores

Food and Beverage Stores
445110   Supermarkets & Other Grocery (except convenience) Stores
445120   Convenience Stores
445210   Meat Markets
445220   Fish & Seafood Markets
445230   Fruit & Vegetable Markets
445291   Baked Goods Stores
445292   Confectionery & Nut Stores
445299   All Other Specialty Food Stores
445310   Beer, Wine, & Liquor Stores

Health and Personal Care Stores
446110   Pharmacies & Drug Stores
446120   Cosmetics, Beauty Supplies, & Perfume Stores
446130   Optical Goods Stores
446190   Other Health & Personal Care Stores

Gasoline Stations
447100   Gasoline Stations (including convenience stores with gas)

Clothing and Clothing Accessories Stores
448110   Men's Clothing Stores
448120   Women's Clothing Stores
448130   Children's & Infants' Clothing Stores
448140   Family Clothing Stores
448150   Clothing Accessories Stores

448190   Other Clothing Stores
448210   Shoe Stores
448310   Jewelry Stores
448320   Luggage & Leather Goods Stores

Sporting Goods, Hobby, Book, and Music Stores
451110   Sporting Goods Stores
451120   Hobby, Toy, & Game Stores
451130   Sewing, Needlework, & Piece Goods Stores
451140   Musical Instrument & Supplies Stores
451211   Book Stores
451212   News Dealers & Newsstands
451220   Prerecorded Tape, Compact Disc, & Record Stores

General Merchandise Stores
452110   Department Stores
452900   Other General Merchandise Stores

Miscellaneous Store Retailers
453110   Florists
453210   Office Supplies & Stationery Stores
453220   Gift, Novelty, & Souvenir Stores
453310   Used Merchandise Stores
453910   Pet & Pet Supplies Stores
453920   Art Dealers
453930   Manufactured (mobile) Home Dealers
453990   All other Miscellaneous Store Retailers (including tobacco, candle, & trophy shops)

Nonstore Retailers
454110   Electronic Shopping & Mail-Order Houses
454210   Vending Machine Operators
454311   Heating Oil Dealers
454312   Liquefied Petroleum Gas (bottled gas) Dealers
454319   Other Fuel Dealers
454390   Other Direct Selling Establishments (including door-to-door retailing, frozen food plan providers, party plan merchandisers, & coffee-break service providers)

Transportation and Warehousing

Air, Rail, and Water Transportation
481000   Air Transportation
482000   Rail Transportation
483000   Water Transportation

Truck Transportation
484110   General Freight Trucking, Local
484120   General Freight Trucking, Long-distance
484200   Specialized Freight Trucking

Transit and Ground Passenger Transportation
485110   Urban Transit Systems
485210   Interurban & Rural Bus Transportation
485310   Taxi Service
485320   Limousine Service
485410   School & Employee Bus Transportation
458510   Charter Bus Industry
485990   Other Transit & Ground Passenger Transportation

Pipeline Transportation
486000   Pipeline Transportation

Scenic and Sightseeing Transportation
487000   Scenic & Sightseeing Transportation

Support Activities for Transportation
488100   Support Activities for Air Transportation
488210   Support Activities for Rail Transportation
488300   Support Activities for Water Transportation
488410   Motor Vehicle Towing
488490   Other Support Activities for Road Transportation
488510   Freight Transportation Arrangement
488990   Other Support Activities for Transportation

Couriers and Messengers
492110   Couriers
492210   Local Messengers & Local Delivery

Warehousing and Storage
493100   Warehousing & Storage Facilities (except lessors of miniwarehouses & self-storage units)

Information

Publishing Industries
511110   Newspaper Publishers
511120   Periodical Publishers
511130   Book Publishers
511140   Database & Directory Publishers
511190   Other Publishers
511210   Software Publishers

Motion Picture and Sound Recording Industries
512100   Motion Picture & Video Industries (except video rental)
512200   Sound Recording Industries

Broadcasting and Telecommunications
513100   Radio & Television Broadcasting
513200   Cable Networks & Program Distribution
513300   Telecommunications (including paging, cellular, satellite, & other telecommunications)

Information Services and Data Processing Services
514100   Information Services (including news syndicates, libraries, & online information services)
514210   Data Processing Services

Finance and Insurance

Depository Credit Intermediation
522110   Commercial Banking
522120   Savings Institutions
522130   Credit Unions
522190   Other Depository Credit Intermediation

Nondepository Credit Intermediation
522210   Credit Card Issuing
522220   Sales Financing
522291   Consumer Lending
522292   Real Estate Credit (including mortgage bankers & originators)
522293   International Trade Financing
522294   Secondary Market Financing
522298   All Other Nondepository Credit Intermediation

Activities Related to Credit Intermediation
522300   Activities Related to Credit Intermediation (including loan brokers)

Securities, Commodity Contracts, and Other Financial Investments and Related Activities
523110   Investment Banking & Securities Dealing
523120   Securities Brokerage
523130   Commodity Contracts Dealing
523140   Commodity Contracts Brokerage
523210   Securities & Commodity Exchanges
523900   Other Financial Investment Activities (including portfolio management & investment advice)

Insurance Carriers and Related Activities
524140   Direct Life, Health & Medical Insurance, & Reinsurance Carriers
524150   Direct Insurance & Reinsurance (except life, health, & medical) Carriers
524210   Insurance Agencies & Brokerages
524290   Other Insurance Related Activities

Funds, Trusts, and Other Financial Vehicles

525100   Insurance & Employee Benefit Funds
525910   Open-End Investment Funds (Form 1120-RIC)
525920   Trusts, Estates, & Agency Accounts
525930   Real Estate Investment Trusts (Form 1120-REIT)
525990   Other Financial Vehicles

Real Estate and Rental and Leasing

Real Estate

531110   Lessors of Residential Buildings & Dwellings
531120   Lessors of Nonresidential Buildings
         (except miniwarehouses)
531130   Lessors of Miniwarehouses & Self-Storage Units
531190   Lessors of Other Real Estate Property
531210   Offices of Real Estate Agents & Brokers
531310   Real Estate Property Managers
531320   Offices of Real Estate Appraisers
531390   Other Activities Related to Real Estate

Rental and Leasing Services

532100   Automotive Equipment Rental & Leasing
532210   Consumer Electronics & Appliances Rental
532220   Formal Wear & Costume Rental
532230   Video Tape & Disc Rental
532290   Other Consumer Goods Rental
532310   General Rental Centers
532400   Commercial & Industrial Machinery & Equipment Rental
         & Leasing

**Lessors of Nonfinancial Intangible Assets
(except Copyrighted Works)**

533110   Lessors of Nonfinancial Intangible Assets
         (except copyrighted works)

Professional, Scientific, and Technical Services

Legal Services

541110   Offices of Lawyers
541190   Other Legal Services

Accounting, Tax Preparation, Bookkeeping, and Payroll Services

541211   Offices of Certified Public Accountants
541213   Tax Preparation Services
541214   Payroll Services
541219   Other Accounting Services

Architectural, Engineering, and Related Services

541310   Architectural Services
541320   Landscape Architecture Services
541330   Engineering Services
541340   Drafting Services
541350   Building Inspection Services
541360   Geophysical Surveying & Mapping Services
541370   Surveying & Mapping (except geophysical) Services
541380   Testing Laboratories

Specialized Design Services

541400   Specialized Design Services (including interior, industrial, graphic, & fashion design)

Computer Systems Design and Related Services

541511   Custom Computer Programming Services
541512   Computer Systems Design Services
541513   Computer Facilities Management Services
541519   Other Computer Related Services

Other Professional, Scientific, and Technical Services

541600   Management, Scientific, & Technical Consulting Services
541700   Scientific Research & Development Services
541800   Advertising & Related Services

541910   Marketing Research & Public Opinion Polling
541920   Photographic Services
541930   Translation & Interpretation Services
541940   Veterinary Services
541990   All Other Professional, Scientific, & Technical Services

Management of Companies (Holding Companies)
551111   Offices of Bank Holding Companies
551112   Offices of Other Holding Companies

Administrative and Support and Waste Management and Remediation Services

Administrative and Support Services
561110   Office Administrative Services
561210   Facilities Support Services
561300   Employment Services
561410   Document Preparation Services
561420   Telephone Call Centers
561430   Business Service Centers (including private mail centers & copy shops)
561440   Collection Agencies
561450   Credit Bureaus
561490   Other Business Support Services (including repossession services, court reporting, and stenotype services)
561500   Travel Arrangement & Reservation Services
561600   Investigation & Security Services
561710   Exterminating & Pest Control Services
561720   Janitorial Services
561730   Landscaping Services
561740   Carpet & Upholstery Cleaning Services
561790   Other Services to Buildings & Dwellings
561900   Other Support Services (including packaging & labeling services & convention & trade show organizers)

Waste Management and Remediation Services
562000   Waste Management & Remediation Services

Educational Services

611000   Educational Services (including schools, colleges,
          & universities)

Health Care and Social Assistance

Offices of Physicians and Dentists
621111   Offices of Physicians (except mental health specialists)
621112   Offices of Physicians, Mental Health Specialists
621210   Offices of Dentists

Offices of Other Health Practitioners
621310   Offices of Chiropractors
621320   Offices of Optometrists
621330   Offices of Mental Health Practitioners (except physicians)
621340   Offices of Physical, Occupational, & Speech Therapists
          & Audiologists
621391   Offices of Podiatrists
621399   Offices of All Other Miscellaneous Health Practitioners

Outpatient Care Centers
621410   Family Planning Centers
621420   Outpatient Mental Health & Substance Abuse Centers
621491   HMO Medical Centers
621492   Kidney Dialysis Centers
621493   Freestanding Ambulatory Surgical & Emergency Centers
621498   All Other Outpatient Care Centers

Medical and Diagnostic Laboratories
621510   Medical & Diagnostic Laboratories

Home Health Care Services
621610   Home Health Care Services

Other Ambulatory Health Care Services
621900 Other Ambulatory Health Care Services (including ambulance services & blood & organ banks)

Hospitals
622000 Hospitals

Nursing and Residential Care Facilities
623000 Nursing & Residential Care Facilities

Social Assistance
624100 Individual & Family Services
624200 Community Food & Housing & Emergency & Other Relief Services
624310 Vocational Rehabilitation Services
624410 Child Day Care Services

Arts, Entertainment, and Recreation

Performing Arts, Spectator Sports, and Related Industries
711100 Performing Arts Companies
711210 Spectator Sports (including sports clubs & racetracks)
711300 Promoters of Performing Arts, Sports, & Similar Events
711410 Agents & Managers for Artists, Athletes, Entertainers, & Other Public Figures
711510 Independent Artists, Writers, & Performers

Museums, Historical Sites, and Similar Institutions
712100 Museums, Historical Sites, & Similar Institutions

Amusement, Gambling, and Recreation Industries
713100 Amusement Parks & Arcades
713200 Gambling Industries
713900 Other Amusement & Recreation Industries (including golf courses, skiing facilities, marinas, fitness centers, & bowling centers)

Accommodation and Food Services

Accommodation
721110   Hotels (except casino hotels) & Motels
721120   Casino Hotels
721191   Bed & Breakfast Inns
721199   All Other Traveler Accommodation
721210   RV (Recreational Vehicle) Parks & Recreational Camps
721310   Rooming & Boarding Houses

Food Services and Drinking Places
722110   Full-Service Restaurants
722210   Limited-Service Eating Places
722300   Special Food Services (including food service contractors & caterers)
722410   Drinking Places (alcoholic beverages)

Other Services

Repair and Maintenance
811110   Automotive Mechanical & Electrical Repair & Maintenance
811120   Automotive Body, Paint, Interior & Glass Repair
811190   Other Automotive Repair & Maintenance (including oil change & lubrication shops & car washes)
811210   Electronic & Precision Equipment Repair & Maintenance
811310   Commercial & Industrial Machinery & Equipment (except automotive & electronic) Repair & Maintenance
811410   Home & Garden Equipment & Appliance Repair & Maintenance
811420   Reupholstery & Furniture Repair
811430   Footwear & Leather Goods Repair
811490   Other Personal & Household Goods Repair & Maintenance

Personal and Laundry Services
812111   Barber Shops
812112   Beauty Salons

812113   Nail Salons
812190   Other Personal Care Services (including diet & weight reducing centers)
812210   Funeral Homes & Funeral Services
812220   Cemeteries & Crematories
812310   Coin-Operated Laundries & Drycleaners
812320   Drycleaning & Laundry Services (except coin-operated)
812330   Linen & Uniform Supply
812910   Pet Care (except veterinary) Services
812920   Photofinishing
812930   Parking Lots & Garages
812990   All Other Personal Services

Religious, Grantmaking, Civic, Professional, and Similar Organizations

813000   Religious, Grantmaking, Civic, Professional, & Similar Organizations

SAMPLE FORMS

Following are forms that are generic in nature. Seek good tax and legal advice before using any of the forms. They have been provided as examples for your use.

Cash-on-Cash Analysis

RECOMMENDED USE

We use the Cash-on-Cash Analysis form three different ways. First, we use the form to do an estimate of return before we make any offer for purchase of a property. Then, we use it after we have purchased a property to determine pricing. Finally, we perform another cash-on-cash analysis after we have rented or sold the property to see what the actual return was. We compare the actual return with the first estimate to help us better hone our estimating skills.

INSTRUCTIONS

Complete each line with estimate (if actual is not yet available) or the available number. There are two cases where the cash-on-cash return will look strange: (1) If you receive from your buyer/tenant a deposit or option equal to the amount you have invested. This will give zero invested in the property; and (2) if you actually receive more back than you have invested. In this case, your cash-on-cash return is higher than 100 percent, and is actually incalculable. Congratulations!

Property: _____

Invested:

Down payment   _____
(Actual, or estimated, based on information
   from your mortgage broker)
Closing costs   _____
(Actual, or estimated, based on information
   from your mortgage broker)
Fix-up costs   _____
(Actual, or estimated, based on information
   from contractor)
Holding costs   _____
(Actual or estimated—usually three months
   times monthly payment)

Total: This is the amount you have invested   _____A

Cash flow in:

Down payment (lease deposit or option)   _____B
(Depending on the type of deal you are doing this
   can be a down payment, a deposit, or an option
   payment. It is the amount you receive from the
   new buyer/tenant.)

Monthly payment received: _____C
(Rentor payment)

Monthly cash flow out:
If sold—mortgage payment _____D
(Buyer has responsibility for repairs, utilities, etc.)

If rented—mortgage payment _____
Taxes and insurance _____
Repairs (generally 5 percent) _____
Property management _____
Other _____
Total cash flow out: _____D

Formula for cash-on-cash ratio:
(C _____ – D _____)/(A _____ – B _____)
   (Monthly Payment Received)   (Monthly Cash Flow Out)   (Amount Invested)   (Down Payment)

Answer will be the percentage return that your money is earning.

Formula for payback period:
(A _____ – B _____)/(C _____ – D _____)
   (Amount Invested)   (Down Payment)   (Monthly Payment Received)   (Monthly Cash Flow Out)

Answer will be, *in months*, the length of time it will take for you to get your investment dollars back.

Worksheet
Brother-Sister Controlled Group Test

PART I:
80% CONTROL TEST

1. List those shareholders (individuals, estates, or trusts) who own voting stock in both corporations and the percentage of outstanding stock each owns.

Shareholders	Corporation X	Corporation Y	Corporation Z
_____	_____%	_____%	_____%
_____	_____%	_____%	_____%
_____	_____%	_____%	_____%
_____	_____%	_____%	_____%
Total	_____%	_____%	_____%

2. Does any combination of five or fewer of the above shareholders own 80% or more of the outstanding voting stock of both corporations?
   Yes _____ No _____
3. If the answer to question No. 2 is no, the corporations are not a brother-sister controlled group and no further testing is required.
4. If the answer to question No. 2 is yes, the 80% has been met. Proceed to Part II to determine the 50% test.

PART II:
50% IDENTICAL OWNERSHIP TEST

1. List the same shareholders whose combination of stock ownership in both corporations met the 80% test and the percentage of ownership in each corporation, and enter the lowest percentage of ownership in Column 4.

	(1)	(2)	(3)	(4)
Shareholders	Corporation X	Corporation Y	Corporation Z	Lowest Percentage
_____	_____	_____	_____	_____
_____	_____	_____	_____	_____
_____	_____	_____	_____	_____
_____	_____	_____	_____	_____

2. Total of Column 4.
3. If the total on Line 2 is more than 50%, the 50% ownership test has been met and the corporations are a brother-sister group.
4. If the total on Line 2 is 50% or less, the test has not been met and the corporations are not a brother-sister controlled group.

Worksheet
Tax Calculation for Members of a Controlled Group

Each member of a controlled group (except a qualified personal service corporation) must compute the tax using the following worksheet.

1. Enter taxable income (Line 30, page 1, Form 1120).　1. $ _____

2. Enter Line 1 or the corporation's share of the $50,000 taxable income bracket, whichever is less.　2. _____

3. Subtract Line 2 from Line 1.　3. _____

4. Enter Line 3 or the corporation's share of the $25,000 taxable income bracket, whichever is less.　4. _____

5. Subtract Line 4 from Line 3.　5. _____

6. Enter Line 5 or the corporation's share of the $9,925,000 taxable income bracket, whichever is less.　6. _____

7. Subtract Line 6 from Line 5.　7. _____

8. Multiply Line 2 by 15%.　8. _____

9. Multiply Line 4 by 25%.　9. _____

10. Multiply Line 6 by 34%.　10. _____

11. Multiply Line 7 by 35%.　11. _____

12. If the taxable income of the controlled group exceeds $100,000, enter this member's share of the smaller of: 5% of the taxable income in excess of $100,000, or $11,750.　12. _____

13. If the taxable income of the controlled group exceeds $15,000,000, enter this member's share of the smaller of: 3% of the taxable income in excess of $15,000,000, or $100,000.　13. _____

14. Add Lines 8 through 13. Enter here and on Line 3, Schedule J, Form 1120.　14. _____

Certified Copy of Resolutions to Liquidate the Corporation

I hereby certify that the following Resolutions were unanimously adopted at a Special Meeting of the Shareholders of _____ held on the ____ day of _____, 20__.

RESOLVED, that the Corporation be completely liquidated in accordance with the provisions of Section 336 of the Internal Revenue Code of 1986, as amended, and be it

FURTHER RESOLVED, that in accordance with such plan of complete liquidation, the officers, directors, and corporate counsel are hereby authorized and directed to see that the following steps are undertaken:

1. that within (30) days of the date of this resolution adopting this plan of liquidation, counsel for the Corporation shall file Form 966 with the District Director of Internal Revenue, together with a certified copy of this resolution;
2. that the services of a disinterested qualified appraiser be obtained to determine the fair market value of the assets;
3. that the corporation shall proceed as far as possible to collect all outstanding accounts receivable and to settle any claims against it;
4. that thereafter, as soon as practicable, the Corporation, by its duly authorized officers and directors, shall distribute all assets, subject to any unpaid liabilities, to the shareholders in redemption and cancellation of all the outstanding capital stock of the Corporation, using their discretion as to how the assets and liabilities will be apportioned among the shareholders, but in no event shall they distribute to any shareholder net assets of a lesser value than is due on a pro rata basis, using the appraisal values obtained in Item 2 of this resolution;
5. that the proper officers of the Corporation shall file a Certificate of Dissolution pursuant to state law;
6. that the proper officers and Corporation counsel shall file all other forms and documents required, including tax returns, as soon as possible after distribution of the corporate assets;
7. that specific authorization is given to _____, counsel for the Corporation, to prepare, sign, and forward to the Commissioner of Internal Revenue, after the final tax return has been filed for the Corporation, a request for proper assessment of all federal taxes due from the Corporation; and
8. that the officers and directors of the Corporation are empowered, authorized, and directed to carry out the provisions of these resolutions, and to adopt any further resolutions that may be necessary in liquidating and dissolving the Corporation in accordance with the expressed intent of the shareholders under the plan adopted.

_____
Secretary

Educational Assistance Program
[Sample Plan for Discussion Purposes Only]

1. **Purpose:** The Company Educational Assistance Program has been established for the exclusive benefit of the eligible employees of the Company. The Company desires to reimburse employees for all or a portion of the cost of attending educational courses related to the employees' success in the performance of their duties with the Company. It is intended that the Program meet the requirements for qualification under Code Section 127 of the Internal Revenue Code, and that benefits paid employees under the Program be excludable from gross income to the maximum extent allowed under Code Section 127.

2. **Plan Year:** The Plan Year is the 12-month period ending on December 31 of each year.

3. **Contributions:** Employees are not required or permitted to contribute to the Program.

4. **Eligibility Requirements:** Company employees meeting the following criteria are eligible:
   (a) Completion of a minimum of six months' service, before the start of the course of education for which reimbursement is to be provided under this plan,
   (b) Attainment of age 18,
   (c) Employed on a full-time basis, and
   (d) Continued employment for one year after satisfactory completion of a course. Any employees terminating within one year will receive a final paycheck adjusted for the amount of the educational benefit received.

5. **Qualifying Educational Programs:** Educational programs qualify under this plan if:
   (a) Participating employees limit their course load to a maximum of two courses or six credits per semester or school period.
   (b) Courses attended during regular working hours must receive prior supervisory approval, so no reduction in participant salary or status occurs.
   (c) The courses in degree programs are pertinent to the employee's functions or skill in performing his or her duties with the Company in a position of advancement to the participant's current position with the Company. An officer of the Company must decide whether an educational course meets this requirement before an employee's enrollment. If it is determined that an educational course does not meet this requirement, the plan will be administered in accordance with Article 11.
   (d) Courses are offered by an accredited school toward a recognized degree program or a definite plan of study. Tuition reimbursement will be at the state educational institution rate in effect at the time of enrollment. However, the employee must meet the requirements for reimbursement in Article 6.
   (e) If the Company specifically requires the employee to enroll in a course, the employee automatically meets plan requirements.

6. **Requirements for Reimbursement:** Upon completion of a prior-approved course, eligible employees must submit to the corporation a copy of the tuition statement and receipts for other items of qualified educational expenses (see Article 7), and a copy of the grade report. No reimbursement will be made without verified tuition and grade reports or if the employee receives educational assistance from other sources (i.e., financial aid or scholarships whether or not such financial aid or scholarships are offered by the company).

Reimbursement will be made according to the following schedule:

Undergraduate Courses		Other Courses	
Grade	Reimbursement	Grade	Reimbursement
A	100%	Pass	100%
B	85%	Fail	0%
C	60%		
Below C	0%		

7. **Educational Expenses Qualifying for Reimbursement:** The following items are reimbursable under this Program as qualified educational assistance: tuition, fees, books, supplies, and equipment related to an approved course of education. Tools or supplies (other than textbooks) that an employee may retain after the course completion are not eligible educational expenses under this Program. Also, meals, lodging, and transportation are not qualified educational expenses.

8. **Limitation on Benefits:** No more than 5% of the amounts paid or incurred by the Company under this Program for any Plan Year may be provided for the class of individuals who are shareholders (or owners) (or their spouses or dependents), each of whom own more than 5% of the stock (or capital or profits interest) in the Company. For purposes of determining stock ownership, the attribution rules of Code Section 1563(d) and (e) (without regard to purposes of determining stock ownership), and the attribution rules of Code Section 1563(e)(3)(C) apply. [For purposes of determining the capital or profits interest of an unincorporated trade or business, the rules under Code Section 414(c) apply.]

9. **Funding:** Qualifying educational expenses submitted for reimbursement by plan participants will be paid entirely from the general assets of the Company. The plan will be known as an unfunded plan.

10. **Plan Administrator:** The Plan Administrator shall be designated by the Board of Directors of the Company.

11. **Plan Administrator Authority:** The Plan Administrator is authorized to develop uniform rules and forms to be used in carrying out the purpose of the Program. The Plan Administrator shall determine all questions relating to eligibility. The Plan Administrator will interpret the terms and provisions of the plans. An interpretation shall be performed in a nondiscriminatory manner and shall be consistent with the purpose of the Program.

12. **Procedures for Reimbursement Denial:** The Board of Directors will review all educational reimbursement requests initially denied by the Plan Administrator. Any decision by the Board of Directors shall be binding on all parties.

13. **Amendment or Termination of Plan:** The Company reserves the right to change the plan provisions by amendment. All amendments, including the amendment to terminate the plan, shall be in writing and acknowledged by the Board of Directors through a resolution. No amendment shall affect the reimbursement of eligible educational expenses incurred by a participant enrolled in an educational course at the time the plan is amended or terminated. Instead, the participant shall be entitled to reimbursement under the terms of the plan at the time the course of study was initiated.

14. **Notification of Employees:** All employees eligible to participate in the Program (see Article 4) will receive written notice of the terms and availability of the Program. Each eligible employee shall receive a copy of the Summary Plan Description. Upon request, each eligible employee shall receive a copy of the plan document.

Notice to Employees
Availability of Educational Assistance Program
[Sample Plan for Discussion Purposes Only]

An educational assistance program has been established for the benefit of the employees of _____. The purpose of the program is to reimburse eligible employees for all or a portion of the cost of attending educational courses related to the employees' success in the performance of their duties.

Only courses offered by an accredited school toward a recognized degree program or a definite plan of study will be considered reimbursable under this plan. To participate in the educational assistance program, contact the Human Resources Department prior to enrolling in class.

Upon completion of an approved course, submit a reimbursement form with a copy of the tuition statement and a copy of your grade report. No reimbursement will be made without verified tuition and grade reports. Reimbursements are tax-free. Tuition reimbursements are made based on the grade attained as described in the plan document. Tuition reimbursements are limited to the rates charged at state universities.

Educational Assistance Program
[Sample Plan for Discussion Purposes Only]

An educational assistance program (EAP) has been established for the benefit of the employees of _____. The purpose of the program is to reimburse eligible employees for all or a portion of the cost of attending educational courses related to the employees' success in the performance of their duties.

Am I eligible to participate? Employees who have worked a minimum of six months prior to the beginning of a course and who are employed on a full-time basis (30 hours per week).

How do I participate? If you have decided on a course of study, submit an Educational Assistance Reimbursement Form for approval before enrolling at the educational institution.

What happens if I terminate employment prior to completing the course? Employees who terminate service with _____ before completing the course will not be eligible for reimbursement under the plan. The plan is for the benefit of employees. Employees who terminate within one year of the satisfactory completion of a course must return any benefits received under this plan. An adjustment for the amount of the educational assistance received will be made to the final paycheck.

Is there a limit on the number of courses I may take? Yes. You are limited to a maximum of two courses or six credits per semester.

What other restrictions apply? The course must be related to your success in the performance of your duties at _____. Only courses offered by an accredited school will be considered reimbursable under this plan. You may attend a private university or college; however, your reimbursement will be at the state educational institution rate. If you are receiving educational assistance from other sources such as financial aid or scholarships, you are not eligible to participate in this program.

May I attend class during my normal working hours? You will need approval from your immediate supervisor before enrolling in a course that meets during your regular hours. However, once approval is received, you should not expect a reduction in pay or pay status (i.e., from full-time to part-time) if you attend classes during the workday.

How do I receive reimbursement? Upon completion of your course, resubmit the approved educational assistance form for payment and attach evidence of completion of the course, such as a grade report. You should also submit your tuition statement to show proof of expenses incurred.

What expenses qualify for reimbursement? Only tuition, fees, books, supplies, and equipment qualify as educational expenses. Any tools or supplies (other than textbooks) that you retain after the completion of the course are not reimbursable. In addition, meals, lodging, and transportation costs are not qualified as educational expenses.

Is there any restriction on the amount of reimbursement I may receive? Under the _____ EAP, you will not receive more than $5,250 during the plan year. The plan year is from January to December. In addition, you will be eligible for reimbursement based on the grades received as shown in the following table:

Undergraduate Courses		Other Courses	
Grade	Reimbursement	Grade	Reimbursement
A	100%	Pass	100%
B	85%	Fail	0%
C	60%		
Below C	0%		

Are any benefits I receive taxable? It is intended that the program meet the requirements for qualification under Code Section 127 of the Internal Revenue Code, and that benefits paid employees under the program be excludable from gross income to the maximum of $5,250.

Is this plan permanent? _____ intends to continue this program as a permanent plan. However, this program shall be subject to termination at any time by a vote of the Company Board of Directors. Any employee enrolled in an approved course at the time of discontinuation shall be reimbursed in accordance with the terms of this program.

Suggested Record Retention List

Type of Record	Suggested Retention Period	On File? Yes	On File? No
I. Correspondence			
General—All	3 Years		
Tax & Legal Communications	Indef.		
Production & Creative	8 Years		
License & Traffic	6 Years		
Sale & Purchase	6 Years		
II. Accounting Records			
Bank Statements & Deposit Slips	3 Years		
Individual Payroll Records	8 Years		
Payroll Time Cards/Sheets	3 Years		
Canceled Dividend Checks	6 Years		
Expense Reports	6 Years		
A/P & A/R Subsidiary Ledgers	6 Years		
Other Subsidiary Ledgers	6 Years		
Trial Balance (Monthly)	6 Years		
Payment Vouchers—All	8 Years		
All Canceled Checks	8 Years		
Audit Reports	Indef.		
General Ledgers & Journals	Indef.		

Type of Record	Suggested Retention Period	On File? Yes	On File? No
III. Corporate Records			
Expired Notes, Leases, & Mortgages	6 Years		
All Cash Books	Indef.		
Contracts & Agreements	Indef.		
Property Deeds & Easements	Indef.		
Registration of Copyrights & Trademarks	Indef.		
Patents	Indef.		
Corporate Charter, Bylaws, & Minutes	Indef.		
Capital Stock & Bond Records	Indef.		
Stock Certificate & Transfer Lists	Indef.		
Canceled Checks on Asset Purchases	Indef.		
Canceled Checks for Taxes & Contracts	Indef.		
Proxies	Indef.		
Labor Contracts	Indef.		
Retirement & Pension Records	Indef.		
Tax Returns & All Work Papers	Indef.		
IV. Insurance Records			
All Expired Policies	4 Years		
Accident Reports	6 Years		

Type of Record	Suggested Retention Period	On File? Yes	On File? No
Safety Reports	8 Years		
Settlement Claims	10 Years		
Group Disability Records	8 Years		
Fire Inspection Reports	6 Years		
V. Sales & Purchase Records			
Sales Contracts & Invoices	3 Years		
Requisition Orders	3 Years		
Purchase Orders	3 Years		
VI. Shipping/Receiving Records			
Export Declarations & Manifests	4 Years		
Freights, Shipping, & Receiving Reports	4 Years		
Bills of Lading Records	4 Years		
Way Bills	4 Years		
VII. Personnel Records			
Daily Time Reports	6 Years		
Withholding Tax Statements	6 Years		
Disability & Sick Benefits Records	6 Years		
Expired Contracts	6 Years		
Files of Terminated Personnel	6 Years		

Note: Indef.—Records must be kept indefinitely. These suggested retention periods for records were developed from IRS and federal regulations. It is suggested that because of the size and volume of business records that such records be inventoried periodically and those records that have expired, according to the retention period, be destroyed.

This is a generic agreement designed to give you an idea of the types of things that you can put into an Independent Contractor Service Agreement. It is not intended to be used without first consulting with an attorney or other qualified advisor.

INDEPENDENT CONTRACTOR SERVICE AGREEMENT

THIS INDEPENDENT CONTRACTOR SERVICE AGREEMENT ("the Agreement") is made as of _____, 20____.

BETWEEN:

(EMPLOYER—*Select the appropriate language and delete the rest*)

(Corporate Employer) _____ (*legal business name*), a _____ (*state of incorporation*) Corporation/Limited Liability Company/Limited Partnership (*select one*) with a business address located at _____ (*address of business entity*).

(Or, if Employer is an individual) _____ (*Employer's name*), an individual who resides at _____ (*address*).

(Or, if Employer is a D/B/A) _____ (*Employer's name*), doing business as _____ (*name of D/B/A*), with a business address located at _____ (*address*).

("Us," "We," or "Our")

AND:

(INDEPENDENT CONTRACTOR—*Select the appropriate language and delete the rest*)

(If IC operates through a legal entity) _____ (*legal business name*), a (*state and type of entity*) with a business address located at _____ (*address of business entity*).

(Or, if IC operates as an individual) _____ (*your name*), an individual who resides at _____ (*address*).

(Or, if IC operates as a D/B/A) _____ (*your name*), doing business as _____ (*name of your D/B/A*), with a business address located at _____ (*address*).

("You" or "Your")

WHEREAS:

A. We are in the business of _____ (*briefly describe Employer's business*) through employees and independent consultants ("the Services");

B. You have represented that You are qualified and knowledgeable in the field of _____ (*briefly describe IC's qualifications*);

C. We have agreed to enter into an Independent Contractor relationship with You to provide Services on the terms and conditions set out in this Agreement.

NOW, THEREFORE, in consideration of the mutual promises, covenants, terms, and conditions herein, and for other good and valuable consideration, the receipt and sufficiency of which are hereby acknowledged by the parties, the parties agree as follows:

1. **Agreement to Engage.** We agree to engage You as a _____
   (insert title or job description) and You agree to be engaged in this capacity.
2. **Project.** We have engaged You to carry out the following ("the Project"):

   _____
   (Set out the details of the project to be accomplished or work to be done by the Independent Contractor. Depending on the project to be completed, you may need to be fairly specific about what will comprise a completed project in satisfactory condition.)
3. **Proper Qualifications.** You expressly acknowledge and represent that You are a qualified _____ *(insert title or job description)* and that You are qualified to undertake the tasks required at all times to complete the Project. You also expressly acknowledge and agree that if You are not able to perform the tasks required to complete the Project, We may terminate this Agreement and You will not be entitled to any compensation other than for that portion of the Project that You may have completed.
4. **Completion Deadline; Satisfaction.** You acknowledge and agree that the Project Completion Date is currently scheduled to be _____, 20___, unless such deadline is extended by Us, in Our sole discretion. You acknowledge and agree to use Your best efforts at all times to complete the Project by the Project Completion Date and to provide Us with a completed Project in a condition satisfactory to Us, with Our satisfaction not to be unreasonably withheld. You further acknowledge and agree that We may request reasonable amendments or refinements to the Project to meet the Project specifications set out in Section 2 above and that all such amendments or refinements shall be included in the compensation to be paid, as set out below.
5. **No Employment Relationship.** You expressly understand and agree that You shall be considered an Independent Contractor, and that no employment relationship shall be formed between You and Us by entry into this Agreement. You shall have no claim under this Agreement or otherwise against Us for vacation pay, sick leave, retirement benefits, Social Security, workers' compensation, disability, unemployment insurance benefits, or any other employee benefits, all of which shall be Your sole responsibility. We shall not withhold on Your behalf, pursuant to this Agreement, any sums for income tax, unemployment insurance, Social Security, or any other withholding pursuant to any law or requirement of any government agency, and payment of all such withholdings and remittances shall be Your sole responsibility. You shall indemnify and hold Us harmless from any and all loss or liability arising with respect to any of the foregoing benefits or withholdings that You fail to remit.
6. **Term.** This Agreement shall be for an initial Term of *(set out the length of the agreement)* ____ months unless terminated by either party in writing, in accordance with the provisions of Section 16 of this Agreement.
7. **Renewal.** This Agreement may be renewed by Us at the conclusion of the Term as set out in Section 6.

8. **Compensation.** We shall pay You compensation of _____ *(if you are using a flat-rate fee, insert this amount)* or at the rate of _____ dollars per hour *(if you are using a per-hour fee schedule)* of billable time worked performing the Services. You shall be paid upon completion of the Services *(if you are paying on a per-job basis)* or on a daily/weekly/bimonthly/monthly *(select the appropriate language and delete the rest)* basis, on the _____ day *(what day)* of each month, for all billable hours worked in the preceding period. Billable time is defined as hours of work that are worked exclusively on performing the Services. In the event of any disputes, We shall have sole discretion to determine what does or does not constitute a billable hour and make payments accordingly.

9. **Additional Compensation.** We acknowledge and agree to pay You additional compensation, at a rate to be negotiated between the parties, for any refinements or amendments made to the Project over and above the specifications set out in Section 2 above.

10. **Time Recording.** You shall be obliged to keep a record of all billable hours worked providing the Services and either include a copy of this record with or integrate this record into all invoices rendered by You. We shall not be required to pay You for any hours that have not been recorded and/or integrated into Your invoices.

11. **Confidentiality.** During the course of performing the Services, You may have access to or receive confidential or proprietary information in reference to Our business. Confidential or proprietary information may include, but is not limited to, trade secrets, techniques, formulae and technical specifications, drawings, models, data, designs, discoveries, software programs, financial data, sales and inventory data, customer lists, supplier lists, and pricing. You expressly agree at all times to maintain the confidentiality of all such information provided and to follow such appropriate procedures as may be put into place by Us to ensure that none of Our confidentiality rights are abridged during the Term of this Agreement or at any time following the expiration or termination of this Agreement.

12. **Confidentiality Obligation following Termination.** The confidentiality obligation outlined in Section 11 above shall continue following termination of this Agreement.

13. **Noncompetition.** You agree that at all times during the Term of this Agreement and following the termination date of this Agreement. You shall not:
    - Use Our confidential information to create a business in direct competition with Us;
    - Provide Our confidential information to any third parties to create a business in direct competition with Us;
    - Attempt to solicit any of Our clients (if appropriate) directly or through a competitor.

14. **Costs of Legal Proceedings.** If We need to commence legal proceedings against You with respect to enforcing either the confidentiality or the noncompetition provisions of this Agreement or because You have breached the confidentiality or noncompetition provisions of this Agreement and We have sustained damages as a result of Your actions, then We shall be entitled to recover from You Our reasonable legal costs, including attorneys fees and expenses.

15. **Indemnification.** If any action is taken against Us by a third party because You have breached the confidentiality provision of this Agreement, or by

Your action or inaction, then You agree to indemnify and defend Us against, and hold Us harmless from, any and all claims, actions, suits, proceedings, costs, expenses, damages, and liabilities, including attorneys fees and costs, resulting from, arising out of, or connected in any way with any act or omission made by You under this Agreement or by Your failure to comply with the provisions of this Agreement.

16. *Termination.* This Agreement may be terminated as follows:
    (a) By either party, for any reason, upon the provision of _____ (*set out a reasonable time to end the agreement, i.e., two weeks, three weeks, etc.*) notice in writing;
    (b) By Us, should You fail to, or be incapable of, providing the Services as agreed, upon the provision of _____ (*set out a reasonable time to end the agreement for nonperformance or inability to perform*) days' notice in writing; or
    (c) By Us, if You breach the confidentiality or noncompetition provisions set out in Sections 11 and 13 above, upon twenty-four (24) hours' notice in writing.

    Any written notice to be provided from one party to the other shall be delivered by either registered mail or courier delivery, to the addresses of the parties as set out at the beginning of this Agreement, or to such other address as the parties may from time to time advise the other, in writing.

17. *Prorated Compensation upon Termination.* Where this Agreement is terminated in accordance with Section 16, You shall receive payment for all billable hours worked by You within fourteen (14) days following Your last day of service.

18. *No Waiver.* If any portion of this Agreement is waived, or if any breach of this Agreement is waived by Us, that waiver shall not equate to a waiver of any earlier, later, or concurrent breach of the same or any other provision. No waiver of any portion of this Agreement or of any breach of this Agreement shall be effective unless made in writing and signed by an authorized representative of the waiving party.

19. *Entire Agreement.* This Agreement contains the entire agreement between You and Us with respect to Your engagement by Us and supersedes any earlier arrangements.

20. *Amendments.* This Agreement may not be amended except by the mutual consent of each party, such consent to be provided in writing.

21. *Governing Law.* Each party to this Agreement expressly agrees that this Agreement shall be governed by the laws of _____ (*insert the state or province where the work is being done, and the country where the work is taking place; BUT, if you are contracting with someone outside of your country, make sure the jurisdiction is YOUR home state, and not the contractor's*). Each party consents to the exclusive jurisdiction of the state and federal courts sitting in _____ (*insert the county and state of the courts that will hear any disputes—try to make sure this is your home county and state*), in any action on a claim arising out of, under, or in connection with this Agreement. Each party agrees that this is a mandatory forum selection clause.

22. **Severability.** In the event of a court ruling that one or more clauses in this Agreement are unenforceable, the remainder of this Agreement shall remain in full force and effect.

IN WITNESS WHEREOF, each party has executed this Agreement as of the day and year first above written.

_____ (Full Legal Name of Employer)

A _____ (State) **Corporation/Limited Liability Company/Limited Partnership**

By: _____
                    (Signature line of signing officer)

Its: _____
                   (Print title of signing officer)

_____ (Full Legal Name of Independent Contractor)

A _____ (State) **Corporation/Limited Liability Company/Limited Partnership**

By: _____
                    (Signature line of signing officer)

Its: _____
                   (Print title of signing officer)

OR, WHERE INDEPENDENT CONTRACTOR IS AN INDIVIDUAL OR D/B/A

_____ (print name of individual), an Individual doing business as

_____ (print name of D/B/A)

_____

Signature

This is a generic agreement designed to give you an idea of the types of things that you can put into a Medical Expense Reimbursement Plan. It is not intended to be used without first consulting with an attorney or other qualified advisor.

[Insert name of your Corporation]'s MEDICAL EXPENSE REIMBURSEMENT AND DISABILITY BENEFITS PLAN

ARTICLE I
ESTABLISHMENT AND PURPOSE OF PLAN

1.1 *Establishment of Plan.* [Name of Your Corporation] ("the Corporation"), hereby establishes the [Name of Your Corporation] Medical Expense Reimbursement and Disability Benefits Plan ("the Plan").

1.2 *Purpose of Plan.* The purpose of the Plan shall be to reimburse the Participants under the Plan for expenses incurred by such Participants for the medical care of the Participant, his or her spouse and dependents not otherwise reimbursed under any other plan of the Corporation or any medical insurance policies, and to provide the Participants under the Plan with the benefits to replace wages lost by reason of absence from work because of occupational and nonoccupational personal injuries and sickness.

1.3 *Coordination of Benefits.* This Plan is an integral part of a coordinated health care benefit program maintained by the Corporation on behalf of its employees. The Plan provides for the reimbursement of payments for health insurance premiums made on behalf of employees and, under certain circumstances, their dependents and spouses. For administrative convenience, the Corporation may elect to pay such premiums directly, in which case such direct payment shall constitute full satisfaction of the Corporation's obligation hereunder with respect to such otherwise reimbursable expenses.

ARTICLE II
DEFINITIONS

As used in the Plan, the following words shall have the meanings indicated in this Article.

2.1 *Basic Compensation.* The term "basic compensation" shall mean the total amount of wages, salary, and commissions of a Participant, exclusive of any discretionary bonuses or overtime pay.

2.2 *Continuous Disability.* The term "continuous disability" shall mean successive periods during which the Participant is wholly disabled, due to the same or related causes, not separated by a return to active employment with the Corporation for ten (10) or more continuous full working days.

2.3 *Dependent.* The term "dependent" shall mean any person who qualifies as dependent of a Participant under Section 152 of the Internal Revenue Code of 1954.

2.4 Diagnostic Procedures. The term "diagnostic procedures" shall mean medical examinations, blood tests, X-rays, and similar procedures which are generally accepted as falling within the category of diagnostic procedures, provided that such procedures are performed at a facility which provides no services other than medical and ancillary services, and shall include ordinary and necessary travel expenses incurred in connection therewith.

2.5 Disability Insurance Policies. The term "disability insurance policies" shall mean all insurance policies providing disability income benefits to a Participant in the event of a disability, on which the Corporation has paid or reimbursed the Participant in accordance herewith for the payment of the premiums during the year preceding the commencement of the disability. Such policies may include individually owned or group disability income insurance policies, or group accident and health, medical, or any other insurance policies that provide disability income benefits.

2.6 Effective Date. The term "effective date" shall mean _____, 20__.

2.7 Employee. The term "employee" shall mean a person who is currently or hereafter employed by the Corporation, but excluding:

(a) An independent contractor or self-employed person;

(b) An employee who is a nonresident alien deriving no earned income from sources within the United States;

(c) Employees who are included in the unit of employees covered by a collective bargaining agreement, unless there is a judicial determination that accident and health benefits were not the subject of good faith negotiations (in which case such employees shall not be excluded from such definition of "employee" if they otherwise qualify); and

(d) Employees whose customary weekly employment is for less than 35 hours or whose customary annual employment is for less than 9 months.

2.8 First Disability Period. The term "first disability period" shall mean the period of time during the continuous disability of a Participant that begins with the commencement of the disability and ends on the last day of the fourth full calendar month following the calendar month during which the disability commenced.

2.9 Medical Care. The term "medical care" shall mean care received for the diagnosis, cure, mitigation, treatment, or prevention of disease. Expenses paid for medical care shall include those paid for the purpose of affecting any structure or function of the body or for transportation and parking primarily for and essential to medical care. Amounts paid for operations or treatments affecting any portion of the body, including obstetrics, expenses of therapy, or X-ray treatments, are included in the term "medical care." Expenses paid for medical care shall also include, without limitation, payments for health insurance premiums, such as Blue Cross and Blue Shield; hospital services; nursing services (including nurses' board where paid by the Participant); medical, laboratory, surgical, dental and other diagnostic and healing services; X-rays; medicine and drugs (as hereinafter defined); artificial teeth or limbs; and ambulance hire. An expenditure that is merely beneficial to the general health, such as an expenditure for a vacation, is not an expenditure for medical care. Expenses paid for transportation primarily for and essential to the rendition of the medical care are expenses paid for medical care, provided, however, that such expenses shall not include the cost of any meals and lodgings while away from home receiving medical treatment. Where a person is in an institution because his or her condition is such that the availability of medical care in such institution is a principal reason for his or her presence there, and meals and lodgings are furnished as a necessary incident to such care, the entire cost of medical care and meals and lodgings at the institution, which are furnished while the person requires continual medical care, shall constitute an expense for medical care.

2.10 Medicines and Drugs. The term "medicines and drugs" shall mean items which are legally procured and which are generally accepted as falling within the category of medicines and drugs, whether or not requiring a prescription. Such term shall not include toiletries or similar preparations, such as toothpaste, shaving lotion, shaving cream, or deodorants, nor shall it include cosmetics, such as face cream, hand lotions, or any other similar preparation used for ordinary cosmetic purposes, or sundry items.

2.11 Limited Participant. The term "Limited Participant" shall mean any employee who has satisfied the requirements for participation in the group health insurance plan maintained by the Corporation and whose participation in this Plan is limited to the benefits provided by Article V, hereof.

2.12 Officer. The term "officer" shall mean an officer or assistant officer of the Corporation.

2.13 Participant. The term "Participant" shall mean any employee who has attained age twenty-five (25) and who has completed three (3) or more years of service prior to the beginning of the plan year. *[You can amend this clause to provide your own required length of service—for example, three months is a common waiting period.]*

2.14 Personal Injury. The term "personal injury" shall mean an externally caused sudden hurt or damage to the body brought about by an identifiable event, provided, however, that such personal injury shall also comply with the definition or definitions contained in at least one policy of insurance providing disability benefits for a Participant.

2.15 Plan Year. The term "plan year" shall mean the twelve (12)-month period coincident with the fiscal year of the Corporation.

2.16 Second Disability Period. The term "second disability period" shall mean the period of time during the continuous disability of a Participant which begins immediately following the first disability period and ends on the last day of the eighth calendar month following the last calendar month of the first disability period.

2.17 Sickness. The term "sickness" shall mean mental illness, diseases, and all bodily infirmities and disorders other than a personal injury, whether resulting from employment or otherwise.

2.18 *Spouse.* The term "spouse" shall mean the lawful spouse of a Participant. In determining whether the status of spouse exists, a Participant who is legally separated from his or her spouse under a decree of separate maintenance shall not be considered to be married.

2.19 *Wholly Disabled.* The term "wholly disabled" shall have the same definition as that contained in the earliest policy acquired of those of the disability insurance policies which provide disability income benefits to a Participant as their principal benefits. If the insurance company writing that policy has determined that a Participant is wholly disabled and is paying or prepared to pay disability income benefits thereunder, the Participant shall be deemed to be wholly disabled for the purposes of this Agreement. In the event that no such disability insurance policy exists insuring the Participant at a time that he or she is alleged to have become disabled, then the Participant shall be deemed to be wholly disabled when, as a result of personal injury or sickness, he or she is so disabled that he or she is prevented from performing the principal duties of his or her employment and is under the regular care and attendance of a currently licensed physician or surgeon. The Corporation, at its expense, may require the Participant to submit to a medical examination by a designated physician or surgeon for the purpose of obtaining an independent medical opinion as to whether or not the Participant is wholly disabled in accordance with the foregoing definition. However, such opinion shall not be binding upon either the Corporation or the Participant with respect to whether or not the Participant is wholly disabled.

2.20 *Year of Service.* The term "year of service" shall mean employment of an employee for thirty-five (35) or more hours per week and nine (9) or more months per year by the Corporation during any of the successive twelve (12)-month periods commencing with the start of such employee's employment with the Corporation or its unincorporated predecessor, including employment as a self-employed person with the unincorporated predecessor of the Corporation. *[As with Section 2.13, this section can be modified to any waiting period you wish, or you may remove both sections entirely if you don't want to have a waiting period.]*

ARTICLE III
REIMBURSEMENT OF MEDICAL EXPENSES

3.1 *Reimbursement.* Reimbursement shall be made by the Corporation to Participants employed on the last day of the plan year or who die or retire during the plan year for expenses incurred and paid by a Participant for disability insurance policies or medical care of the Participant, his or her spouse and dependents, provided such expenses are not reimbursed to the Participant under any other plan of the Corporation, including any insured or partially insured plans requiring the payment of premiums by the Corporation, under any privately financed insurance, or under Medicare or any other federal or state law. If an expense for medical care is partially reimbursed under any other plan of the Corporation, privately financed insurance, or any federal or state law, that part of the expense which is not so reimbursed shall be reimbursed to the Participant under this Plan.

3.2 *Determination of Status.* For the purposes of this Plan, the status of a person as a Participant's spouse or dependent shall be determined at the time the expense for the medical care is incurred.

3.3 *Covered Period.* This Plan shall provide reimbursement for those expenses for medical care incurred on or after the effective date, provided, however, that this Plan shall not provide reimbursement for such expenses incurred by a disabled Participant, or his or her spouse or dependents, for which payment is made after the second disability period.

3.4 *Maximum Payment.* Notwithstanding anything contained herein to the contrary, the aggregate amount to be paid by the Corporation hereunder in connection with expenses incurred and paid by a Participant during any plan year for medical care of the Participant, his or her spouse and dependents, shall not exceed the lesser of the following amounts:

(a) An amount which, when added to the Participant's other compensation from the corporation, equals the fair value to the Corporation of past and present services performed as an employee by such Participant.

(b) $5,000 or such amount as determined from time to time by the Board of Directors of the Corporation. [*You can change the provisions of the entire Section 3.4 as you choose, or, if you don't want to put a cap on paid expenditures, you can remove this section altogether.*]

ARTICLE IV
DISABILITY BENEFITS

4.1 *Wage Continuation.* In the event that a Participant who is an officer shall become wholly disabled, the Corporation shall pay to the disabled Participant during the first disability period the same basic compensation that he or she was receiving immediately prior to the commencement of his or her disability, reduced by any disability benefits which are payable to him or her under any disability insurance policies on account of disability during each respective pay period during the first disability period. If the period of his or her continuous disability extends beyond the first disability period, the Corporation shall thereafter pay to the disabled Participant during the second disability period an amount equal to seventy-five percent (75%) of his or her basic compensation, reduced by any insurance benefits which are payable to him or her from any disability insurance policies on account of disability during each respective calendar month of the second disability period. If the period of continuous disability of a Participant extends beyond the second disability period, he or she shall be entitled to continue to receive wages only to the extent of the benefits that he or she receives under any disability insurance policies.

4.2 *Partial Disability.* In the event of partial disability of a Participant who is an officer, the Corporation shall pay to the disabled Participant during such period of partial disability the same basic compensation that he or she was receiving prior to the commencement of his or her disability, reduced by any disability benefits which are payable to him or her from any disability insurance policies on account of disability during the respective pay periods. Notwithstanding the foregoing, if the disabled Participant is absent from work for sixty (60) working days which are not separated by a period of ninety (90) consecutive days during which the Participant worked on a full-time basis, the Participant shall be entitled to continue to receive wages thereafter only to the extent of wages due to him or her for work actually performed during the period of partial disability, together with any benefits which he or she receives under any disability insurance policies.

4.3 Covered Period. This Plan shall provide disability benefits for disability commenced after the date hereof.

ARTICLE V
BENEFITS OF LIMITED PARTICIPANTS

Notwithstanding any provision herein to the contrary, the benefits payable with respect to any Limited Participant who neither is an officer of the Corporation nor otherwise satisfies the requirements of being a Participant in the Plan shall be limited to payment by the Corporation of the premiums for health insurance in accordance with the terms and conditions of the group health insurance plan, if any, maintained by the Corporation.

ARTICLE VI
GENERAL

6.1 Funding with Insurance. In connection with the Corporation's obligations to reimburse medical expenses and continue wages as provided herein, the officers of the Corporation are authorized to purchase and pay the premiums for, or reimburse Participants for the purchase of and payments of premiums for, such insurance policies as may be determined by the directors of the Corporation to be advisable to fund the said obligations.

6.2 Funding from General Assets. To the extent that benefits provided under this Plan are not funded by insurance as provided in Paragraph 6.1, such benefits shall be funded by payments from the general assets of the Corporation.

6.3 Excepted Injury and Sickness. In no event shall any benefits be paid under this Plan for any injury or sickness:

(a) Incurred when an employee was engaged in, or resulting from his or her having engaged in, a criminal enterprise.

(b) Resulting from an employee's habitual drunkenness or addiction to narcotics, or

(c) Resulting from an employee's self-inflicted injury.

6.4 Administration. The Administrator of this Plan shall be _____ or such other person or persons as may be designated from time to time by the directors of the Corporation. The Administrator will be responsible for the control and management of the Plan and, except as otherwise provided herein, any action on the part of the Administrator shall be final and conclusive on all Participants.

6.5 *Claims Procedure.* The claims procedure hereinafter set forth shall be applicable with respect to the Plan.

(a) *Filing of a Claim.* Not later than thirty (30) days following the last day of each Plan Year each Participant shall submit to the Administrator an itemized list of the expenses for medical care for which the Participant is claiming reimbursement on account of the payment thereof during the prior plan year or any portion thereof, together with a signed statement specifying the reimbursable transportation and parking expenses. In the case of a Participant who is an officer, the itemized list shall identify those expenses incurred for diagnostic procedures. The Administrator may require a Participant to furnish notices, bills, or other evidence in connection with any one or more of the itemized expenses or the payment thereof.

(b) *Notification to Participant of Decision.* If a claim is wholly or partially denied, notice of the decision, meeting the requirements of subsection (c) following, shall be furnished to the Participant within a reasonable period of time after receipt of the claim by the Administrator.

(c) Every Participant who is denied a claim for benefits shall be provided by the Administrator with written notice setting forth, in a manner calculated to be understood by the Participant, the following:

(i) The specific reason or reasons for the denial;

(ii) The specific reference to the pertinent Plan provision on which the denial is based;

(iii) A description of any additional material or information necessary for the Participant to perfect the claim and an explanation of why such material or information is necessary; and

(iv) An explanation of the Plan's claim review procedure as set forth in subsection (d) following.

(d) *Review Procedure.* A Participant (or his or her duly authorized representative) may request a review of the denial of the claim by filing a written application for review with the directors of the Corporation at any time within sixty (60) days following receipt by the Participant of written notice of the denial of his or her claim. The directors may hold a hearing or otherwise ascertain such facts as it deems necessary and shall render a decision which shall be binding upon all parties. The decision of the directors shall be in writing and a copy thereof shall be sent by certified mail to the Participant and the Administrator within ninety (90) days after the receipt by the directors of the notice of review, unless special circumstances require a reasonable extension of such ninety (90)-day period. The written decision shall include specific reasons for the decision, written in a manner calculated to be understood by the Participant, and specific references to the pertinent Plan provisions on which the decision is based.

6.6 Nonalienation. No benefit payable at any time under the Plan shall be subject to alienation, sale, transfer, assignment, pledge, attachment, or encumbrance of any kind.

6.7 Amendment of Plan. The Corporation reserves the right at any time and from time to time to amend in whole or in part all of the provisions of the Plan by resolution of its directors, and each such modification or amendment shall become effective as of the date specified by the directors in said resolution.

6.8 No Waiver. If any portion of this Agreement is waived, or if any breach of this Agreement is waived by the Corporation, that waiver shall not equate to a waiver of any earlier, later, or concurrent breach of the same or any other provision. No waiver of any portion of this Agreement or of any breach of this Agreement shall be effective unless made in writing and signed by an authorized representative of the waiving party.

6.9 Entire Agreement. This Agreement contains the entire agreement between the Corporation and the Participants and supersedes any earlier arrangements.

6.10 Governing Law. Each party to this Agreement expressly agrees that this Agreement shall be governed by the laws of _____ *[insert the state or province where your entity was formed]*. Each party consents to the exclusive jurisdiction of the state and federal courts sitting in _____ *(insert the county and state of the courts that will hear any disputes—try to make sure this is your home county and state)*, in any action on a claim arising out of, under, or in connection with this Agreement. Each party agrees that this is a mandatory forum selection clause.

6.11 Severability. In the event of a court ruling that one or more clauses in this Agreement are unenforceable, the remainder of this Agreement shall remain in full force and effect.

DATED this _____ day of _____, 20____.

[INSERT NAME OF ENTITY]

By: _____
Signature of President

Index

Meet Diane Kennedy

Diane Kennedy, the nation's preeminent tax strategist, is owner of D Kennedy & Associates, a leading tax strategy and accounting firm, and the author of *The Wall Street Journal* and *Business-Week* best sellers, *Loopholes of the Rich* and *Real Estate Loopholes*.

Diane's extensive teachings have empowered people throughout the country to minimize their tax liabilities through the use of legal tax loopholes.

Diane has written for *The Tax Savings Report*, *Investment Advisor* magazine, *Personal Excellence*, the Money & Finance section of *Balance* magazine, and *Healthy Wealthy n Wise*, where she has a regular column. She's been featured in *Kiplinger's Personal Finance*, *The Wall Street Journal*, *USA Today*, and the Associated Press and on CNN, CNNfn, Bloomberg TV and Radio, CNBC, *StockTalkAmerica*, and numerous regional TV and radio shows.

A highly sought-after international speaker and educator, she has dedicated her career to empowering and educating others about financial investments and the tax advantages that are available. Through Diane's knowledge and execution of legal tax loopholes in her business and real estate investments, she and her husband Richard are able to contribute to special life-changing projects and charities in the United States and third world countries.

Diane provides critical tax law updates, advice on the latest tax loopholes, as well as tax-advantaged wealth building resources on her web site: www.TaxLoopholes.com (821 North Fifth Avenue, Phoenix, AZ 85003, 1-888-592-4769).